AGILE ARTIST

Life Lessons From Hollywood And Beyond

COLIN EGGLESFIELD

net worlding
PUBLISHING

AGILE ARTIST

Life Lessons from Hollywood and Beyond By Colin Egglesfield

eBook: 978-1-944027-29-2

Print: 978-1-944027-30-8

Copyright ©2019 by Networlding Publishing www.networlding.com

To artists everywhere.

Even if you don't know you are.

Yet.

TABLE OF CONTENTS

Preface.. 1

Chapter 1: Run, Don't Walk.. 5

Chapter 2: Everyone Is An Artist.................................. 61

Chapter 3: Carpe Diem.. 89

Chapter 4: Free Ballin'.. 123

Chapter 5: Every Breath You Take 175

Chapter 6: Success... 207

Chapter 7: Share Like Your Life Depended On It...... 251

Before You Go: The Great Invitation 285

Acknowledgments... 287

Paying It Forward.. 289

Englewood 291

About The Author 293

PREFACE

It was a relatively normal nothing Thursday afternoon in Los Angeles when I got a phone call from a producer friend of mine named Alex.

"Yo, what's up?!" I answered.

"Hey, are you around in the next week?"

"Uh, yeah, I think so, why?"

"I was calling to see if you wanted to work with Sylvester Stallone."

It took me a second to register this and gauge if he was bullshitting or not.

"Uh...yeah," I responded, half thinking his next response was going to be "Ha, gotcha, fucker! "

The next thing out of his mouth, however, was, "Okay, great. The only thing is you're going to have to leave on Saturday to fly to

Savannah, Georgia because we start shooting on Monday." Holy shit. This was real.

"Hold on a sec, let me check my calendar," I said back, half testing him.

"Okay, just let me know ASAP so we can book your flight and let your reps know."

It took me all of a half second to say, "I'm kidding! Yeah man, are you serious? Sylvester Stallone? I'm there! "

Four days later, I was on set in Savannah, working with my boyhood idol. Hollywood icon Sylvester Stallone has transcended industry norms and remains the epitome of what it means to be an Agile Artist.

For more than twenty years, my career has taken me to Hollywood and beyond. I've often found myself in many of these surreal situations. I wonder how the hell they happened, and yet, half intuitively understand that I have consciously manifested them from the inner depths of my dreams.

Whether it's been Giorgio Armani personally fitting me with his latest runway show creation, dining with Elton John and Donatella Versace in Lake Como, or working with Academy Award–winning actors on a movie set, I realize I have truly lived a blessed life, despite having to overcome some life altering events.

We all dream and aspire to do great things. As life sets in, however, sometimes these goals get diluted. Even worse, they may diminish to the brink of disappearing. My hope is that by sharing some of my stories, you will be inspired to dream again, perhaps bigger than you ever imagined, and to create the life you have always hoped to realize.

Life can bring us all to our knees and kick us while we're down. It kicks some of us harder than others, but we all experience valleys at some point in our lives. When we fall, it can feel like there's no hope, no "how," and no one who can help. Having lived through some pretty harrowing experiences that include 9/11, twice overcoming cancer, and making it from Small Farm Town, USA to the biggest stages in Hollywood, I hope I can share some wisdom I've developed along the way. The obstacles I encountered not only helped me to realize my dreams, they gave me the strength to always pick myself back up and keep putting one foot in front of the other. I have been humbled throughout, but as a result, have been blessed with the opportunity to work with and learn from some of the most talented, well-respected people in the world.

One of the most important lessons I have learned is that I wouldn't have been able to survive without the encouragement, love and faith of so many amazing people in my life. They have pushed me when I needed to grow, leveled with me when I needed some truth, and believed in me even before I did. They lent me a shoulder when I was broken, and offered a hand up, not a hand out, when appropriate. Because of their tremendous support, I am able to dedicate this to each and every one of you dealing with any adversity you might be facing in life. Know this: you are not alone.

To travel this path, the inspired path of the Agile Artist, means tapping into the innate resourcefulness that all of us possess. It's not only necessary, it's required to effectively move through these challenges with ease, purpose and fulfillment. I'm not a therapist. I'm not a psychologist and I'm certainly no self-help guru. But… from my own experiences, I have become more nimble and efficient not only with recognizing, but also manifesting new opportunities and connections. It's these inspired paradigm shifts that have made all the difference in my life.

This is not to say that this path is going to be easy. Pursuing anything worthwhile almost never is. As high as the highs can be, we all eventually meet disappointment that can be absolutely devastating…especially when what we're pursuing is motivated from the depths of who we are. The key is to be able to deal with challenges and disappointments and not be stopped by them.

To live as an Agile Artist is to rise above the noise, the disappointments, and the negativity, every single day, as you wait for special people and opportunities to present themselves. It's these inspired intersections that can make all the difference.

Call it paying it forward, or repaying the generosity of all the people who have helped me along the way. Whatever it's called, I've been fortunate enough to have the opportunity to share what I've learned along the way. Now, with this book, I'm excited about pulling back the curtain once again. This time I've organized the insights and wisdom that have helped me identify what I wanted out of life. I've taken time to reflect on how I overcame the fears and obstacles in my life to make my dreams happen.

In writing this book, I'm not only sharing the secrets of an Agile Artist. I'm also inviting you to join the Agile Artist community so we may help each other manifest the inspired lives that we want to wake up to each and every morning. We are all artists in one way or another. Art doesn't, by definition, limit itself to painting, writing, or creating new works. Art and artists are those people who authentically support, motivate and give who they are with each other. When we support the creative process, be it networking, supporting, encouraging, or promoting each other, we not only have the opportunity to make our own lives better but we also have the opportunity to make the world a better place.

One of my favorite quotes is from Charles Bukowski, a poet, novelist, and short story writer. It reads, "Find what you love and let it kill you." To me, this is the perfect metaphor for how we should live our lives. Do what you love until the day you die. What I love to do is to create and to make a difference.

I understand and appreciate that everyone has their own unique situations. And I'm not here to compare experiences about who has had it better or worse than anyone else or attempt to elicit pity. I'm simply mentioning my experiences and what I have learned from them in hopes that they may be of value to you. If what I say here resonates, great. If not, then by all means, throw it way. Either way, I look forward to hearing about what you gain from this book and invite you to continue the discussion of bringing more creativity and fulfillment everyday, living the life of the Agile Artist.

01 RUN, DON'T WALK

"Life is not a dress rehearsal."
–Rose Tremain

"Oh my God! It's another one!" I yelled into the phone. A flash of light and a descending spray of metal and glass exploded out the back of the South Tower just a few hundred feet in front of me as a narrow and high-pitched bang reverberated through the columns of buildings forever into eternity.

Not even an hour earlier, it was a picturesque morning. The sun sprayed bright beams of light into my studio apartment, beckoning me to begin a new day of big promise and hustle. Because I lived on the eighteenth floor of a building in New York City that faced the World Trade Center towers, it was normal for me to wake up to the muffled sounds of horns honking, people yelling, and cars whizzing by on the West Side Highway that separated us below. Today, however, was different.

As I lay in bed negotiating with my alarm clock to let me sleep for a few more minutes, I started to notice the whirps of police cars along with fire trucks and ambulance sirens echoing between the buildings outside. The urgent sounds of emergency vehicles enroute to someplace nearby kept getting louder and more frequent. I got out of bed and groggily walked to my windows to see what was happening. What was normally six lanes of bumper-to-bumper traffic below my window was now devoid of cars. This was the first thing that seemed off. As I watched, more and more fire engines, police cars, and ambulances arrived, and I started to notice the steady smacking of debris onto the street. The firetrucks and police cars weren't just on their way to an accident or fire. They were grouped below me, and in front of the Twin Towers.

Then I looked up from my window. I saw a gaping hole about a quarter of the way down from the top of the North Tower. Flames licked out of the void in the tower. The damage didn't look that bad at first. Then I noticed that I could see people with their heads poking out of the windows above it, indicating that this might be worse than what the hole belied. I stood there in awe, trying to comprehend what I was seeing. Black smoke steadily wisped out of the hole, then grew stronger and thicker. After watching the scene in front of me for a few moments, my confusion prompted me to turn on my television. I couldn't figure out what was happening, but I thought maybe the local news had an explanation for what was happening. When I flipped to NY1, I only remember the broadcaster saying something about a plane having hit the World Trade Center.

My first thought was that a Cessna had accidentally run into the tower because from my perspective, the damage didn't look that substantial. Little did I know what I was looking at was the less invasive, residual blast from the remnants of the plane being shot out the back side. The north side of the tower had taken the brunt of the carnage, but I couldn't see that from my apartment.

As a side note, during this time in New York, I always had my Sony video recorder with me. I loved to make short movies while running around the city, so when I realized what was happening, my natural reaction was to grab my camera and hit record. After pushing that little red button, what I witnessed was something that will haunt me until the day I die: people leaping out of the windows from the top floors of the towers.

Looking back now, I realize this was one of the most defining moments of my life. To watch someone decide that jumping out of a window from a thousand feet in the air was a better option than remaining trapped in a scorching inferno is to this day, something still incomprehensible to me. I remember starting to shake and my knees getting so weak that I had to kneel down on the floor of my apartment. I was literally getting nauseous. Partially startled out of my paralysis by the ringing of my phone, I answered, "Hello?"

It was my best friend, Lisa, my New York partner in crime. To this day I share an incredibly special bond with her. "Are you okay!?" she asked with pointed concern. After a brief pause to collect myself, I told her I was fine, but that what I was seeing was horrendous. I huddled in the corner of my apartment with my back against one wall, looking out of my window, horrified by what I was seeing, but unable to look away. I remember eventually sliding the window open a bit which allowed me to actually hear the voices of the first responders and the cacophony below. This only made the scenario more intense. As I continued to stare at the flames and the thickening smoke, the clear blue sky and warm sun seemed to disguise the terror that was unfolding.

As I knelt there, I described to her what I was seeing… people hanging half of their bodies out of the tower above the smoke and flames. Horrified, my voice would crack as I would intermittently say to her, "Oh my God, Lisa! Another person just jumped!" I remember being so angry from experiencing such helplessness. I felt lame, unable to do anything except watch as countless people decided to take fate into their own hands and free themselves from Hell. At a certain point I couldn't keep watching. I mustered the nerve to get up and move to the middle of my apartment. Only a few feet from the windows, I continued watching while listening intently to see if the news had any more information about what had happened.

I just remember standing there, looking at the TV with my phone in one hand and my video camera in the other. At the time I didn't realize the camera was still recording. What happened next nearly knocked me off my feet and forever seared another horrific image into my brain.

The flash bang from the second plane hitting the south tower jerked my head from the TV, back to my window. The tempered concern I experienced up until that point was now a full blown panic. When I re-watch the video recording of everything that transpired that morning, it's almost as though I'm hearing another person on the camcorder. "Oh my God! It's another one!" The next moment, I responded to Lisa in an eerily subdued voice, saying, "I'm okay, I'm okay. I've gotta go." What I didn't realize at the time was that my body was starting to slip into the dulling effects of fullblown shock.

I hung up the phone, threw on a pair of jeans and a T-shirt, and ran down eighteen flights of stairs in a few seconds. I was literally jumping down five stairs at a time for fear the ceiling was going to collapse on top of me.

When I got down to the lobby level, I burst outside to the front of my building to find a large group of people standing there, moving their gaze up to the sky. From street level, the towers seemed so massive, so broad, so solid, even with cragged holes and black smoke billowing out. I think, collectively, this huddled group of strangers felt a sense of safety even though we were only roughly five hundred feet away from impending chaos.

At a certain point, I noticed my modeling manager, Roger, standing among this throng of people, wearing an expression of awe. When he saw me, we walked toward each other, both of us at least somewhat comforted in recognizing someone familiar. I remember standing there together, looking up in horror as more and more people inside the tower could be seen sticking their heads out of the windows, trapped by the melting metal below them. We stood there as a steady stream of people migrated toward my building, only to be occasionally halted by the screaming of people as another poor soul leapt from one of the floors above the flames.

The police started yelling at us to move back, and a sense of fear began to take hold. I don't think we really knew what to do as we witnessed person after person leaping to their death. The real breaking point seemed to be when, what we thought was another person falling, turned out to be two people who were actually holding hands, tumbling together. At this moment, I remember Roger saying he couldn't watch anymore. He suggested we walk up the sidewalk to get away from the mass of people steadily getting larger.

As we made our way toward Chambers Street, the sun began its late summer blaze. I quickly dipped into a deli to grab some water as a relief from the heat and to quell my nerves. I made my way into the middle of the store that, for any other random Tuesday September morning, seemed completely normal. It was normal except for the moment I reached into a large display bucket to grab a bottle of water. I remember that the instant my fingers wrapped around the ice cold plastic, the ground began to violently shift and shake. The lights flickered then went out, followed by a low rumble that quickly escalated to the point of a deafening roar.

I immediately ran to the front of the deli and out the front door where I was met with the sight of men and women in full business attire, running and screaming. Roger was nowhere to be seen. Because my view of the towers was blocked by the close proximity to the buildings next to me, I didn't really know what was happening. I guess my instincts kicked in because I found myself running up the street with everyone else.

Now, for anyone who has never had the chance to see the original Twin Towers in person, the idea that anything could happen to these behemoth, 1,368-foot-tall structures that spanned over sixteen acres was just unfathomable. When I heard a woman scream, "The tower just fell!" I thought she was referring to the antenna spire on the top of the North Tower, but as I sprinted farther up the West Side Highway, I got to a clearing in between buildings where I could actually see toward the towers again. Except this time, when I looked, something seemed oddly wrong. It was almost like a visual effect or a trick, because only one tower was visible. In the place of the other was a giant, mushrooming cloud of debris and dust headed our way.

To say this was surreal is a gross understatement. I just knew that I had to keep heading north to keep far enough ahead of the swiftly moving cloud of churning darkness. As we trudged up the highway, I heard someone yell out that a plane had hit the Pentagon as well. Then a lady shouted that Los Angeles had been bombed and that America was under attack. It was hard to know what to believe at the time because in the moment, my immediate focus was getting to someplace safe. The idea of all of this happening at once was too much to comprehend. In the meantime, all the cell phone coverage was down, so every time I tried to call my parents and let them know I was still safe, my call wouldn't go through.

As we approached Houston Street, about a mile north of Ground Zero, the sound of a faint crack and dull rumble prompted us to turn around. When I looked back toward where we had come from, the second tower began to crumble right in front of my eyes. I remember people shrieking and crying, but for some reason I just stood there, paralyzed. I don't remember being able to feel anything. The only thing I remember was how oddly similar it looked to so many films I had seen where New York City gets destroyed by some sort of natural disaster or robots or Godzilla. The only difference was, *this* was terribly real. There was no walking out of any movie theatre back to the way things were.

I eventually made my way across town to my friend's apartment in Union Square where a group of us reconnected. We were thankful to see each other again. I still hadn't been able to reach my parents on my cell phone because the networks were jammed. I had no way of letting them know I was okay. My parents later relayed to me they were absolutely beside themselves, fearing the worst, knowing that I lived so close to the towers, yet with no idea of their son's fate. When I did finally reach them, I just remember my mom being overjoyed and grateful and both of my parents telling me how much they loved me. It made me truly realize how much we meant to each other, something that has gone a long way in my life to say the least.

With no way to get back home to my real family for the next few weeks, I hunkered in front of the TV with my good friends, waiting, fearing what might come next. Looking back, it seemed like the closest thing to living a real-life Armageddon. Everyone and everything seemed to revolve around survival. What made it even more odd, though, was that I don't remember feeling many emotions other than a heightened sense of alertness or hypervigilance.

It's not that I remember feeling afraid so much as being in a constant state of apprehension. The first few days after 9/11, I remember going to the grocery store and it being like a scene in a movie about the end of the world. We were hoarding things from the shelves and piling up grocery carts, buying everything we could get our hands on because we didn't know how long this was going to last.

It was two weeks before those of us who lived down near Ground Zero were told by the authorities we would be allowed back to our homes to check the damage and see what we could salvage. To do this, I had to go to Chelsea Piers Sports Complex where ten people at a time were loaded up into the back of a pickup truck, given surgical masks to protect us from the smoke and debris, and then told we would have to wait in line again once we got through the barriers of tanks and military vehicles. With masks and anxiety in place, we proceeded to head south.

Once we pulled up to my building, we were off- loaded and had to wait for a National Guard soldier to take us, individually, into the building. When it was my turn, the soldier led me up the eighteen flights of stairs in pitch blackness with only a single flashlight guiding the way. Making our way through the stairwell and subsequent hallway, we finally arrived at my apartment door where he asked me to hold the flashlight as he fumbled with some keys. I quickly noticed my door frame was bent and a padlock and latch were bolted onto the door.

He shared with me that the FBI had broken into all of the apartments that face the World Trade Center, including mine, to look for the black boxes from the airplanes. Hearing this was just one more unsettling aspect of this nightmarish experience.

Walking into my apartment was like entering the aftermath of a bomb having gone off. My windows facing the towers had been completely blown in, and there were debris, dust, parts of metal beams, broken glass, pieces of carpeting, and several documents from financial institutions lying about. Standing in the wreckage that had been my home, I walked to what used to be my windows. I heard the sound of crunching glass with every step. What once stood stoutly in front of me, greeting me every morning, anchoring me to the city I loved, was now two massive craters bleeding smoke and emitting the rancid smell of burning chemicals. I could see straight down into the carnage where the first responders were crawling around, pulling out chunks of debris in search of bodies and evidence.

I stood there for a few moments just staring in disbelief at the aftermath. I'm sure the soldier had seen others experience a similar reaction that day. He reminded me that I only had ten minutes to grab whatever I could put into a suitcase and his urgency snapped me out of my trance. I dusted off whatever residue I could from some shirts and pants in my closet, grabbed some socks, underwear, and some toiletries, and threw them in my suitcase. Then we left.

From the day this happened, my parents beckoned me to come back to Chicago. What's weird is that leaving New York City, as chaotic and hectic as it was, was not something I wanted to do. I guess at the time I felt a sense of camaraderie with the millions of other New Yorkers who had just gone through something with me that no one else could possibly understand.

Over the next few weeks, being in the city felt increasingly like being in a war zone. There were battle tanks, army personnel carriers, helicopters, and jet fighters flying overhead. It wasn't just the devastation around us. It was the presence of the military and first responders and the stench of death and chemicals as well. So I finally agreed to return back to Chicago for a bit of peace. Before I left, however, I visited my place one more time. I was able to grab some more clothes and some other items that were important to me and headed off to Newark Airport in a taxi. As the driver made it through the Holland Tunnel and we got onto the New Jersey Turnpike, from the left side of the taxi, looking across the Hudson River, I could finally see the magnitude of the damage and the amount of smoke that still billowed from the World Trade Center site.

This was about a month after the towers had fallen, and still, there was residual, undeniable evidence that something horrible had occurred. We continued to speed down the turnpike in silence, and as my eyes locked on Lower Manhattan, I noticed a small crack in my stoic veneer. I could feel something starting to well up inside me, almost as if my subconscious was beginning to realize that I was out of danger. It was as if the psychological walls that had been erected from the devastation I had witnessed were slowly starting to give way, and my buried feelings about what had happened were finally surfacing.

Once I got to the airport, it was incredibly hard for me to hold myself together. I checked in and got my ticket, and as I went through security, I could sense myself feeling real emotions again for the first time in over a month. I struggled to hold back what was starting to feel like a huge wave inside me. I knew I just needed to sit down. I went into a restaurant and was led to a table by the hostess, and as soon as I took a seat, I began to sob uncontrollably. It was almost as if my body had finally realized I was in a safe enough space to release what I had stifled for the past four weeks. I sat there for quite a while with my head bowed, buried in a napkin, releasing the fear, sadness, anxiety, and anger that had been shackled inside me.

I don't really remember even getting on the airplane, or anything about the flight. All I remember was that when I landed in Chicago, my parents were waiting for me right after I exited through security. The second we saw each other, I immediately ran to them. The three of us stood there in the middle of the airport, holding each other forever. It made me truly realize how much my parents really meant to me, how fragile life really is, and just how quickly it can change.

THE IMPERMANENCE OF LIFE THAT REVEALS YOUR AGILE ARTIST

> *Rocky Balboa: "Let's do it tomorrow."*
> *Apollo Creed: "There is no tomorrow! "*

Witnessing the events of the World Trade Center lifted any veil of doubt or uncertainty about what was important in my life. The fear of moving out to LA to pursue my budding dream of becoming a professional actor paled in comparison to the fear I had just experienced just a few months prior. Because of this, I could not get life's impermanence out of my mind. I used this wake-up call, if you will, to change my focus. I stopped thinking about all the reasons why becoming a professional actor was a ludicrously stupid idea to thinking, how can I make this happen?'

Whenever I think back to that time, the image of the people I saw trapped on those burning floors forces its way in front of anything else I might be worried about. I can't help but think about what must have been going through their minds. Was there something they had always wanted to accomplish but hadn't because they were too afraid to fail? Was there a place they had always wanted to visit but didn't because they didn't think they had the money? Maybe they just wished they could have told their parents, family, and friends that they loved them one last time but took it for granted because there would be another opportunity to do so.

The idea of lost opportunity and regret presented to me in such a distinct, urgent manner threw me into overdrive. Fear of failing didn't matter anymore. My determination to pursue my passion and what I absolutely love to do was now galvanized in my whole body, mind and soul.

In the weeks after the Trade Center attack, I decided I was never going to look back on my life with regret for not having truly lived. I felt like I owed that, not just to myself, but to all the people who perished that day. There's a scene at the end of the film *Saving Private Ryan* when Tom Hanks' character speaks to Private Ryan after Hanks' character is shot. Hanks has spent days—weeks, even— looking for Private Ryan, losing some of his men and then himself to save Ryan. Private Ryan (played by Matt Damon) approaches Hanks as they both recognize Hanks' impending death. Hanks then says to Damon, "Earn this."

Living through the Trade Center experience made it very clear to me that life is not something to be taken for granted. It motivated me to go out and pursue all the amazing things life has to offer and to "earn" my place in it. From then on, I was going to live life unabashedly, unapologetically, with all my heart and soul, and nothing was going to stop me.

CREATIVE QUESTIONS

"It's only after we've lost everything that we're free to do anything." – Tyler Durden, Fight Club

I stayed in Chicago from October through December of 2001. Up until that point, I had been in New York for four years. I was starting to flirt with the idea of heading out to Hollywood to test the waters of pursuing a full-time acting career. I still felt connected to New York on an emotional level, especially after what had just happened, so I headed back in December to evaluate what I was going to do.

After being away from New York City for about two months, it was almost as if the city was unrecognizable. The resident buzz, energy and color that normally permeated the streets during the holidays was replaced with a blanket of somberness and gray. The once-varied mix of people's emotions and moods was now a shared, muted expression of sadness. It was as if everything and everyone was moving in slow motion. I couldn't quite grasp my bearings about the city's current identity and where I fit in it. The first place I went to was my apartment to ascertain its condition and see what, if anything, I could salvage.

When I arrived, there were workers milling around, and I was told by one of the building managers that all residents were required to vacate so repairs could be made and inspections conducted. Since the land that my building rested upon was actually the earth that was dug out from the base of each of the towers, city officials needed to assess the structural integrity of the foundation. This area of New York City is presently called Battery Park City. Before 1968, however, when the first shovel broke ground for the construction of the towers, it was actually part of the Hudson River. I was told that because Battery Park was a man-made plot of land, the city had to make sure the area was still habitable.

Knowing I would have to move out of my apartment regardless of what else I decided to do, I began to take stock of what I had to do next. For all intents and purposes, the building looked relatively normal. As the elevator dinged at the eighteenth floor and I stepped out, a flood of anxiety started to rush through my body. The building manager led me to my apartment and opened up the padlock that was still bolted to the door. The door creaked open, and I stepped in. I was surprised to find my apartment eerily devoid of any major evidence that anything on the scale of what I witnessed had actually happened.

Gone were the metal beams, the broken pieces of concrete and glass, and the papers and gray dust that had made my home look so monochrome the last time I was there. I slowly walked to the new windows that had been installed. The new windows had replaced the cracked and jagged edges of the previous ones that had been blown in when the towers fell. Rather than comfort me, they added to the surreal-ness of the room. The building manager left me there, staring out the windows down into the two gigantic pits that were still smoldering.

I wasn't quite sure what to do. I knew I had to leave this place, but I didn't know where I was going to go. I proceeded to call a couple of real estate agents and have them show me some new apartments. I wasn't enthused at all. I felt as if I were just going through the motions. It was hard to feel connected to anything anymore since my life and the world as I had known them were now completely different. That night I remember going back to my hotel room, sitting on the floor next to the bed, closing my eyes, and thinking about what I was going to do next. Inevitably, thoughts of moving out west to Los Angeles kept rearing up, beckoning me to say yes.

Up until this point, whenever I had a decision to make, there were plenty of people who I could seek advice from. Whether it was my parents, teachers, friends, or, most recently, entertainment industry agents and my manager, there was always someone around to be my sounding board. This was the first time, however, that I knew only I would be able to decide what was best for me. As a member of a small group of people who had actually witnessed firsthand what happened at the Trade Center, there weren't many people I knew who were in a position to understand how I was feeling. I was considering a career that very few other people I knew currently maintained or wanted to pursue. I had to look inward to find the answer. I couldn't think of anyone else who would quite understand my situation and what I was contemplating doing. This would be the first major decision I would make entirely on my own.

Prior to 9/11, whenever I seriously considered heading out to Los Angeles, I would get this nervous twinge of excitement thinking about how incredible it could be. As quickly as those feelings of aspiration and excitement surfaced, along came that voice in my head that would chime in and say all kinds of things about why it was a horrible idea.

"You're crazy! "

"You don't know anyone in LA! "

"You don't know where you're going to stay! "

"You barely have any money. How are you going to survive?"

"You have only ever booked two acting jobs, and there's no guarantee that you will ever become a professional actor, let alone book another acting job. LA has hundreds of other actors who have way more experience than you do."

"Who the hell do you think you are?!"

It's times like this, when faced with a big decision, that our brain will try to talk some sense into us. In reality our brain isn't thinking about what's best for us. It's simply trying to keep us 'safe.' No matter how many "reasons" your mind comes up with, it's important to take a critical look at these "reasons" and see them for what they are instead of letting them stop you.

Negative thoughts exist for one reason: to protect us from perceived (not actual) danger. I'm not saying that the voice in your head should be ignored altogether since it very well may be protecting you from experiencing actual bodily or psychological harm. What I'm getting at is this. When I've examined my thoughts and taken a critical look at why they occur, I've recognized that most of the time, they're not actually serving a real purpose with regard to "saving" me from real, imminent danger. In other words, our brains often times inaccurately perceive a threat when the reality is anything but.

The mammalian brain has evolved over thousands of years through natural selection to protect us from the danger of being eaten by whatever lurks in the night. This is useful when you're trying to survive in the jungle. However, our brain still operates similarly when faced with what it perceives as the same kind of lifethreatening danger. It will invent every excuse as to why something is a bad idea or won't work to prevent us from being exposed to this 'perceived' danger. Unless...you frame what you are deciding on in a different context by presenting your brain with a better set of questions.

It's important to recognize that the little voice in your head *is not based in current reality*. It's essentially like 'Alexa' or 'Siri' except it's operating on software that was programmed by your brain in response to *past* trauma when you were younger. It does so to "protect" you by preventing you from taking action that could result in another emotionally traumatic experience. Most of the time it's not software that was programmed to make you feel empowered or to succeed. It's messaging that you decided was "true" when you were a kid, and unfortunately we carry this same false messaging into our adult lives.

When that voice comes up, and it will, it's very easy to let it stop you, simply because you don't have a good reason to refute it or have a solution to focus on right then and there. What I have learned to do is twofold. First, I write these thoughts down on a piece of paper. By getting them out of my head and onto paper, I can start to see them for what they are, reasons for keeping me 'safe.' I then transform these thoughts into creative questions. By turning a negative thought into a creative question, I no longer feel stopped.

That night in my hotel room, while I sat on the floor sorting my thoughts out, galvanized by my desire to pursue my acting career, I realized that to get control of my thoughts, I had to make my brain 'work' for me instead of letting it "decide" for me based on outdated programming. I recognized that I was going to have to "update" the software in my head by adding a question onto the original thoughts that originally popped up. Little did I know at the time that this change in my thought process would serve as the seeds that would bear fruit years later.

"You're crazy. This is never going to happen" became "This is totally doable. Now, how can I make this happen?"

"You don't know anyone out in LA" became "You do know people who know people who live in LA. You can you ask them to introduce you."

"You don't know where you're going to stay" became, "Who can I call to ask if I can stay with them for a bit until I figure out my own place to live?"

"You barely have any money" became, "I can ask my agent how can I book as much work as possible, and I'll find a part-time job once I get out there to get me by."

"You have only ever booked two acting jobs, and there is no guarantee that you will ever become a professional actor, let alone book another acting job. LA has hundreds of other actors who have way more experience than you" became, "There are hundreds, even thousands of other people who have done this. Why can't I at least try?"

"Who the hell do you think you are?!" became the trigger to remind myself of one of my favorite quotes by Marianne Williamson, which reads:

"Our deepest fear is not that we are inadequate. Our deepest fear is that we are powerful beyond measure. It is our light, not our darkness that most frightens us. We ask ourselves, Who am I to be brilliant, gorgeous, talented, fabulous? Actually, who are you *not* to be? You are a child of God. Your playing small does not serve the world.

There is nothing enlightened about shrinking so that other people won't feel insecure around you. We are all meant to shine, as children do. We were born to make manifest the glory of God that is within us. It's not just in some of us; it's in everyone. And as we let our own light shine, we unconsciously give other people permission to do the same. As we are liberated from our own fear, our presence automatically liberates others."

By asking the right creative, positive questions when doubts and negative questions arise, your mind becomes engaged in the challenge to find an answer. Because by its very nature, the brain is hardwired to find solutions to your questions, it will provide you with the answers if you let it. Our brains are more powerful than we can possibly fathom, not just by providing answers but also by actually influencing your reality and helping you manifest the life you want to live. A lot of the lessons I have learned by pursuing the life of an artist over the past few years are incredibly powerful and practical. I'm really excited to be sharing them so you too can create the life you truly want.

What's liberating about recognizing how to reframe your thoughts is learning that instead of being paralyzed by fear and the unknown, answers will emerge that empower you. We literally have the ability to ask our brains how to accomplish. It's up to us then to actually manifest solutions, by taking action based on the answers that emerge and replace the negative thoughts that were originally taking up the same brain space.

It's ironic to me how we update the software on our phones and computers whenever a new version is released in order to fix bugs and keep our devices working but how rarely we focus on our own updates. The question I'd like to ask is this: when is the last time you updated your brain's software and considered what version you're still running on? Maybe it's time?

THINKING VS. BEING

"Emancipate yourselves from mental slavery.
None but ourselves can free our minds."
– Bob Marley

It's important to recognize that *you are not your thoughts*. Our thoughts are an amalgamation of a myriad of sources of information filtered through our upbringing. What we have learned from our parents, school, culture, religion, and what we have seen on TV and in the movies has all affected us. Not one thought in and of itself is bad or good. It's the *effect* that our thoughts have on us that is important to look at. What I've learned is that as powerful as our brains can be for creating and making things happen, if left unchecked, our thoughts or, more precisely, that little voice in our head, can be incredibly disempowering and destructive. When we allow that thought or voice to become our inner critic and let it dictate to our true self, what it says will make us happy, then we're trapped.

People who have achieved massive success have taught me it's neither the money nor the fame nor the private jet that truly makes the difference in life. First and foremost, it's security and having our basic needs met, followed by the fulfillment that comes with having a purpose in life. It's being able to fully express who we are as a result of our success that we crave, not the success itself. If the by-product of your being fully self-expressed in the pursuit of your dreams includes lots of money and fancy cars and jets, then great, but the pursuit of these things in and of themselves will always lead to disappointment and a feeling of emptiness.

Jim Carrey has continually inspired me not only for what he's accomplished but also for the unabashed freedom he allows himself to be completely self-expressed. Can you think of anyone else in the world more self-expressed than his character in *Ace Ventura* or *The Mask?* He's someone who believes heavily in the power of manifestation and has talked extensively about the meaning of life, success, and accomplishing one's goals. One of my favorite quotes from him is this: "I think everybody should get rich and famous and do everything they ever dreamed of so they can see that it's not the answer."

When we see a famous actor, singer, or athlete driving around in a Rolls Royce and wearing gold chains with lots of beautiful people around, it's hard not to think that all our problems would be solved if we were to trade places with them. As someone who has experienced a certain level of industry recognition as a fashion model and as an actor, and has made decent money on television shows and had the fancy cars and gone to all the Hollywood Oscar parties, I agree with Jim Carrey—these are not the answers to those seeking happiness.

Someone else's happiness and fulfillment is not necessarily yours. Deep down, when we go beyond our thoughts and connect with ourselves on a spiritual level, the answers to all of our innermost and fundamental questions emerge. Whenever I connect to this place, I feel a sense of calm, purpose, and confidence. This allows me to look at a situation without the noise of external influences getting in the way. I'm then able to take intentional, thoughtout action instead of making decisions from a place of fear, worry, or scarcity.

When I was sitting on that hotel room floor in New York, contemplating what to do next with my life, I allowed myself to experience what it would feel like to live in LA and live my dream life as a professional actor. Imagining myself being on set, working with Daniel Day Lewis, Tom Cruise, and Anthony Hopkins, telling stories, and giving service to the words and inspiration of incredible writers, directors, and producers helped make my decision to move out to LA that much more realistic.

You are whatever you decide to be. How you figure out what to decide is by taking the time to be quiet with yourself and explore what emerges in your thoughts and feelings. Whatever excites you, makes you feel nervous, and motivates you to take action is a good start. You don't have to know how it's going to happen—that's the job of the universe. The important part is having the impetus, the beginning thought that starts the fire inside you. Then ask yourself, "What action can I take to begin?"

TRUSTING YOUR INSTINCTS

"Creativity comes from trust. Trust your instincts."
– Rita Mae Brown

Learning how to curb my inner critic has proven to be invaluable. It was during those first few years in Los Angeles when I started to become more open, relaxed, and confident on stage and in front of the camera that sparked my overall growth as a person. That confidence started reinforcing my love for the craft of acting. As my love for acting continually grew, my desire to get better at it was constantly fueled. No matter what was happening on any given week—whether it was a bad audition, being stuck on the 405 for three hours, or having to endure another nightmare first date, listening to a girl talk about the vitamin content of kale juice or how hot it was at Coachella—whenever I got into my acting class, all my real-world problems disappeared.

To me, walking into an acting class is like walking into a sacred temple. There is something magical, mystical, and mythical about theatre that lights me up and makes me feel alive! I knew from the moment that I stepped into my first acting class that it was something I wanted to do for the rest of my life. The more I studied and became engrossed in the craft, the more it ignited a desire within me to be able to act in movies like my idols, Montgomery Clift, Marlon Brando, Paul Newman, and Daniel Day Lewis.

As I started to become more proficient as an actor, I was fortunate to have landed with an agency that sent me out on auditions. One of the hardest things to have happen when you're first starting out as an actor is finding reputable representation to secure auditions for you. What makes it equally difficult is that most productions are sanctioned by the unions. At the time I started it was the Screen Actors Guild and The American Federation of Television and Radio. They have since merged. As a performer, for the most part, you aren't able to work for a sanctioned production unless you're a member of the union, but the catch-22 is that you can't become a union member unless you have worked for a union production.

The way around this is be so good in the audition that the producers and director want to hire you even though you aren't a member or have exactly what the producers are looking for that no other union performer has. Luckily, I got my union card by doing commercials. (My first commercial was for Folgers Coffee where I had to dance on a New York subway—the commercial never ran probably because my dance skills were *too good*.) However, it just so happened that as I started to book a few commercials in a row, the agents started to take notice and asked if I would be interested in going out for any "legitimate" auditions, meaning auditions for theatrical film and TV projects.

This was a big deal and one that I didn't take lightly. For each audition I went on, I would hire my acting coach to work with me, which is pretty standard in the business. The problem is that coaching can get expensive and start to add up. For a normal acting class, the cost for a month, which usually includes 1 three-to-fourhour class per week, ranges from about $250–$400. If you would like private coaching to work on a specific audition, coaches range from $80 per hour all the way to $600 per hour.

Because I wanted to make sure I was prepared and ready for my auditions when I first started going out, I decided to spend the money to get coached for almost every audition, which normally came out to about $200 a session. In my mind it was worth it because I had originally planned on spending roughly $200,000 on medical school, so I figured I was investing in myself and my professional career.

My first few experiences of auditioning were nerve-wracking. I was new to LA, and GPS and smartphones hadn't been invented yet. This meant you had to have this big bible of a map called the Thomas Guide, which would require you to juggle this thing on your lap while changing lanes so you wouldn't miss your turn. Then you'd have to flip through several different pages when you got to the edge of the page. When you still couldn't find where you were going, you'd have to pull off to the side of the road while people were honking at you because you'd made a wrong turn.

Auditions were often held in these hole-in-the-wall offices in East LA or in the Valley. You'd be buzzed in through a back door and instructed to walk up some old creaky steps to another door, which led to a small room the size of a closet with a video camera and one casting director who would ask you to start the audition over halfway through because he ran out of tape.

The other side of the spectrum involved going to one of the major studios. This felt like trying to penetrate Fort Knox; after 9/11, the security at the majors had been beefed up. When you pulled up to the front gate, five guards would walk around your car, asking you to open your trunk, and would use poles with mirrors to view the underside of your car, presumably searching for explosives. Hey man, I'm just here to audition for Cappuccino Guy Number 2. I'm not trying to blow up your studio.

Notwithstanding it taking an hour just to drive five miles in LA, by the time you arrived at the studio, you had to find the right gate, then find parking, then turn around because you weren't allowed to park in the A or B lot, but you could park in the C and D lot, which is a half mile down the road, but then you have to walk back the way you came from in the blazing LA sun to show the security guard your ID. Then they gave you a map to zig-zag through the studio lot, which was really amusing, actually, because you'd see gladiators and zombies walking around headed to the cafeteria. All this made it fun to try to guess what was being filmed and only further inspired me to get the job. Finally, once I'd reach the casting office, I'd walk in, and inevitably there would be ten to fifteen other guys that looked similar to me, including five who were on my favorite TV shows. Oh, and make sure you wipe the sweat off your face and look camera ready when you walk in!

After a few of these experiences, your resolve to become a working actor gets tested, and you learn very quickly that all the red carpet premieres and awards shows belie the immense amount of work and sacrifice that goes into it all. My first acting teacher told us that it would take ten years to become a professional working actor and twenty years before we became good at it. To be successful at anything, it helps to be talented, but if you want any sort of lasting success, I've learned that the love for the process of what you're doing is the most important component.

You have to *love* what you do because if you don't enjoy the process, the ups and downs of any career are going to make you miserable. I've always been someone who has enjoyed a challenge, but what has kept me pursuing the life of an artist for as long as I have is simply because I love the process. This is definitely not the easiest or most stable way to make a living, and I can't tell you how many crappy auditions I've had, especially when I was just starting out. In the back of my mind, though, I just knew that if I kept with it, and kept going to auditions, kept going to acting class, kept striving to get better, that eventually my time would come. And sure enough, I started to get closer and closer to actually booking the principal roles.

During the years I was going through the bulk of what I consider my 'pound-the- pavement' acting baptism, I'd see certain actors, like Ashton Kutcher, book shows such as *That '70s Show* right out of the gate, after only two auditions in their life. Instances like this happen, but are few and far between. It's definitely possible, but from having been around enough working actors and reading about and watching interviews with successful actors, I knew that you had to pay your dues. One quote that has always stuck with me is this: "It's easy to make it to the top. It's harder to stay there." This is the brutal truth and something that I've had my fair share of experience with. This business can chew you up and spit you out faster than you can imagine. What you have to learn how to deal with is a lot of "no's." You also have to learn how to not take things personally, which is a lot easier said than done.

As I started to get closer to booking the job on my auditions, I began to develop more confidence in the reality of my actually becoming a professional actor and the idea kept getting more and more exciting to me. At this time, I had a part-time job building furniture, and made money to go toward rent. I also booked the occasional commercial here and there, which kept me afloat. To say the least, I definitely wasn't in the place to be too picky about what I auditioned for. There were a few occasions, however, where my agent would send me something that I just didn't think I was right for.

Once, after rehearsing with my acting coach and realizing that I was not going to audition well for this particular role, I called the agent that was handling this project and mentioned to her my reservations.

This was my first taste of the clear delineation between the business side of show business and the artistry side. A lot of the times, surprisingly, they come into conflict with each other. Instead of having a conversation with me about why I didn't connect with the role, and perhaps nurturing a novice artist's instincts, she let it be known how disappointed she was, asking whether I realized how difficult it was for her to get this audition for me.

"Opportunities like these don't come around very often," she made clear.

She reiterated her disappointment and then got off the phone. I sat there in my car, half amused that a grown women I barely knew was "disappointed in me" as if I'd gotten a 'D' on my social studies test, and half concerned she might be right and that I wasn't good enough as an actor to make it work. Being new to the business, I wasn't sure whether this was the norm, but I began to question my instincts about my decision-making as an artist. I started wondering if my agency was going to let me go because I hadn't booked anything of real substance, and here I was, telling one of the agents that I didn't want to go on an audition that hundreds of actors would have killed for.

I began questioning whether I had made a terrible mistake and considered calling her back to let her know that I had changed my mind. Thoughts started coming into my head, such as "you're an idiot", "what did you just do", "she's gonna fire you", "you might as well move back home". I knew they were only thoughts, but in the moment, I was sitting there stewing on them because I had no context to compare them to. It's times like this when I have felt the most alone. I had been honest about how I felt and it seemed to have backfired. I wanted to be a professional actor more than anything, and now it was feeling as if I had pissed away the opportunity I had been working toward for years because I couldn't make an audition work.

To take a step back for a second, I'm incredibly grateful for so many things in my life and for the upbringing I had. My parents worked very hard to provide for us and always lived an amazing example of what it meant to be kind, generous, hardworking, and disciplined. They always supported me and made me feel cared for. I was blessed with many opportunities that I recognize a lot of people in the world don't have. I've come to recognize, however, that there are certain personality characteristics through no fault of anyone's, that for some reason or another, don't get focused on. They just sort of slip through the cracks of adolescence, and we have to nurture them when we get older. One of those characteristics, for me, was to listen to and trust my instincts.

Call it Midwest ethic, or perhaps the result of a traditional Catholic upbringing, but growing up, I saw adults as the authority on all matters. They knew best since they were older and had more experience. That doesn't mean that I always listened to them, but for the most part, I grew up without truly honing my ability to trust my instincts.

I think this led me to rely too heavily on whomever I thought was the authority in a given situation, whether it was my acting manager, my lawyers, or in this case, my agent. Essentially, anyone who had been working in the business for a while in a professional capacity. In other words, I wish I had listened to my own instincts when I knew something didn't feel right instead of following other people's advice.

I ended up caving, calling my agent back and telling her I would go on the audition, which made her happy. When I went into the audition, however, sure enough, I fell flat on my face. I couldn't honestly bring this character's words to life, no matter how hard I tried. I had saved face in the eyes of my agent, but in the eyes of this casting director, I was a shitty actor who wasn't going to be called back anytime soon.

To reiterate this point, there was another instance when I went on an audition for the TV show *Battlestar Galactica*. They were bringing the show back to TV as an updated version of the original that first aired in the seventies. It just so happened to be my favorite show when I was a kid—that and *Buck Rogers*. I'd fantasize for years about flying through the universe, shooting at Cylons and saving the galaxy. Now here I was twenty-some-odd years later, the same age as the guys I watched when I was younger. It was slated to air on the Sci-Fi Channel, which at the time was still a bit of a fledgling network. It didn't have the pedigree of respectable shows that it has now. In other words, originally, it wasn't the most respected show to come through on the breakdown services (what the agents use to find out what projects are being cast).

Needless to say, I went on the audition and it went amazingly well. I loved my character and I could tell the producers really liked me. It seemed like they were leaning toward actually casting me on the show, which would have been a huge break. Being the principal character on a show that was already picked up for a series and also on one I would have loved to have acted on was an amazing possibility. At one point they had me come in and audition with the final few actresses who were going to play opposite me. I can't tell you how excited I was! Until...

At this point I had switched agencies and was now working with a different agent named Larry Taube who is still, to this day, one of my favorite people in the business. What I loved about Larry was that he made the effort to get to know me well enough to understand what projects resonated with me and which ones he thought I'd have a legitimate chance at rather than just throwing spaghetti on the wall to see what stuck, so to speak. During the time the *Battlestar* audition process was going on, Larry informed me about a show slated to air on Fox. The show revolved around a family in which one of the sons dies. I'd be playing his brother, and it was all about how this family would deal with his death and how we would try to pick up the pieces and move forward. I read the script, really liked the material, and decided to audition for it. You know how they say, when it rains, it pours?

For years, I couldn't get a decent acting job in the entertainment industry to save my life. Wouldn't you know it that after auditioning for this Fox show called *Still Life*, the producers and the network chose me as one of the final two actors that they liked for the role in this show. This meant that the studio and network executives wanted me and this other guy to do a screen test for the role. This is what all actors live for! Here I was about to test for two network shows! WTF?! The issue was that the screen test was set for a Friday and the *Battlestar Galactica* producers needed an answer about whether or not I was committed to their show. They needed an answer before that Friday because they were going into production.

Ahhh, what do I do?! In my gut I really wanted to do the *Battlestar* role, but after talking to my agent, I agreed that being on a FOX TV show would be a smarter career move than one on the Sci-Fi Channel. The wrinkle was that the FOX show was not guaranteed because I still had to audition for it against the other actor. I thought about it and after seeing his 'reasoning,' even though I felt more connected to the *Battlestar* role, I decided to lean toward what my agent suggested and bought into going for *Still Life*.

We turned down the *Battlestar* role, and on that Friday, I went to the screen test, acted my heart out, and—didn't get the part. Furthermore, the Fox show never went to air while *Battlestar Galactica* went on for a total of five seasons and garnered a wide range of critical acclaim.

This was a tough one. I don't blame my agent at all because ultimately, I was the one who made the decision. I realized, though, that I let my decision get swayed, not only by someone else's opinion, but because I had also ignored my gut instinct. I was creatively excited about the role and I knew it was something I would have loved to have acted in. I knew in my heart what I wanted to do, but I simply didn't trust my instincts. From experiences like these, I've learned that the only thing you can do is recognize the insights learned and then let them go. It does no good to dwell on the past because it's not something you can change.

MANIFESTING YOUR DESTINY

"1995. Seven bucks in my pocket. I knew two things: I'm broke as hell and one day I won't be." —Dwayne "The Rock" Johnson

After toiling around Hollywood for almost two years with only varying degrees of success, I'd booked a few roles here and there. I played the spring break dude on *Gilmore Girls* and a half-dead zombie who tries to kill Alyssa Milano on *Charmed*. I also shot a Victoria's Secret commercial, with Gisele Bundchen, shot by Michael Bay, in the Hollywood Hills that involved a Ferrari, a helicopter, torches of fire, a steamy pool and, of course, Gisele in lingerie. This was sadly one of the coolest things I've shot but that ended up on the cutting room floor. Apparently, my assets weren't as good as Giselle's. Other than that, not much else was happening to make me feel like I was making serious headway toward booking my first big break.

According to the US Bureau of Labor Statistics, of the 160,000 SAG/AFTRA members nationwide, roughly 90 percent are unemployed at any given time (only about 3 percent are consistently working full time). Even though I didn't know the exact statistics at the time, it wasn't a surprise that I wasn't securing consistent work. However, try telling that to your landlord when rent is due or to the door guy at the Skybar who would gladly let you in for $50 to then pay $16 a drink.

Since most of us actors frequently find ourselves in the "starving artist" category, we are constantly doing whatever we can to increase our odds at winning The Role. For me and a lot of other serious actors who I know and have worked with, it can become an allconsuming endeavor. Often I found myself ceaselessly strategizing how to get my next acting job. This prevented me from being able to enjoy simply having lunch with a friend or to go for a hike in Malibu's beautiful hills. If something wasn't business related, I wasn't able to justify what I deemed as "wasting the time." Enter Wendy Spiller.

Wendy Spiller is a life and career coach who a friend of mine mentioned to me one day after telling him about my situation and how I felt my acting career was going nowhere. Since desperate times call for desperate measures, I was pretty open to speaking with anyone who could help me create some sort of momentum or, at the very least, a plan. I decided to give Wendy a call.

The way my friend described her was that she helps manifest the things that you want to have happen in your life, something I hadn't really heard of before. In the past, when people used the word 'manifest,' to me it sounded like hippie-dippie, wishful, or positive thinking, which I didn't give too much credence to. I'd always been of the mindset that if you just put in the work, you will eventually start to see results. After all, I *was* noticing in my acting classes and in *some* auditions that my work was having some sort of effect with regard to getting callbacks. However, I wasn't booking anything. Basically, I wasn't sealing the deal, so I was open to hear more about Wendy and what she could do.

On the day of my appointment, I drove through the winding Hollywood hills until I reached her front gate, which had a big iron heart on it. Nice touch, I thought to myself as I buzzed her keypad. The gate slowly opened up. I drove up a steep driveway and parked my car. I knocked, and within a few seconds I heard a cacophony of barking dogs followed by the door opening up. Wendy is a beautiful, blonde woman with amazing energy, and she welcomed me in with the biggest and warmest of smiles, and then led me into her study.

I have to say, it was pretty magical. She had crystals everywhere and beautiful art on the walls and a big plush purple couch, which she encouraged me to sit on. It felt very inviting and incredibly calming. She started out by asking me questions about where I came from, my childhood, what led me to Los Angeles, my relationships, and why I was there to see her. As I was telling her about my life, I found myself talking for about two hours as she wrote on a piece of paper. Before I knew it, she gave me the paper; I thought she was just taking notes, but what she did was turn every negative thing I had said into a positive.

She turned "I can't find work, I can't get an acting job, I can't seem to find a girlfriend, and I'm broke" into "I work all the time on acting projects that inspire me, I'm so grateful and happy to have found the woman of my dreams, I'm making a ton of money, and I live in the house that I've always envisioned." There were about fifty such declarations. She then had me look into a mirror with blinking lights built into the frame and read the declarations to myself in this mirror. It felt stupid and embarrassing at first, but I had gone up there willing to try something new. I thought, "I don't have much to lose."

So, I went along with Wendy's process and wholeheartedly started to say these phrases to myself. To be honest, after I finished, it did help begin to change my perspective and uplifted my mood a bit. She kept reiterating that it was important to focus on gratitude. She taught me that it's a gratitude mindset, perspective, and feeling that needs to be present in order to attract whatever you want to bring into your life.

As I started to read more about manifesting and what Wendy was opening me up to, I began to become present to the fact that everything in this world is made up of energy. Everything. Because our thoughts and mindset are energy, we can actually influence the physical universe with our thoughts. What I didn't realize was that my mindset was mostly focused on the lack of things in my life such as work, fulfillment, money, and so on. I learned that when you are constantly focused on what you don't have, you are sending that energy out into the physical world, and the universe simply responds and brings you more of that. Conversely, what Wendy opened my eyes and mind to was that by focusing on gratitude and repeating the declarations she had written down on that paper, I was changing my reality. By speaking those positive things into the mirror, I would be sending signals out to the physical universe that I, in fact, was ready to welcome these things into my life.

She then had me write down five goals that I wanted to achieve in life. She instructed me to make sure I wrote them in the present tense, as if they were already happening. So, I wrote some things such as, "I'm a working actor on a hit TV show! I work on a major motion picture with A-list actors! I live in the house of my dreams! I contribute to society and people appreciate my work!" After I wrote these down, she mentioned that I should create a vision board, a collection of inspirational quotes, goals, and pictures that I'd put together and hang on my wall. The purpose was that every day, I fed my mind and reminded my subconscious of the things that I wanted to manifest.

Wendy also suggested I buy a copy of *GQ* magazine, cut out a picture of myself, and tape it onto the cover of the magazine, replacing who was actually featured on the cover. It may sound weird, but doing all these exercises was incredibly helpful because it made me get specific about what I wanted to manifest.

After I had written out my goals with Wendy and she explained to me about vision boards, she had me close my eyes and she asked me what my dream acting job would be. I said, "Working on a World

War II film directed by Steven Spielberg."

She asked, "Where is it shooting?"

I said, "In Paris."

She pushed on with, "Who is your co-star?"

I replied, "Gwyneth Paltrow."

She said, "Okay, so you're on set in Paris. What color is the sky?"

"Bright blue."

"What does the air feel like on your skin?"

"It's a balmy 60 degrees."

"Good," she said. "Now, what do your surroundings look like? What is Gwyneth Paltrow wearing? What color is her hair? What is the scene about?"

I answered her, creating this fictitious scene in my head, and all the while it started to feel as if I were really there!

Wendy then proceeded to say, "Steven says, 'Action!,' You're doing your scene with Gwyneth. Describe it to me." I did this in full detail.

She then said, "Stephen yells, 'Cut!' He walks over to you and Gwenyth, he puts his arms around both of you and says, 'Amazing work.' You and Gwenyth are smiling at each other because the film is complete and you know you made a beautiful movie. What does that feel like?" It was exhilarating! It was hard not to be completely swept up in the emotion of what I was imagining.

Wendy proceeded to then say, "Keep your eyes closed. Now encapsulate this whole scene you have created into a golden ball of light. Imagine this ball of light illuminating and emitting all the energy of the scene, and now, breathe that in through your nose. Breathe that into your body, down into your lungs. Breathe it down into your fingers, down into your legs, and all the way down into your toes. Breathe it into every single cell of your body so that every part of you experiences what it feels like being on set in Paris, working with Steven Spielberg and Gwyneth Paltrow."

For ten minutes, I just sat there breathing all of this in. It was incredible, and it completely changed my outlook and my perception as to why I wasn't booking anything. I realized I was focusing too much on nothing happening and not enough on what I wanted to bring more of into my life. I left there with a renewed sense of resolve.

I didn't really tell anyone about my going to see Wendy, but I was reading my declarations every day, before I went to bed and when I woke up every morning, and I started writing in a journal about things I was grateful for.

Within two weeks, I got a call from my agent saying that he had gotten me an audition. I went to pick up the script at my agency, went to a coffee shop, and started to read it. This may sound crazy but it was a World War II love story called *Beautiful Dreamer*. I flew through the script, started memorizing my lines, and went in the next morning for the audition. My agent called me later that day saying that they really like me for the part, and that I was one of three guys being considered for the role.

This was starting to get a little creepy, having just created this in my mind two weeks prior on a purple couch in a complete stranger's house, but I thought, "hey, if it means I get to act in this film, I'll take it"! My agent then let me know that I was scheduled to go back in a couple days and this time, I'd be doing a chemistry read with the main actress, Brooke Langton. It wasn't Gwyneth Paltrow, but she was cute and had a similar essence, and at this point I was just grateful to be going back in. It was a Friday when I went in for this chemistry audition and Brooke and I hit it off exceptionally well. We had a great read together and I was really excited about potentially getting this role.

I went home after the audition, feeling like the work Wendy and I had done together was really paying off. Unfortunately, a few hours later, I got a call from my agent saying that they had chosen one of the other guys for the role, but "they really liked me." Great consolation.

Through the weekend, I was disappointed. I was encouraged, however, with this "manifestation stuff" which seemed to be something I could actually start doing more of. So, I continued repeating my declarations and writing in my gratitude journal. This is where it gets even weirder. Monday comes around and I get a call from my agent, saying the actor that they had chosen for *Beautiful Dreamer* had just gotten word that he got hired on a Steven Spielberg film. He dropped out of *Beautiful Dreamer* and the producers wanted me to come back and read one more time with Brooke because they were considering another actor as well and wanted to compare the two of us.

I went back for that third time and decided the role was going to be mine. I did, however, walk in with a "take it or leave it" attitude. I knew I was this character regardless of whether the producers saw it or not. In my heart and in my gut, I was the guy.

A few hours after walking out of the audition, I got the call from my agent saying I had won the role. Who can really say if this was a coincidence or not? However, when you look at where I was two weeks before, sitting on Wendy's couch, manifesting a World War II love story directed by Steven Spielberg and that I was now about to start shooting a World War II love story with a Steven Spielberg component to it, it was all I needed to recognize the power of what Wendy shared with me… the power of manifestation.

THE SECRET ABOUT THE SECRET

"Anyone who doesn't believe in miracles is not a realist."
—Audrey Hepburn

When I met Wendy, she had also mentioned the book and movie *The Secret* to me. If you haven't seen or read it, I'd highly recommend doing so. The premise of *The Secret* is similar to what Wendy had me do in our session together. By changing one's perception from a negative mindset to a place of gratitude, you feed your subconscious the appropriate programming necessary to attract whatever it is you want to manifest in your life. I'd actually recommend watching the film over reading the book. Hearing first-hand accounts and testimonies from the numerous authors, meta-physicists, psychologists, and researchers about how this process works, in my opinion, is much more impactful.

I've heard many people scoff at the concept of *The Secret* and write it off as wishful thinking or some new age scam. What I've discovered is that their misconception is based on the belief that just by wishing for or having positive thoughts about something you want such as a million dollars, it will suddenly appear. What I think people miss is that to manifest something, you not only have to think it and believe it, you also, must really *feel* and *experience* it even before it has happened. It's when you put yourself into your dreams and continually take action toward manifesting them that they come true. It's about the combination of thought, feeling, *AND* action.

Had I not gone to acting classes and had I not gone to my agency to pick up the script for *Beautiful Dreamer* and had I not read it and gone in for the audition three different times to actually win the role, my dream of acting in a World War II film would not have been realized. By sitting down and taking the time to visualize what it was I wanted to create and feeling it down to the core of my being, I was more likely to take the actions necessary to make it happen.

One example of manifesting is to go test drive your dream car. By being up close and actually experiencing what it is you want, it becomes more real to you and less of a far-off idea. Open the door, get in the car, smell the leather, turn the engine on, take it for a test drive and feel the way it corners and hugs the road. By tapping into your primal senses and feeding your subconscious with the raw materials for what you want to manifest, the universe will naturally respond. Another example would be to wear a ring on your finger if your desire is to find a life partner, and create the feeling of what it means to you to be married.

Author Jack Canfield, a huge proponent of the Law of Attraction, made a cameo appearance in *The Secret* movie. Jack has written many books. Among his first was *Chicken Soup for the Soul*, written with Mark

Victor Hansen. In fact, they wound up writing an entire series of these books. In *The Secret,* he talked about how when he was in his late 20s, his mentor, W. Clement Stone, instructed him to set a goal that was so big and so unbelievable that if he achieved it, he would know that it was a result of following his program for success.

At the time, Jack was a schoolteacher, making about $8,000 per year. So he set a goal of making $100,000 in the next calendar year. To reinforce this to his subconscious mind, he took a $100 bill, and using a projection screen to make it bigger, traced it and added three zeroes so it looked like $100,000. When he was finished, the bill was two by three feet. He then taped it to the ceiling above his bed. Every morning when he woke up, the first thing he would see was that $100,000 bill. Understanding a lot about the Law of Attraction, he also would say several abundance and prosperity affirmations, then he would close his eyes and visualize living a $100,000 lifestyle, including his ideal car, house, and the charities to which he would contribute. He understood how crucial it was to *feel* the power of living his dream.

At that time, he was selling his first book (before *Chicken Soup*) and making about $2,000 a year from it. He was inspired to put an ad in the *National Enquirer*, and his sales shot through the roof. He also started charging more than he ever had for speaking engagements. To make a long story short, he didn't make $100,000 in the next year, but he came pretty darned close. He reports he made a little over $92,000—way more than he'd ever previously manifested. That's just one story that resonates with me about the power of the Law of Attraction and visualization. What is that you want to manifest? Try it!

His story, coupled with my own experience with *Beautiful Dreamer,* made me start to realize that life can be shaped towards what I want for it to be more than I had thought possible. Looking at it this way, you can begin to find an opening to be more of an artist, the creator of what you want for your life, and that you really do have the ability to "order" whatever you desire. If what you want is not on the menu, you really do have the ability to request a special order. The universe responds to the energy you resonate with. By deciding what you want in life and living that decision with passion and enthusiasm, you can truly be the artist that creates your own life, even if you didn't grow up thinking that way.

Manifestation is not, however, something that happens overnight. And so it's important not to let our daily survival routine get in the way of continually nurturing what it is that we want to manifest. The process of manifesting must be practiced every day. Whether it's journaling in the morning or, at night, before you go to bed, as I do, or having a vision board in view most of the day, or reading declarations of who you need to be into the mirror, it's got to be an integral part of your life. You must feed your mind and subconscious with visual, mental, and audio cues that inspire you. Every day it's essential to renew your conviction and gratitude that what you want is not a 'want,' but something already present in your life.

An analogy someone shared with me: this law is similar to a seed that you plant in the ground. If you keep watering it for a few weeks but still don't see anything, it's easy to give up and stop watering because you're not seeing any results. Little do you know that the seed was just on the brink of breaking through the dirt and blossoming when you stopped watering it. If you get discouraged and stop watering too soon, your dream will wither and die.

I'm a firm believer that if you commit to the process, you can create and manifest whatever it is that you want to have in your life. I have learned, and experienced first-hand, that by aligning the essence of who I am with who I need to be in order to manifest my dreams, that this process truly works. I'm excited to hear about what you manifest for yourselves!

HOW TO BE A TRANSPLANTED, UNABORTED FETUS

"Think left and think right and think low and think high. Oh,
the thinks you can think up if only you try."
– Dr. Seuss

After seeing Wendy and putting into practice what she taught me to do, things started happening that I can't explain. There was no explanation other than that these things were a result of the ideas I was focusing on and manifesting. One of the declarations I had written down with Wendy was, "I work on a major motion picture with A-list actors." After I finished shooting *Beautiful Dreamer*, out of the blue I got a phone call from my agent saying that the casting director for a film called *Must Love Dogs* starring Diane Lane and John Cusack wanted me to play a role in the film and I didn't even need to audition for it. It was a straight offer! The role was small, but it was something, and more importantly, I was starting to generate momentum by continually practicing looking at the world from a place of creative manifestation and gratitude.

Before I knew it, my agent sent me another audition for a role on the long-standing ABC soap opera *All My Children*. This was one of the most popular daytime shows on television at the time. It also happened to be my mom and my sister's favorite soap while I was growing up. I remember seeing the likes of Erika Kaine, Adam Chandler, and Tad Martin flitting around the TV in our living room while I was playing with my G.I. Joes and Matchbox cars. There were about eight other daytime shows on air at the time. The irony that the one I grew up with and had an emotional connection with was the very show "requesting me", was not at all lost on me at this point.

By now I was starting to feel more confident in my auditioning. I was actually beginning to go into my auditions with more of a sense of ownership than anxiety. Normally, I would find myself walking into auditions, signing in, and noticing the other ten guys in the waiting room who looked similar to me, including popular working actors who I had seen on TV and in films. Often times, I would get so intimidated that I was auditioning against much more experienced actors that I'd unwittingly allow my insecurities to sabotage my performance. A lot of the time, I was just grateful that I even got the audition—actually booking anything would have been a farfetched dream.

As I consistently practiced the attraction process, however, I began to feel more confident in my classes and auditions. I was beginning to recognize that my ability as an actor was becoming better and my talent, more refined. I attribute this to the fact that I had created the expectation for myself that "I am a working actor." It was as if my talent began to follow suit with the mindset I had created and, in turn, was manifesting daily. I felt the universe was meeting me in this space, and we were conspiring together to make magic happen. This is an incredibly exciting place to live your life from. It's one I work to recreate daily. As a result I started to look at my auditions less from a place of fear, nervousness, and intimidation, and more from a perspective of curiosity, excitement, and exploration. I was able to show the casting directors my particular take on the role without thinking or worrying about my competition.

I also was immersing myself in the lives of actors I admired. I read biographies of actors like Montgomery Clift, Paul Newman, and Robert De Niro. I'd consume magazine and TV interviews with actors I wanted to be like. I started to realize that their thought processes were very similar to mine in the beginning of their careers. It seemed they too had started to shift their mentality at a certain point when it came to auditioning. This made me realize that everyone starts somewhere and that anything worthwhile is a process and a journey. What I was also starting to recognize is that everyone has their own path and pace of progress and growth.

It was becoming evident to me, as well, that it does no good to compare yourself to anyone else. No two people are on identical paths.

Poet and writer William Blake once said, "I will not reason and compare: my business is to create." To further this point, twotime Academy Award–winning actress Hilary Swank, who was one of the producers on a film I did called *Something Borrowed*, writes, "We often find ourselves comparing, especially on social media. It's really impossible and fruitless to compare without knowing everyone's whole story. We are all on our own unique journey, each in a different place on that journey than any other…let's remember to keep our head in our own game, working towards our unique purpose."

Another quote I found years ago was from Sam Worthington, the lead actor in *Avatar*, who commented on auditioning "Me turning up to an audition is me saying, 'I'm interested.' You're not there going, 'I'm scared whether you're gonna give me the part or not.' You're there going, 'I'll dedicate myself to it. But what've you got? What am I gonna get out of this? Is this gonna be something that we can both grow from?' [At the *Avatar* audition] that was the best thing. I didn't really give a fuck whether I got the job or not."

Another one of my favorite actors is Anthony Hopkins. Hopkins won an Academy Award for his mesmerizing and powerful turn as Dr. Hannibal Lecter in Silence of the Lambs despite only being on screen for fifteen total minutes. He says similarly, "My philosophy is this: It's none of my business what people say of me and think of me. I am what I am and I do what I do. I expect nothing and accept everything. And it makes life so much easier." Reading as much as I could about how other actors had "made it" and learning how they dealt with the same issues and struggles that I found myself contending with helped immensely. It helped not just with my acting but with my mindset as a young person finding my way and learning to deal more effectively with other aspects of my life.

I guess one of the big reasons why I cherish acting so much is because the craft has forced me to contend with obstacles in my life I knew I wanted to overcome. I knew I was lacking in my ability to communicate or in possession of the wisdom to contend with certain life challenges. I wanted to learn to better communicate so I could connect on a deeper and more meaningful level both with my family and in relationships. I also didn't want to feel small and insignificant anymore. I desired to be able to confidently and wisely make a difference in other people's lives, to be of value and have purpose. With acting, I found a path towards all of this.

One of the most fulfilling things for me is to know that I have made someone feel better. I knew I had some growing to do as a person in order to do this at the level I desire to. I also want to be a great husband and father someday, and I knew I needed to learn more about responsibility and to deal more effectively with adversity to do so. Acting, for me, has been the playing field and the practice court for my development, both as an actor and as a person. Regardless of whether or not I ever win an Academy Award, I know in my heart that, through it, I have gained much more in terms of my personal growth.

All of this is possible for you as well, but it takes leaving your comfort zone and taking some risks. You're going to fail and look stupid sometimes, but by putting yourself out there and daring yourself to overcome shortfalls, eventually you will hit the benchmark you seek and reap amazing rewards.

As such, when I got the call from my agent that the producers of *All My Children* were interested in doing a screen test, I was elated and at the same time, I had this sense of calm and ease, knowing in my heart that the role was mine. It was as if I had already booked the role without even having screen tested. This is the place from which I've realized you can be unstoppable. It's a place where intuition and confidence and gratitude start to emerge within the depths of your being. That place, that calm comes as a result of an immense amount of hard work coupled with an immense amount of faith and trust in something that is beyond what we know exists in our physical bodies.

At this point in my career, I had been studying acting for seven years. My hours of experience in acting classes and auditions were now finally melding with my newly discovered ability to tap into the world of manifestation, or what I also like to call the world of miracles.

This led me to feel that every aspect of my being was being pulled in the direction of *All My Children*. They were offering me a three-year contract to move back to New York and be a principal actor on the show, meaning I would be one of the leads. I was very excited about the offer on both accounts. My agent, Larry, however, told me he felt the amount of money they were offering me was not commensurate, in his opinion, with what they should be. I didn't know any soap actors at the time, but I did know a ballpark range of what an average soap actor makes, which was not bad at all. However, compared to the prime-time television and feature film work that my agent felt I was very close to booking, the pay was not nearly as high.

Larry laid out what he thought we should do. Because he was highly respected in the industry and I really liked and trusted him, when he said he felt I shouldn't do the role for less than a certain number, I was again faced with a hard decision—take the advice of an experienced professional or listen to my instincts. Stay where I was or heed the fireworks going off inside me, take the damn role, and get my ass back to New York, pronto.

This is where I realized there are several different factors required to create a successful acting career and, for that matter, similar career paths. There are the artistic and technique-related aspects, such as learning to become proficient enough to work on a professional Screen Actors Guild project. There are the business and career components, including all the politics. Publicity and marketing are next, which involves needing to stay relevant, not only in the public eye, but also in the eyes of all the casting directors, directors, producers, and studio heads. And lastly, there's the networking and relationship side of the business. The most successful actors in the business, the ones who have created longevity for themselves and consistently work, have mastered all four of these.

At this point in my career, I was starting to get my sea legs when it came to acting techniques and booking jobs. I was networking quite a bit at industry functions and parties, and new that once I began working, I would learn to do publicity and interviews. However, the business and career perspective of acting was something I had no real clue about. In other words, how does one construct a successful acting career and end up on the A list. As such, I relied heavily on my representatives for advice as to what they felt was the best course of action to take.

I had also had a manager at the time and he concurred with Larry. These two experienced representatives who I felt had my best interest at heart advised me to stand firm at the number my agent thought the producers of *AMC* should come up to in order for us to say yes. As much as I wanted to trust my reps, I began to get that feeling, again, that the direction we were heading in was against my intuition. For me it wasn't about the money so much as it was about the opportunity to do something that seemed incredibly exciting. I waited for a couple days. The casting director even called me directly, trying to convince me to do the show for the amount of money they were offering. This is wholly unconventional in the entertainment industry, but because I had decided to listen to the voices of "authority," I didn't budge. And...neither did the producers.

I wasn't surprised when my agent called to let me know they had passed on me. As confident as he was that I was going to book something bigger and better, I couldn't help but be disappointed knowing I had just let a tremendous opportunity go. Not only had I said no to something I was excited about, but also, and probably even more so, I was disappointed because I felt I let myself down by not listening to and heeding my intuition. Again. I had ignored my instincts. By doing so, I had ignored myself, when what we should always be doing is honoring ourselves. This is, ironically, one of the first pieces of advice I got from my first acting teacher, and one of my greatest mentors, Jacqueline Segal.

This experience shook me quite a bit and made me realize how profound a life-altering decision can be and what the consequences, regardless of the outcome, could be. I even called my agent back a couple days later to ask if they had booked the role yet. He informed me they had. It was time to just move on.

The only thing I could do was to go back to acting class, keep rehearsing, and keep trying to manifest. If you fall off the horse, the only thing to do is get back on, right? So, I jumped back into my daily routine of classes, rehearsals, and auditions, and a couple months later the *AMC* experience was over and in my rear view mirror. Or so I thought.

It was now July 2005, two months after the whole *AMC* decision. I remember getting a call in the morning from my agent saying the producers of *All My Children* had just contacted him again. He relayed that they didn't like the actor they hired to play the role I auditioned for and they wanted to fly me to New York for the screen test to replace him. I was dumbfounded and ecstatic. I told my agent to negotiate whatever amount of money he felt they would come up to without losing the deal. Luckily, I had a second chance to decide on a major life change—something one rarely gets the opportunity to do. To me, this was another sign that it was my role and that the acting gods were conspiring to make this happen because it was what I had manifested!

A couple of days later, I was on a flight to New York. I just kept thinking in my head, *this is my role and no one else's*. I felt it was a done deal before I even stepped on the set, I was that confident. Don't get me wrong - I was still nervous. There was still no contract or assurances that they were going to hire me because I still had to show up and perform for them. What I knew I had on my side, though, was the feeling that the role was already mine.

There have only been a handful of times I've been that confident about things in my life. They haven't always worked out but, the one thing I do know is that I never would have stood a chance at making any of these things happen if I didn't at least walk into these situations with a high degree of confidence. From what I've learned, decision-making comes down to two important ingredients: preparation and then taking action. There is no way you can do anything without having enough reasons and leverage to take action. Secondly, by writing in your calendar the action that you intend to take, you actually make it real. I had prepared for this moment for seven years. All my acting training, my manifesting practices, it all came together in that moment. I had a high level of confidence and then I took the action regardless of how I was feeling or what the outcome would be. I could do this because I had put this in my calendar: *I book the role of Josh Madden on AMC.* It was my time to go to that screen test and make it happen.

It was a warm and balmy Friday morning as the bright yellow taxi I was riding in pulled up to the corner of 66th Street and West End Avenue on the Upper West Side of Manhattan. As I got out of the cab, I just stood on the sidewalk looking up at the ABC Studios logo for a few seconds, and a rush of excitement started to set in.

There was also a huge line outside waiting to get in to see a taping of *The View*, which I came to learn filmed right across the hall from *AMC*. I made my way through the throng of people to the front security desk, showed my ID, and was told to go to the third floor and that someone would be waiting for me. Walking down the hall, I had this sense that I was in my new home. It just felt right and it was my job now to just go do what I knew I could.

I was greeted by the casting director, Judy Blye Wilson, an incredibly sweet and warm woman, who immediately made me feel welcome. She escorted me to the soundstage where I was introduced to a very talented and beautiful actress named Connie Fletcher. Of course, whenever you turn on a soap opera, there are good looking people abound, but now I was there in the real Pine Valley, meeting them in person. All I could think was, *Let's do this!*

We had to act one scene on the soundstage with all four cameras to simulate an actual taping. This was new to me because when filming a movie or a primetime television show, there are usually only one or two cameras being used to film a scene. On a film or regular TV show, the shot order is usually a wide master shot of the scene, then they move in for some medium shots, then close-ups, and sometimes they'll want to come in even tighter for an extreme close up, if it's an exceptionally emotional scene.

Before each set up, the lighting has to be adjusted accordingly. That can take anywhere from a few minutes to a few hours, so there's a lot of down time and waiting on sets for the new setup to be ready. In addition to the particular aspect of the shot, when filming close-ups, the cameras will be set up for each one of the actors at a time. Once they complete one actor's close-up, then the cameras and lighting have to be moved to the complete other side of the set to get the other actor's close-up.

This whole process can take hours. This is one of the main reasons that a one-hour primetime show takes about 7 twelve-hour days to film. A normal, hour-long television show is really about 43 minutes of actual show time and 17 minutes of commercials (for half-hour shows, it's 21 and 9 minutes). An hour long script is usually about 50 to 65 pages, which means that each day, about 7 to 9 pages are filmed.

As far as movies go, a normal film script is about 80 to 120 pages in length, where each page generally equates to about a minute of on-screen time. Most independent films, because of tight budgets in the range of $15,000 to $500,000, will try to film in two to four weeks.

This means that each day, about 7 to 12 pages are filmed. In contrast, the major studio blockbuster films such as the superhero films and fantasies such as *Batman,* the Marvel films, *Lord of the Rings,* and *Transformers,* whose budgets are upward of $200 to $300 million, can take over a year to film because they shoot around onethird of a page a day due to the complexity and amount of coverage being shot. Daytime TV is a whole other beast. It's almost insane what the producers of daytime are able to do in a day because a onehour episode of daytime (43 minutes) is filmed in one twelve-hour day. That's 60 to 80 pages *every day.*

To be able to shoot this much material, four cameras roll at once with all aspects shot at the same time. This means the master wide shots, the medium shots, and the close-ups are all shot in one take. Most of the time each scene is shot in one or two takes. Primetime TV and films will have three to seven takes on average. David Fincher (*Fight Club, Social Network*) and the late Stanley Kubrick (*Eyes Wide Shut, 2001: A Space Odyssey*) are known to have done as many as one hundred takes for one scene. The single opening scene of *The Social Network* for example, in which Rooney Mara's character breaks up with Jesse Eisenberg's in the bar, was shot over a day and a half and consisted of ninety-nine takes.

Because of the speed at which soap operas film, the producers need to make sure that the actors they hire are not only believable in their roles, but are also capable of memorizing 10 to 20 pages of material every day. Each scene is about 5 to 10 minutes long, and in an hour-long soap such as *AMC,* each actor is in about four to five scenes. The scenes are shot back to back, so you have to have all your lines memorized for each scene and be ready to shoot for about an hour to two hours straight.

For an actor who has never done this before, it can be incredibly intimidating and nerve-wracking, to say the least.

Once I got exposed to this process and the amount of content produced and put on air so quickly, I gained a huge appreciation for the actors and everyone involved with making it all happen. I don't think daytime actors get the type of recognition they deserve for the amount of skill they have and what they do on a daily basis. Daytime actors are some of the most talented and hard-working actors in the business. This level of work was something I was about to get my first taste of.

When I was brought to the set, I was incredibly excited to finally see the real Pine Valley that I had grown up watching on my TV at home. Connie was exceptionally sweet and made me feel completely comfortable, which helped make the process as fun and exciting as it was. I put my whole heart and soul into that screen test. I made every effort to connect with Connie, to truly listen to what she said, to let it affect me and simply go on the journey with her.

In the scene, I had to be all the aspects of what you know soap characters to be. I was trying to convince Connie's character to be with mine because I was in love with her even though she was in love with someone else. I had to be charming, seductive, playful, honest, vulnerable, and in the end, disappointed that she decided not to be with me.

I just remember being on that sound stage, moving around in the blocking they had shown us and feeling like I owned it. It was amazing! Connie's and my energy felt like it expanded from us all the way up to the control booth on the floor upstairs where the director and producers were watching.

The screen test only lasted about twenty minutes, but it seemed like time didn't even matter.

Afterward, I thanked Connie and everyone else and said goodbye. I flew back to LA and one week later, I got the call confirming I had booked the job. This is one of the few times in one's acting career where the feeling of excitement and gratitude is unparalleled; it's simply the best feeling in the world!

SOMETIMES YOU'RE NOT WHO YOU THINK YOU ARE

"Don't think. Thinking is the enemy of creativity. It's self-conscious, and anything self-conscious is lousy. You can't try to do things. You simply must do things." —Ray Bradbury

I packed up my stuff at my apartment on Genesee Avenue, between Melrose and Beverly, and had a moving company load it all up and drive it to New York. My brother, Sean, flew out to LA, and we decided to road trip together to Chicago, where I would drop off my car and fly to New York a few days later. I was thirty-two years old and in many ways, I felt like my life was just starting because I had been waiting for this moment for eight years. It had been almost a decade since I started my first acting class in New York with Jackie, and now I was finally seeing my hard work starting to pay off.

I had finally booked my first real, consistently paying acting job. I couldn't have been more excited. Showing up on set for my first day of work was one of the most thrilling days of my life. I was now on set with Susan Lucci, "The Erika Kaine" and "The Queen of Daytime." This was the woman whom I had grown up watching in my living room since I was a kid, and now I was acting with her. Everyone was very welcoming, including Susan, who is one of the sweetest and hardest working actors I've ever had the pleasure of working with. I couldn't have been happier knowing this was going to be my home for at least the next three years.

When I got hired, they didn't really say much about the character I would be playing. It didn't matter because on my first day of shooting, I got to punch a guy out who had tried to molest one of my good friends which, in my opinion, was a great way to make an entrance onto daytime. Before I knew it, I was the producer of Erika Kaine's talk show, and shortly after getting hired to do that, I ended up trying to poison her so that I could take over her talk show. She found out about it and fired me, but that was fine because shortly thereafter, I discovered that I was a doctor, having gone to medical school like my father, Dr. Greg Madden, played by the incredibly talented and versatile Ian Buchanan.

Thus, I then played a doctor for a while until I found out that my real mother was indeed Erika Kaine. That's right, I was Erika's son! Hold on though, not just a normal son! Let me now take you inside the incredible world that is soap opera:

Oh my God! I'm the son of the Queen of Daytime, and she didn't even know she had a son! But wait! I also learned that my dad was secretly in love with her thirty years prior when she came to him to have an abortion, but instead of performing an abortion, he stole me (as a fetus) out of Erika and implanted me into his own wife. As a result, I was born to Dr. Madden and his wife. For years I thought they were my real parents, but in actuality, Erika was my biological mother. She found out about this later, of course, after Dr. Madden had been buried underground by Tad Martin.

Apparently, Tad was trying to get Dr. Madden to tell him the whereabouts of the daughter who Tad had given up for adoption. Dr. Madden had helped facilitate the adoption, but because Dr. Madden had made an oath agreeing to never let anyone know who had adopted baby Kate to protect the adoptive parents, Dr. Madden was left to die underground. Of course, Tad was not going to let him die and was only trying to scare Dr. Madden into revealing the whereabouts of baby Kate, but wouldn't you know it, there was an earthquake in Pine Valley and the underground box that Dr. Madden was buried in caved in near where I was playing basketball. When I heard the screams of a girl, I ran to see what was the matter. I arrived to see a man's hand sticking out of the ground with what looked like my dad's watch.

As I dug him out under the glare and sounds of fireworks because it was the Fourth of July, I began to sob uncontrollably, sinking quickly into a profound depression. In the midst of my grief, I went to the local bar and club where all the cool people in Pine Valley hang out at, and, over the loudspeaker, the voice of my dad— or Dr. Madden, who I *thought* was my real dad—came on. Because he thought he was going to die in this underground box, he revealed that he was not my real dad, but that Erika was my real mother.

Erika knew about this and hadn't told me. I was mad about that and ran out and kidnapped JR Chandler's wife, Babe, who I was in love with, and stole my dad's private jet. When we were flying over the Bahamas, the plane ran out of gas and we crash-landed and woke up on a deserted island with our clothes almost completely burned off. We had to huddle together to keep warm on the beach that they had created in the sound stages of *AMC*, which was really impressive complete with papier mache mountains and a waterfall.

This created the setting for Babe and I to start falling in love. But love was not to be, as Babe was rescued by her husband, JR, and so, sadly, my dreams of being with Babe were *dashed.* In the midst of my heartache, I decided to become the marketing director of a cosmetics company. Then, when we were all at a Mardi Gras ball and "Janet from Another Planet" decided to blow up the venue, Erika and I got trapped in a small, caved-in section of the building.

But I was able to save her life using a pocket knife and a straw because she had a pneumatic embolism that needed to be relieved. Even though I hated her, I did what I needed to do to save her. Then once we were rescued, she tried to make amends with me. But I was still angry, so I went around Pine Valley being angsty and mad. During that time, I also tried to hook up with Greenlee. While trying to figure out why her name was Greenlee, I got tired of trying to chase an unavailable woman, once again. Additionally, being the marketing director of a cosmetics company was no longer doing it for me, so I became the manager of my brother-in-law Zach's casino until I got tied up at gunpoint and mixed up with another crazy lady.

My character apparently was attracted to crazy, unavailable women.

Did you get all that?

Toward the end of my contract with *AMC*, one day while I was walking down the street in Soho, our executive producer called and asked me how I was doing. I replied, "Hey Julie, I'm good! How are you?" She said she was doing fine and then shared with me that they were going to be *killing my character off* in a couple of weeks. I stopped in the middle of the street and just stood there as she relayed to me how they were going to do it.

This was it. The end. I knew it was going to come at some point, but I guess I wasn't really ready for the reality of it. I did my best to finish the call with Julie without sounding too distraught with this news, but inside, I was starting to feel unsettled and sad, which I truly didn't expect. It took me some time to begin to accept the fact that the job that I had for the past three years was about to end, but as they say in show business, the show must go on. I did my best to adopt this motto and look forward. So, to wrap up Josh Madden's tenure on the show, the writers decided:

Because I was feeling like an outcast and an unaborted fetus, I figured I'd steal twenty million dollars from Zach's casino and take my lesbian sister Bianca's girlfriend hostage. But Zach wasn't having any of that, so he shot me.. As I lay on the floor with a bullet in my head, I got to say goodbye to Erika and tell her I loved her. I wasn't actually dead though, just brain dead, so they brought me to the hospital, and wouldn't you know it, there was another earthquake in Pine Valley. Or maybe it was a hurricane. I couldn't remember. My other sister, Kendall, got caught in her house when it collapsed. She was also dying of heart failure. They brought her into the hospital. Then later, as we were lying side by side, Erika walked in, and the doctor mentioned to her that there was a chance to save Kendall by transplanting my heart into her, which they did, then I really died...but Kendall lived on. Oh, and I did come back, as a ghost, for one episode...and that was my last day on *AMC. Phew!*

OLD ENDINGS, NEW BEGINNINGS

"If you want a happy ending, that depends of course, on where you end your story." —Orson Welles

It was bittersweet filming that last day on *AMC*. I was happy that I was able to conclude my three-year stint by shooting my last scene with Susan Lucci, who was as sweet and gracious and loving as any real mom could be. I'm not going to lie, it was a struggle to hold back some tears because I was genuinely sad to be leaving what I considered my family. That's one of the very difficult parts of acting, or any transient job for that matter, in that you work closely and intensely with these people day in and day out for years, and then for the most part, they are gone. For all the great and fulfilling things that living the life of an actor can provide, there are several aspects that make it incredibly difficult. Saying goodbye is one of them.

Not only was I going to miss my "family," but for the first time in three years, I was going to be unemployed. I was thirty-five years old and had moved to New York for this job, one that I hoped was going to last much longer than three years. Now I found myself without work and with a healthy case of anxiety about deciding what to do next. As an actor, I have found myself in these situations several times during my career. I've come to realize there are always going to be situations in life where we can feel helpless because we don't know what our next step is going to be. It's very easy to get stuck in this place of fear and anxiety when we focus and obsess about the unknown and our lack of control. What I've always tried to do in these situations is to refocus both my attention and actions on the things I can control, which in this case was doing whatever I could to book my next acting job.

My final scene with Susan involved our characters saying goodbye to each other, so it was a nice and rather fitting way to end my time there. When we finished the scene, we gave each other the biggest hug. I thanked her for all her love and support over the past three years, and she wished me the best on my journey forward.

At the conclusion of our scene, the studio broke for lunch. After Susan and I said our goodbyes and I said my farewell to some of the other cast and crew members, I found myself alone on the set and able to just take it all in one more time. I stood there and relished in all the great memories that I had been fortunate enough to create in that space and with so many amazing people. It was hard not to hold back feelings of sadness and for a few minutes, I just stood there and reminisced, knowing that this was the last time I'd probably see this set and most of the folks who I had become so close to.

After a few minutes, I don't know if it was the acting gods or the universe giving me a sign, a crew member strolled onto the empty set where I was standing and mentioned to me that my brother was next door over at *The View*. I thought, my brother? My brother was living in Chicago, so I was confused at first by what he was talking about. Curiously, I walked across the hall to *The View* soundstage to see none other than the guy I get compared to five times a day: Tom Cruise. One of my all-time favorite actors, Tom, was promoting his latest film and was just wrapping up his interview. What was remarkable about him was that you could easily tell he had star quality. After his interview, he stepped off the stage to meet members of the audience who had come to see the taping. He quickly became surrounded by people, and as I stood there and watched, he signed autographs and took pictures for about twenty minutes with every single person who asked him to.

After he was finished with the last photo, I walked up to him and introduced myself. He was wearing that famous Tom Cruise grin and with an intense but personable expression, looked me in the eye and said, "It's great to meet you, Colin." I told him I was an actor across the hall at *All My Children,* and that today was my last day. I then thanked him for being such a huge inspiration to me for wanting to become an actor.

He politely said "thank you" and asked if I'd like to take a picture together. Are you kidding? Hell yeah! Afterward, I told him I was probably going to be heading back out to Los Angeles to keep pursuing my acting career, to which he responded by wishing me the best of luck. Even though it was a brief exchange, it was a special and uplifting moment that I definitely appreciated at this downward turn in my career, one that helped me move on with hope even though I had no idea what would happen next.

Three Take Away Action Tips:

1. When you find yourself doubting your choices, ask yourself empowering questions to change your perspective and give you leverage. For example: "What is one thing I can do to feel better today?" and "What would it look like if what is not currently working would start working for me?"

2. Don't get stuck worrying about the things you can't control. Focus on the things you know you can impact: your *attitude* and your *effort.*

3. Focus daily—hourly, even—on what you know in your heart to be what you want to manifest in your life. Do the work to feel confident about it. Write down your dreams in your calendar to make them real. As Walt Disney, one of the best dreamers ever, once said, "If you can dream it, you can do it."

EVERYONE IS AN ARTIST

*"Every child is an artist. The problem is how to remain
an artist once he (or she) grows up."*
— Pablo Picasso

rt can move you, it can humble you, it can leave you in awe.

On a primal level, it is the way in which we as human beings communicate and express who we are. Whether we're aware of it or not, art (in any form, whether it be a painting, a movie, or architecture) is important because it's the medium through which we are able to connect to something that is grander than ourselves. Ultimately, art allows us to discover and communicate to others who we know ourselves to be. Artistry also frees us from linear thinking. When we're free to think in any and all directions, our own creativity is able to kick in and offer solutions to problems in unique and unpredictable ways. Too often we think problems can only be solved by focusing brute, analytical brain power on the problem. We fail to appreciate the power of the creative within.

We may identify as a doctor, a mother, an actor, or a businessman, but on a more spiritual level, art is our connection to and the purest expression of who we are. That's why when we see good art, it acts as the conduit into the world of myth, into a spiritual realm beyond our normal, benign existence. It takes us to a place subconsciously where we feel connected to source, the universe, God, or whatever you may refer to this force as. It is this connection that makes us feel whole and complete. Whether we realize it or not, *this is vital to our existence as human beings!*

A lot of us may say we can identify art and appreciate it when we see it or hear it, but as we get older, few people would say that they are indeed artists. This is a complete departure from when we were kids. Kids have a natural proclivity to use pretty much any medium they can get their hands on to create, whether that medium is finger paint, markers, or spaghetti sauce. To kids, art and creativity come as naturally to them as breathing. So what happens as we get older?

Edward Boches, a professor of advertising at Boston University's College of Communication who teaches a course called "Fundamentals of Creative Development," writes that at the beginning of each new semester, on the first day of class, he poses this question to his new college students: "Do you think of yourself as creative?" He says on average, only half the class raises their hands. If we were so inclined to "express or apply our human creative skill and imagination" when we were kids, what makes only half of us as adults feel like we still are connected with that aspect of ourselves?

WHERE DID OUR CREATIVITY GO?

"To be an actor, you have to be a child."
– Paul Newman

A favorite author and speaker of mine named Ken Robinson gave a great TED talk about how kids, even if they don't know the answer to something, "will at least take a chance and give it a go." He went on to say that "they are not frightened of being wrong." He follows it up by adding that if you're not prepared to be wrong, you will never come up with anything original.

By the time kids become adults, most of them have lost this capacity to be wrong. What Robinson talks about resonates with me because growing up, I was incredibly sensitive to being wrong and looking stupid. Where this begins and how it originates varies from person to person and culture to culture, but many, including

Robinson, say it starts in school. The outdated industrial age paradigm of education where children sit in organized rows, working individually to figure things out for themselves, moving from class to class at the sound of a bell, competing with each other in math, reading, and science to get the best letter grades, can severely hinder their ability to discover and nurture what they're best suited for in life. It can also inadvertently cause anxiety and long-term psychological issues.

For the most part, structured learning in today's school systems is not at all conducive to supporting individual identities. Kids in these environments can often feel less than competent if they don't measure up to others in their classes.

I fell into this trap myself, and many times felt as if there were something wrong with me. Some may argue that we, as a culture, have become too soft on kids these days, because everyone seems to get a trophy and is acknowledged as a winner. In my opinion, it's not about being a winner or a loser nor is it about being the smartest or the best.

I believe we, collectively, are out of touch with our basic human need to feel connected to who we know our true selves to be, and to nurture that same feeling in others and be accepting of it. In other words, we are hung up with trying to make ourselves and others 'fit in.' We have lost our ability to confidently express and share ourselves through creativity because it has been systematically educated out of us.

Not everyone is born the same, but we, as a society, unrealistically expect everyone to measure up to the same standards. In the process, we are creating generations of people who have lost touch with their authentic selves, whom they once knew themselves to be. This often causes us to pursue both careers and relationships that end up broken and disappointing simply because it was never what we, in our hearts and spirits, wanted to do in the first place. It's what we thought we were 'supposed to do.' The amount of pressure we place not only on our kids but, also on ourselves, to be perfect is insane. It's no wonder there are so many depressed, medicated people, not just in America, but around the world. The evidence is staring us in the face. What we expect of ourselves and others is unrealistic and it's making us feel that it's wrong for us to be our authentic selves.

I'm not a field expert in either education or psychology, nor do I claim to have all of the answers. What I do know, however, is that in today's day and age, where people change jobs more frequently than ever, creativity and the ability to be agile have become more important than ever. As such, it's important that both kids and adults alike be prepared for the way 'real world' exists today. Exposure to different ways of thinking and doing will help accomplish that.

There are schools that are taking more innovative approaches to learning, such as those that follow the Montessori method. Here, students are not separated by grade or age, and are allowed to choose their focus of study from a collection of options and learn together in small groups. This teaching style tends to lend itself as a better fit for a lot of kids. The bottom line is, one size does not fit all. From my volunteer work reading to kids in elementary schools and speaking with lots of teachers and principals, as well as my own experience as a student, the most effective teaching method is the one that fits the individual. The most powerful way to keep kids engaged and motivated is to recognize and cultivate kids' individual needs and strengths.

Because a lot of kids don't necessarily know what they want to do with their lives, it's important they are provided with opportunities to explore their interests. They must then be supported in learning the tools required to create the mindset that is necessary to turn ideas into reality. Some kids really enjoy mathematics, and that inspires them. Others really enjoy biology and looking at slides. Still others love being onstage, acting, singing, and/or dancing. No matter what their passions or interests are, they should be supported in what they love most.

Robinson tells the story about Gillian Lynne, a famous choreographer who rose to prominence for her choreography of the musicals *Cats* and *Phantom of the Opera*. When Gillian was eight years old, her teachers wrote to her parents saying that they thought Gillian had a learning disorder because, they said, she couldn't concentrate, was fidgeting all the time, and was disrupting the other students. Today, she would have probably been diagnosed with ADHD. This was the 1930s, however, and ADHD and many other psychological labels had yet to be identified, so Gillian's mother brought her to a doctor to find a cure for her condition.

After Gillian's mother spoke at length with the doctor about her daughter's issues, the doctor told Gillian he needed to speak with her mother privately. He said they were going to leave the room for a few minutes. Before they left, however, the doctor turned some music on the radio that was sitting on his desk.

After they left the room, the doctor told Gillian's mom to watch her daughter. When they looked back into the room, Gillian was dancing to the music. The doctor turned and said, "Mrs. Lynne, your daughter isn't sick. She's a dancer. Take her to a dance school."

Fortunately, Mrs. Lynne did just that. Gillian describes how wonderful it was when she arrived at the dance school and was amazed to see so many kids just like her—kids who had to move to think. Gillian went on to the Royal Ballet School, became a member of the Royal Ballet, went on to form her own dance company, and ended up working with Andrew Lloyd Webber, being responsible for some of the most successful musical runs in history and becoming a multimillionaire.

Robinson finalizes his point by saying, "Somebody else may have put her on medication and told her to calm down."

How many kids nowadays are facing the same situation? It reminds me of the quote by Einstein, "If you judge a fish by its ability to climb a tree, it will spend its entire life believing it's stupid."

How many kids are we prescribing medication for and labeling stupid for the wrong reasons?

FINDING YOUR "SELF"

"It's better to be hated for who you are than to be loved for someone you're not. It's a sign of your worth sometimes, if you're hated by the right people."
– Bette Davis

My mom says that when I was a kid, I didn't start speaking until the age of four. I'm not sure if she or my dad were ever seriously concerned that perhaps I had fallen off my Big Wheel one too many times, or if they just thought I was naturally a bit slow. Considering my two siblings were unabashedly vocal, they may have wondered why I was so quiet. I remember always sitting there in awe of how Kerry and Sean could make a compelling case for why they deserved more Fruit Loops or why an eleventh Cabbage Patch Kid needed to be adopted into the Egglesfield household.

It was frustrating, watching them give my parents a run for their money (especially since my brother is four years younger than me). Realizing that I didn't possess the same verbal dexterity to articulate what I was trying to say and how to truly express myself was even more frustrating. What I was good at, however, was being able to harness these same feelings and emotions and use them to create. For as long as I can remember, nothing has fulfilled me more than the process of creation, of putting things together in different and random ways. Being able to create something that gave others a glimmer of inspiration, or reminded them of who they truly are, or that something meant more to them on a deeper, subconscious level than they realized, energized me.

For lack of a better description, it's almost as if my soul has the truest experience of its own self when I'm creating, which, I think, is the most satisfying experience one can have.

Growing up I would regularly lock myself in my bedroom, spending hours on end building model airplanes, assembling Lego spaceships, and drawing pictures of sports cars and the Millennium Falcon—things that made me use my imagination. This in turn transported me to exciting new worlds. I felt more closely connected to these imaginary worlds than to the real world. The real world was the place I very often struggled to fit in to. This was especially magnified by living with a hyperactive little brother who seemed to have invented *Punk'd* twenty-some-odd years before Ashton Kutcher did.

Secluded up in my private little nook, I felt safe to tap into the random impulses that would come to me. Because I had eliminated distractions and judgments, which allowed my mind the freedom to explore, my creativity blossomed. In other words, at a very early age (even though I wasn't necessarily conscious of it then) you could say that I made it a priority to create the space for creativity to grow and develop. As I've gotten older and the demands of the day tend to creep in and take over my life, what I have continued to maintain is my priority for allowing myself to create. I have always had this insatiable desire to do so.

Like most students around the world, though, I didn't learn at school that art was a priority. For better or worse, the message I received was that it was important to get good grades in math, reading, and science, to continue on with schooling, and to eventually get a "decent job." I remember plenty of people commenting that they liked what I had drawn or created in my art classes, but no one ever mentioned that I should professionally pursue my affinity for creating.

The idea of being an artist or creating for a living was never seriously supported. Since I didn't know any professional artists, actors, or creative types, I simply wrote creativity off as something that was nice to do as a hobby, but not a viable means to make a real living. I dismissed it somewhere during my teenage years, even though it was the very thing that inspired me and made me feel fulfilled on the deepest levels. As much as I loved being an artist, I never truly felt there was a way to make a sustainable living doing just that.

Once I got to college, armed with a "responsible" mindset, I thought the "good boy" thing to do was pick a major that seemed safe in order to get to get a job after I graduated. So I found myself choosing engineering as my field of study. My thinking was that it might allow me to have some sort of creative outlet; perhaps I might learn how to design something. After a few semesters...well, to put it bluntly, it sucked. Not just because I was terrible at it or found it exceptionally uninspiring trying to solve for the coefficient of friction. It just sucked altogether.

I remember sitting in Dr. Jaggi's Physics 101 class with an omnipresent pit in my stomach as he and his star pupils gleefully waxed poetic about the polarity of light and centrifugal forces. All the while they were geeking out doing experiments with magnets, I'd find myself drawing cityscapes and sports cars in my Trapper Keeper.

After my sophomore year and two years of angst and frustration with a field of study I couldn't see myself working in for the rest of my life, I started to entertain the idea of following in my father's footsteps to become a physician. Being able to help people seemed like a good reason to pursue a career in medicine, so by reason of default more than anything, I decided to change majors to biology/pre-med. Since it was required to take electives in addition to my biology classes, I signed up for an art class, mainly because I had to. At least now, if I had to suffer through organic chemistry lab, I had something to look forward to in between my "real" classes.

Looking back, I can say there was definitely a difference between the students in my art classes and those in my others. The students in my art classes, especially the ones who were art majors, for the most part, dressed differently, wore their hair differently, and seemed to have an overall disregard for what the latest trends in fashion were and the need to fit in.

There was something very authentic and unique about how they seemed to be able to express themselves in a way that didn't appear to be filtered or tainted by what society dictated as cool or acceptable. There I was in my Ralph Lauren button down, J. Crew pants, and trendy Caesar haircut (a la George Clooney circa his ER days) sitting in my life drawing class. I remember staring at a naked, sixty-year-old lady-model, surrounded by my fellow creatives, a couple of whom looked borderline homeless. This only further cemented my false belief that if you wanted to be an artist, you had to commit to a life of humble means and forgo having a "normal" lifestyle and being able to provide for a family.

As haphazard as some of the artists in my classes looked, I had feelings of admiration for them. I'm not sure where this thought came from, but in my ignorance, I also felt a sort of pity. I couldn't help envisioning the life of an artist as someone living in their parents' basement well into their forties, waiting tables and occasionally trying to sell a picture of a cat they had painted at a local coffee shop just to make ends meet. I couldn't help but draw comparisons to famous artists who I had read about and studied, who struggled mightily during their careers in pursuit of their life's passion. It's crazy and ironic to think that Van Gogh's *Irises* sold for $54 million in 1987, but that during his lifetime, he was mostly broke, dealing with mental illness, and like a lot of his contemporaries, looked down upon as a misfit of society.

Similarly, Rembrandt was generally considered one of the greatest painters and printmakers in European art, and among the most important in Dutch history. Unfortunately, his life was fraught with tragedy. After his wife died and his friends deserted him, he was pushed into bankruptcy and unable to find any more work. He died in obscurity and poverty in 1669.

Paul Cézanne's father encouraged him to be a lawyer or banker, like himself, but Cézanne saw himself instead as a famous painter, like so many other bohemians living in Paris. Receiving some of the harshest criticism of the Impressionists of the time, he left most of his works unfinished and supposedly destroyed others before he died of pneumonia in 1906. Little did he know that his posthumous success would see his painting *The Card Players* bought by the State of Qatar in 2011 for $259,000,000, which at the time, was the most expensive painting ever sold.

Anyone who has seen the film *Ferris Bueller's Day Off* will remember George Seurat's painting from when Ferris, Sloane, and Cameron go to the Chicago Institute of Art. While Ferris and Sloane have stolen themselves away for a romantic moment in front of the Marc Chagall stained glass windows, Cameron is seen staring at Seurat's *A Sunday Afternoon on the Island of La Grande Jatte,* where Parisians are lazing on the banks of the River Seine, women with parasols and men in top hats. This is Seurat's most famous work and is a leading example of the pointillist technique that he was a master at. He utilized only the tip of the paintbrush to apply dots of paint on the canvas. This painting has become so iconic that the original, currently hanging in the Art Institute of Chicago, has an estimated value of $100 million. In late-nineteenth-century France, however, Seurat's influence was mostly overlooked. He lived a quiet, sleepy, reclusive life until he died from an uncertain combination of illnesses in 1891.

Our friend Vincent Van Gogh only sold one painting during his lifetime. Can you believe that? It sold for today's equivalent of approximately $109. Although he is famous for works such as *The*

Starry Night, he battled mental illness most of his life. Unfortunately he finally lost this battle, cutting his ear off in 1888 and committing suicide not long after by shooting himself in the chest. His last words were, "The sadness will last forever." He died broke and destitute, a bonafide tragedy. Yet he left an amazing legacy.

Becoming a "starving artist" was not something that seemed to fit into Big Ten collegiate life and what I thought, at the time, was the path I was supposed to take to become a productive member of society. Needing to make enough money to raise a family and go on vacations and be able to afford putting my own kids through college was the priority. The idea of becoming an artist and living the life of one instead of focusing on a career that would make serious money was not realistic, at least in my mind at the time.

It was in this art class that I began to recognize a budding duality inside myself. I did like learning from my biology and anatomy classes and I did like the discipline required and the structure of the courses that would lead to the path of becoming a doctor. However, when it came to my art classes, there was something very primal, authentic, and satisfying to my soul about taking a piece of chalk or a brush and dragging it along a blank sheet of parchment, in whatever direction or manner I wanted, as a pure expression of whatever impulses flowed through me.

This duality made me feel like two completely different people at different times. It's almost like Dr. Jekyll and Mr. Hyde were hiding in the wings of my brain, waiting to alternately appear on stage, depending on what environment I was in or what people I was with. The artist in me has always liked to look at the world from an unusual and interesting perspective with a bit of a playful mischievousness. My analytical side, on the other hand, has always loved structure, has always had a thirst for knowledge, figuring things out like a puzzle, and strategizing about how to solve problems.

During these college years, I would vacillate between trying to do the "responsible" thing, which required contorting my personality to fit in while stressing out about getting good grades to win approval from my parents and teachers, while conversely wanting to escape all of this by surrounding myself with my art classes, where I felt accepted for who I was no matter what I wore, or how many Latin words I could regurgitate.

In my art class, I felt free to experiment, think outside the box, and challenge the status quo. What I found, however, was that if I stayed in that space for too long, I would start to isolate myself from my friends and family to avoid judgment. This would ultimately lead to losing my connection to the things and people that kept me grounded in reality. I have always swung back and forth between these two worlds, sometimes further than I'd prefer. Whenever I would swing too far in either direction, my life seemed to either shut down or spin out of control.

This is what I had struggled with for as long as I can remember…having to shrink my personality to fit in, or being brave enough to follow my own path at the risk of being labeled "different" or "weird" and isolating myself from the world. While I was growing up, it appeared to me there was no middle ground. It was one or the other. Toe the line, make money, get the house with the dog and 2.5 kids, and ultimately create a predictable and secure life for myself. It was that, or maintain the freedom to create at any moment, in any instant, which has always made me feel the most alive and most fulfilled albeit living a life of unpredictability, devoid of any semblance of conventional security.

As much as being comfortable and knowing where the next paycheck is coming from can offer peace of mind, for the longest time, I have most often pursued the unknown and adventure. I chose the option where I wasn't certain how things were going to turn out. It's in this realm where I feel there is neither judgment nor right or wrong.

A favorite quote of mine by the poet Rumi says, "Out beyond ideas of wrongdoing and rightdoing, there is a field. I'll meet you there." That field is where I have always felt free to express who I truly am, which is why I have always needed to create.

YOU, THE AGILE ARTIST

"When you get older, you realize it's a lot less about your place in the world but your place in you. It's not how everyone views you, but how you view yourself." – Natalie Portman

From my experiences, no matter how much I tried to deny something or ignore it, if it was the truth, it always kept nudging, gnawing, and poking me until it was acknowledged. It wasn't until I stumbled into an acting class that the my restless truth was finally able to be recognized.

Until I became an actor, I was always jealous of artists or entrepreneurs who were able to find a way to make a living as professionals doing what they seemed to love. I would (and still do) find myself walking through museums such as the Met in New York or the Art Institute of Chicago, looking at paintings of blotches and splashes of what appear at first glance to be the creative catharsis of a four year old. I have watched with awe as one tech startup after another produced twenty-something-year-old wunderkind millionaires, while I, at the same age, printed out MapQuest directions to find a bar where I could watch a Chicago Bulls game. I would find myself sort of half-appreciating, half-judging as that little voice in my head said, "I could do that." However, I wasn't putting myself out there, taking chances, or actively pursuing my life's passion. Deep down I knew that, which made me both confused and restless.

It wasn't until after I answered a radio ad for a model/talent search that I traveled the world, landing in New York and finally ending up in this small, dingy, makeshift second-floor studio in the

East Village. There, Jackie Segal taught acting classes. This turned out to be the epicenter of my discovery that the art of acting and this exact studio was what I had been seeking for twenty-four years. As soon as I got up to do my first monologue, as nervous and sweaty as I was, it felt like I had finally found the place and the thing that lit me up, challenged me, scared me, inspired me, and made me feel fulfilled.

I had found a place that felt almost like coming home, where I felt safe, accepted, and challenged. It was a place that resonated within my whole body and made me feel excited to show up, where I didn't feel like I had to be perfect and where I could take chances and risks. It was a place I could channel all my restlessness, confusion, and every other emotion that would push on me from the inside, angling to be released, which up until that time, I would do my best to suppress. I finally felt like I had found the place where I could let loose and feel free to express my authentic self.

After I started regularly attending acting classes, I realized that for as long as I could remember, I was playing small with my life. I recognized that I was afraid to share too much of myself, especially what really mattered to me. Growing up, I felt the need to ignore certain feelings I had because I didn't want people to see me vulnerable. In Jackie's class, however, I had found an outlet and a place to express anything that I chose to put into my work which was cathartic and empowering to say the least. In a word, it was thrilling!

Having the chance to bring life to words crafted by geniuses such as Tennessee Williams, Shakespeare, Eugene O'Neill, August Strindberg, and Chekhov was, and still is, in my consideration, an honor. And as I started to delve a bit deeper into the world of acting, I realized that it wasn't just an art form, it truly was a craft requiring an insane amount of discipline to achieve success. I found it also to be a welcome challenge because I discovered that acting is a living canvas that requires all of one's faculties and being in order to bring art to life in a very fluid, dynamic, and in-the-moment way.

As I began to pursue my newly discovered vocation in earnest, I started going to all kinds of theatre in New York, from Broadway to Chinatown. I would seek out lectures given by professionals working in the industry. I'd make it a point to meet and speak with them about their careers and ask for advice. In doing so, for the first time in my life, I found the clarity to make the connection between being an artist and making a living at it. Discovering acting made me realize that I could potentially become a professional artist and create for a living. I knew it wasn't going to be easy, but at least I knew now there was the possibility!

Once I discovered acting, I fully realized no matter how hard you try to subdue and contort yourself to fit into a job, a relationship, or whatever, the truth of who you are will always be there to remind you of your authentic self. Eventually, your truth will find its way to express itself, and the harder you try to ignore it or push it down, the harder it will push back and find some way to manifest.

One of the difficult parts about this for me, however, was that once I discovered this truth, that I am most engaged, inspired, happy, and fulfilled when I'm acting, was to consider how the people in my life, especially my family (specifically my parents) were going to react. My parents had spent thousands of dollars to put me through college, and here I was running around stages in New York City wearing fake mustaches, practicing different accents, and learning how to cry on cue.

The fear of the unknown, especially in regard to how people might react to something you share with them about yourself, can be paralyzing and can prevent you from expressing your authentic self. My love of acting was something I knew I simply had to be truthful about regardless of the consequences, because I had realized there was no denying what I wanted to be doing. Finally, I had found something I felt deep down made me truly fulfilled and was worth pursuing. This definitely wasn't easy, though, because growing up, as I mentioned, I wasn't very self-confident, which made me want to avoid criticism and judgment as much as possible. I was so self-conscious about looking or saying something stupid that the last thing I wanted to do was draw attention to myself for fear of being ridiculed.

The more I performed and was able to create on stage, the more I started to become in tune with myself, and I realized that by honoring what was my truth, I started to develop more self-confidence and self-approval instead of seeking outside recognition. Whether it was getting good grades, doing what my teachers and parents wanted of me, and suppressing my real feelings about things, I now realized that I was putting the needs and desires of other people above my own. In the process I was not truly acknowledging the real me.

As soon as I discovered I was studying acting because my decision came from a place of pure joy and fulfillment, where I truly know who I am, the less concerned I was with what people thought. It became easier to share with my family that acting was what I wanted to pursue. My parents have always been incredibly supportive, but the problem is that I wasn't always honest with them about what really mattered to me. Acting has essentially helped me to become the person I have always wanted to be - someone who can announce with confidence to the world "This is truly me."

What I found very interesting was that frequently, business professionals, doctors, and lawyers would join one of my acting classes. A lot of them were in their thirties and forties. When I would get to know them, they would all say that despite having a good job with good pay, they felt unhappy and unfulfilled. They said things like, "I did what I thought I was supposed to do, and now I want to do what I *really* want to do, which is act. I've always wanted to act." The truth will always find its way and set you free. Even if you don't think of yourself as one, you are an artist.

As acclaimed novelist James Baldwin once observed, "The role of the artist is exactly the same as the role of the lover. If I love you, I have to make you conscious of the things you don't see." This is the daily mantra by which the Agile Artist lives. It's bringing to the forefront of one's consciousness those things whose presence we weren't aware of and sharing them with the world.

When we own the Agile Artist within us, we can constantly tap into reservoirs of creativity, bringing them to our consciousness, and thus, our everyday existence. Our creativity is a resource to enrich our lives! To inspire us! To allow us to overcome the challenges we face to accomplish the things that are truly important to us and to simply make us feel alive!

We can sometimes go through life almost robotically, performing our day-to-day routine just to survive. But by implementing a bit of creativity into even the smallest and most mundane of tasks, you will start to open up a part of your brain that is receptive to inspiration, more connection, and in some special cases, miracles. Since I found acting, I have been able to bridge that gap between having a professional purpose and acknowledging myself as a true artist who must create. Even though it's not easy and there are plenty of ups and downs, every day I am able to honor the true artist within myself by utilizing all my faculties to create, to inspire, and connect with people. This has made my life incredibly rewarding and one I wouldn't change for anything.

DO THE WORK

> *"The more you do your homework, the more*
> *you're free to be intuitive.*
> *But you've got to put the work in."*
> *– Edward Norton*

Whenever I have wanted something badly enough, it almost seemed like I would put so much pressure on myself to make it happen that I would end up self-sabotaging. I can remember doing gymnastics in fifth grade, and how fun it was to run around, tumble, and do flips and cartwheels and the like. As soon as my mom would show up toward the end of practice to pick us up, however, I remember wanting to impress her with my newly learned skill, and inevitably, it wasn't as good as only ten minutes prior when I was just doing it for fun. I have found a very similar pattern when I'm acting. Whenever I have gone into auditions to try to impress the casting director or show off an interesting choice I had made for a line, it always backfired.

The thing with acting is that when it is great, it can be absolutely beautiful. It can move us, inspire us, change us, and take our breath away. From my extensive acting training, however, I've learned that much like anything else, trying too hard to accomplish an end result can prevent us from being in the moment and therefore preclude us from being as effective, productive, and truthful as we have the potential to be. This is why acting and other performance-centric actions or activities are such a zen process. Whether it's trying to hit a baseball or giving a lecture in front of three hundred people, trying too hard to be "good" more often than not has the opposite effect.

Similar to someone learning a new skill, such as playing golf for the first time, there are a myriad of different components that must be mastered in order for all of them to work together in concert to achieve the desired result. When learning to golf, for example, one must be cognizant of the angle of the club, whether the grip is too tight, the speed of the backswing, and making sure one's hips and legs are in the right position. By practicing hitting hundreds and hundreds of golf balls, the act of consciously thinking of each individual aspect of the swing begins to blend together into the single act of hitting the golf ball.

Many people refer to this as being "in the zone," when one is completely "unconscious" of the actual components of performing a task and everything just flows in the moment. I remember watching game One of the 1992 NBA Finals where Michael Jordan, after hitting his sixth three-point basket in the first half against the Portland Trail Blazers, turns to jog back to the other end of the court. As he does, he shrugs, puts his hands in the air and has this look of amazement himself, as if there were some omnipotent force working through him, not of his own accord.

One definitive truth about acting is that the camera never lies. When watching a TV show or film, it's easy to see when an actor is fully present and committed to their role, similar to "being in the zone." As such, we, the viewers, become captivated and are transported into their world. Conversely, bad acting can make us feel disconnected and annoyed. There are many distinctions that go into a great performance, arguably the most important of which is being completely present and "in the moment".

One of my favorite acting coaches, Margie Haber, teaches an audition technique class. When I was in it, she would have us students come into the room, and one by one our 'auditions' would be taped. After all of the students had their turn, we would, as a class, then watch everyone's tapings and offer constructive feedback. It's one of the most naked, uncomfortable and honest experiences one can go through. I'd also say it's one of the most beneficial with regard to an actor's development. One key discovery I found from doing this, very early on, is that you could tell when I was too "in my head" about remembering my lines or self-conscious about how my performance was. After watching the playback of my audition in front of the class, it was quite evident when I was fully in the moment and when I wasn't. This exercise pointed out for me the glaring distinction between a good performance and one that made you want to vomit.

I remember watching my earlier performances with twenty of my fellow acting students, cringing in my seat, seeing when I wasn't fully present. In a similar vein, we all know that when trying to multi task while simply spending time with a friend or partner it prevents the person you're with from fully being able to connect with you. It's possible to multi-task and seem to accomplish several things at once, of course, but when you split your focus between multiple activities, your attention becomes scattered. In doing so you are more apt to be less effective and make mistakes than when being fully present with just one activity. This is the same phenomenon that happens when we are focused on looking good or trying to be perfect in the eyes of whoever happens to be watching us: it prevents us from being in the moment. When we are distracted with text messages, phone calls, emails, or other people, it's impossible to fully connect and therefore be able to drop into "the zone," where we are most effective, with the least amount of effort.

How do you get there? There are a lot of different components that go into being able to drop into that "zone" space where you are completely out of your own way and able to channel the creativity and wisdom of the universe, so to speak. When it comes to becoming good at anything and the concept of mastery, it all starts with putting in the work. Regardless of whether we're talking about a world-class athlete, an Academy Award–winning actor, or the CEO of a Fortune 500 company, the best and most effective performers in their field are the ones who make it look easy because *they have put in the work.*

When it comes to acting or real estate and community development, which are the fields that I know best, I see it as my job to continually seek to master my craft. There is never a time when I rest on my laurels and stop seeking out growth. I strive to maintain my skill as an actor at a high level by continually rehearsing so that I am able to pick up a script, break it down into its component beats, and mine the emotional aspects of the character with no judgment or concern for the outcome.

Since venturing into real estate, I'm constantly going to investment club meetings and visiting my properties and the neighborhoods I work in. I seek out collaboration with other real estate brokers and investors and attend networking events whenever I can. By doing so, I pick up insights and knowledge which fuels my confidence and ability to be present, authentic, and intentional. This is where the magic happens.

One of my favorite playwrights and one of the most famous of them in American history, David Mamet, (*Glengarry Glen Ross*, *American Buffalo*) writes in his book *True and False* that the most important job of the actor is to simply show up, be brave, and say the lines truthfully. He goes on to say, "Invent nothing, deny nothing, speak up, stand up … Art is an expression of joy and awe. It is not an attempt to share one's virtues and accomplishments with the audience, but an act of selfless spirit."

As James Cagney said, "Find your mark, look the other fellow in the eye, and tell the truth." Along these lines, my dad sent me a newspaper clipping one day describing Sam Shepard talking about Marlon Brando. Shepard said, "I don't think Marlon Brando ever set out to be an icon. But he said one of the best things about acting I've heard. He said, "Just because they say, 'Action,' doesn't mean you have to do anything." Shepard continues on to say, "And he's absolutely right. In other words, if you can reveal some glimmer of truth, whatever that might be, however that's interpreted, people recognize it when they see it. If you can do that, then you become an inspiration in some kind of a way. But you don't set out to become an inspiration: you just set out to do something simple and truthful." When people see "some glimmer of truth" it can be truly inspiring. This is one of the primary reasons I find acting so compelling.

Nothing worthwhile comes easy, and the only way to truly be able to be in the moment is to do the work for you to able to show up and just play. Robert Downey Jr., for all of his charm and nonchalance in his acting style, is one of the hardest working actors in the business. Not only does he memorize his lines, he memorizes *all* the lines of the other actors that are in the scene and then will write them out on a piece of paper until he is able to do so from memory. This, he says, allows him to then show up and play.

Anthony Weiner, the Emmy Award–winning creator and writer of *Mad Men* (which also happens to be one of my favorite shows ever produced) did not allow actors to have scripts on set. You were expected to have your lines memorized by the time you arrived on set so you were able to be present and simply show up and play.

Much like learning anything new, it took me a while to become comfortable enough in front of the camera to be able to be in the moment. I remember directors coming up to me, reminding me to not let all the distractions on set get in the way of doing the most important job I have as an actor—to simply listen to the other actor. When I was just starting out, the more work I put into preparing for a role, the greater was my desire to show off this work instead of simply being in the moment. I have since recognized the key to any success is to prepare, prepare, prepare, which enables you to be to show up and be the best you.

Again, one of the biggest tenets actors are taught is that listening is everything. I'm stressing it here because it really is the key to everything. True, active listening allows us not only to hear another person's words, but to feel and take in another person's energy. This allows for an authentic connection that makes people feel subconsciously safe.

Similar to bad acting, you can tell when two people are not truly actively listening to each other. Their body language is usually closed off or uncomfortable-looking and their facial expressions look forced and inauthentic. Watching bad acting often demonstrates how the necessary work hasn't been done, which I admit to having been guilty of. Whenever I have failed to do the proper amount of work necessary to perform or execute at a high level, I noticed right away that I'm too in my head. When I'm self-conscious about how I appear, it completely ruins the performance and I feel like a fraud. The only thing that makes a difference is putting in the work.

As actors, we traffic in the world of emotions. We learn how to tap into our psyche to elicit specific emotions for the scenes that we are acting in through techniques such as sense memory and emotional recall. These techniques entail conjuring up memories from your past that at the time resulted in a specific emotional state, such as when your dog died when you were eight or when you and your significant other broke up for the thirteenth time. By closing your eyes and having your acting teacher guide you to recreate the environment and circumstances related to the event, your body will start to allow those emotions to be felt again, depending on how willing you are to let yourself delve back into that memory.

Just to give you a little background about this, The Actors Studio in New York, founded in 1947, is best known for its work refining and teaching method acting. Some of the best actors of the day were members of the Actors Studio, including James Dean, Paul Newman, Marlon Brando, Marilyn Monroe, Robert De Niro, and Al Pacino. This type of acting was revolutionary in the 1950s when films like *Cat on a Hot Tin Roof* and *East of Eden* hit the big screen. Contrasted with the suave and stoic acting style of someone like a Humphrey Bogart in *Casablanca*, Clark Gable in *Gone with the Wind,* and John Wayne in most anything he starred in, the acting that came out of the Actors Studio was applauded for its realism, authenticity, and vulnerability. James Dean's performance in *Rebel without a Cause* and Marlon Brando's tour de force display in *A Streetcar Named Desire* unapologetically featured passion, vulnerability, and angst.

Some actors and teachers don't subscribe to this technique because they feel it's both manipulative of your psyche and unnecessary. One such defector from the sense memory/Actors Studio camp was an actor and eventual acting teacher named Sanford Meisner who popularized the Meisner technique. Meisner was instrumental in teaching such notables as Dylan McDermott, James Caan, Steve McQueen, Robert Duvall, and Jeff Goldblum, to name a few. This approach was developed to get the actor out of their head through the use of repetition exercises to help the actor become fully present. This in turn would allow him or her to be able to experience the emotions that would naturally emerge from the circumstances of the scene. Meisner stressed "the reality of doing," in which you are focused on the objective you want to accomplish in the scene and also able to actively listen, having done the work enabling you to do so.

I have studied both methods and have a repertoire of tools that I use for various purposes and scenarios. Some techniques may work for some and not for others. It's interesting to hear stories like how Elizabeth Taylor and Paul Newman had a difficult time working together on *Cat on a Hot Tin Roof* because of the contrasting styles in their approach to acting. Newman was a method actor and loved to rehearse because through it he would discover new aspects of his character that he would incorporate into his performance. Elizabeth Taylor, on the other hand, felt that too much rehearsing would make her on-camera performance stale and less spontaneous. She relied more on the text and the scope of her imagination in the moment to create her character and bring the scene to life.

Regardless of whatever style an actor subscribes to, the common theme to both is the emphasis on authenticity…being real. To bring your true essence to a character without holding anything back and without having to hide aspects of who you are that you may feel are ugly or embarrassing. As I started to do scene work and audition for TV shows and films, I began experiencing the fact that the more open and vulnerable I was in these situations, the more work I started to book. I started to feel confident in who I was despite all my perceived imperfections.

Soon, I recognized that acting class, for me, was a sanctuary of sorts. There, I felt I could fall on my face, create, try new things, experiment with different aspects of my personality, discover what my limits and triggers are, and not feel like I had to pretend to be anything other than myself. As Ryan Gosling says, when he is preparing for a role, he doesn't pretend to be someone else. Instead he "turns up and tones down" aspects of his own personality that he feels are appropriate for whatever character he is playing, but he still brings who he is to the role.

I grew up struggling with self-esteem issues and feeling like I had to achieve certain things in order to gain approval, such as getting As on my report card and scoring touchdowns. By contrast, acting class felt like a place where there was no pressure to be anything other than who I am. One of my favorite quotes by Sanford Meisner encapsulates this beautifully: "To be an interesting actor— hell, to be an interesting human being—you must be authentic, and for you to be authentic, you must embrace who you really are, warts and all. Do you have any idea how liberating it is to not care what people think about you? Well, that's what we're here to do." I couldn't have said it better.

Years of study have made me appreciate acting more and more, and every year there are certain performances that absolutely blow me away. Most of the time they are so subtle, so real, and so natural that all the hours of rehearsal and preparation are completely disguised and wholly undetectable. These are the best performances —when the audience is pulled into the story and brought on a ride without even knowing how they got there. It's all because of the work that went into it.

STEALING THE CREATIVE CONNECTION

"Every artist gets asked the question, 'Where do you get your ideas?' The honest artist answers, 'I steal them.'"
— Austin Kleon

What is it about creativity that makes some people think they have it and others think they don't? Why do some people seem to have ideas and creativity oozing out of every pore of their skin, while others feel as if writer's block permeates every aspect of who they are? In Austin Kleon's book *Steal Like an Artist,* he describes some key ingredients necessary for creativity to flourish. I'm going to honor him now, yep, by stealing.

Kleon champions the idea that nothing is original and that "all creative work builds on what came before." He talks about how collecting ideas and knowledge from the world around us is actually the impetus for generating our own ideas and sparking creativity.

Speaker and author Maria Popova adds, "In order for us to truly create and contribute to the world, we have to be able to connect countless dots, to cross-pollinate ideas from a wealth of disciplines, to combine and recombine these pieces and build new castles." She mentions the analogy of Legos, in that "the more of these building blocks we have, and the more diverse their shapes and colors, the more interesting our castles will become."

If we're to use the example of Professor Boches' polling of his students as any indication of whether people consciously think of themselves as creative, it would appear that half the population doesn't think so. If this is indeed the case, those who don't think of themselves as creative could plausibly ask, "If I've gotten along just fine without looking at life from an artist's perspective, why does it matter now?"

I would argue that all people have within them the sensibility of an artist, even if they are not consciously aware of it. Being an artist doesn't necessarily mean picking up a paintbrush or sculpting clay on a potter's wheel. Being an artist is to look at any situation, task, or relationship and ask, "What can I do to make this work better or more efficiently or be able to derive more fulfillment?" How can I be a better parent or husband? How can I be more efficient at work so I have more free time to do the things I really want to be doing? How can I throw the best birthday party ever for my best friend?" I would further this point by saying any sort of problem-solving involves a high level of artistry.

Thus, seeking out new experiences and exposing yourself to inspiration can help give you the seeds for new ideas that can make your life better. This is why I am always making an effort to attend concerts, go to museums, and travel. It's not just places and things that inspire me. I'm always seeking opportunities to meet new people and hear new ideas and thoughts. Getting set in your ways and in the same daily pattern can prevent creativity from blossoming. Even if it's just getting outside and going for a walk down a street you've never been down before or watching a new TV show, you may discover something new that you can borrow or steal and, therefore, use for whatever purpose you need it.

Kleon also suggests carrying around a notebook for jotting down thoughts and observations so you don't forget them, and also for doodling, which stimulates the creative right side of your brain. He also keeps a "swipe" file for all the things that he's "swiped" to refer to when he is looking for inspiration. As Pablo Picasso himself was noted as saying, "Good artists copy, great artists steal."

A researcher named Dr. Duezel explains that "only completely new things cause strong activity in the midbrain area," which is your brain making new connections and rewiring itself. So, you can indeed teach an old dog new tricks, so to speak. Popova continues by saying that "trying something new and forcing a gentle brain overload can make a dramatic improvement for your brain activity," which can spark creativity.

When someone invites you to go to an event or to a play or museum, just say "yes!" Wear your watch on the other wrist, take a new way home from work, check out a new restaurant you've never been to. Go out and explore and allow your brain to be filled up with new and interesting content for you to steal and make something of your own!

Three Takeaway Action Tips:

1. Bring more curiosity to everything you do. Curiosity is born out of focus and intention to seek out something unique or different from what others might see with regard to almost anything. Getting curious might be as simple as asking yourself a question like, "What is different here that others might not see?"

2. Seek out new experiences and new ways of doing the things you already do. This is another way of discovering something new in daily life that can grow into something that is art, and further, something that might even grow into a career or new business venture.

3. Steal or riff off of anything that inspires you creatively. There is often, if not always, a way to riff off of some idea to form something that's unique to only you. If you need help riffing, get a friend, coach, teacher, etc. to help you. It can be just the thing to set you on a new path, a better path in your life!

03 CARPE DIEM

"Carpe diem. Seize the day, boys.
Make your life extraordinary."
– John Keating, Dead Poets Society

During my senior year at the University of Iowa, I was waiting tables at the esteemed University of Iowa Athletic Club. This is the place for Hawkeye fans to gather, watch games, eat brunch and dinner, and regale the stories of Iowa's yesteryears and the promise of the upcoming season. Waiting tables isn't one of my favorite things to do because, well, it's waiting tables, and because we had to wear these cheesy polyester tuxedo outfits. *And* I hated my boss. For the most part, the clientele and my fellow servers were great. As much as I didn't like serving, it made me realize that having a job just to make a living was not what I wanted to do for the rest of my life. I knew I needed to be doing something more fulfilling.

I was majoring in biology/pre-med and studying to take the MCAT, the test to get into medical school, but even so, deep down I wasn't quite sure if becoming a doctor was my life's passion. My dad was a gynecologist/obstetrician and what I noticed about him was how much it meant to be able to bring new life into the world and how many people he was able to make a difference for. He loved what he did and it showed. The best example he provided to me and my siblings was his passion for what he did and how impactful his work was to so many.

Even though I wasn't completely convinced being a physician was my life's calling, I went to classes, moving in that direction because I didn't know what else to do. When I heard about Doctors Without Borders, an international program where physicians travel around the world to places in need of medical help, I felt something spark my inspiration. From that moment on, the idea of traveling to far off and distant lands kept nudging me from within.

As they say, be careful what you wish for. After finishing a shift at the UIAC one bitterly cold February night, I was driving home, cruising down Dubuque Avenue in my brown Toyota Camry, when an ad came on the radio that blasted, "Next Tuesday night, come to the Paula Palm model search at the Davenport Holiday Inn! Come see if you have what it takes to become a fashion model and travel the world." As far-fetched and ludicrous as that sounded, the idea of traveling the world and exploring life outside of the Midwest resonated with me. I had always dreamed of adventures to the far off and unknown but didn't know where or how to start. Since the idea was always top of mind for me, it seemed as if the universe were answering what I was truly calling out for.

I didn't tell anyone what I had heard on the radio or that I was seriously thinking about going to the event, because I didn't want to open myself up to judgement. It was something I wanted to investigate for myself and I decided that no one else needed to know about it.

I pulled into the Davenport Holiday Inn, about forty-five minutes from The University of Iowa. I parked my car, went inside, and was shown into a small event space where about forty other people were milling around. At a certain point, two beautiful women asked us all to sit down. One of them introduced herself as Paula Palm, a former model who now went across the country to scout for models and place them in agencies around the world. The other woman introduced herself as a being a former model as well. She described for us, in detail, what the industry entailed and how traveling to, and living in, Paris, Milan and New York was a very common practice for industry professionals.

After they finished outlining the particulars of the fashion industry, the women talked about the upcoming model convention that they were sponsoring in Chicago. Paula informed us that they would be inviting some of us in the room that night to the convention to meet modeling agents and possibly be signed to a contract. Because there were certain height and size requirements for what the agents would be looking for, Paula said that not everyone would be invited to come. They mentioned that the typical height requirement for a male model was six feet tall, and that the ideal height was 6'1" or 6'2." Because I'm barely 5'11", I wasn't sure if they'd think I was too short.

I waited as, one by one, they invited us to the front of the room until it was my turn. Looking back, I remember how it was similar to *American Idol.* There I was, nervously standing in front of these gorgeous women who sat behind a table and started to ask me questions about who I was and where I was from. Because *ER* was one of the hottest shows on TV at the time and George Clooney was "the man," I was sporting the Caesar haircut, much like other guys at the time. I also wore glasses for nearsightedness, so if you can picture that combination, I wouldn't necessarily say it was the recipe for what they were looking for. However, Paula asked me to remove my glasses and mess up my hair, which I did.

I had never really been scrutinized like this, and I found it a bit amusing, to be honest, but after our brief exchange, they politely smiled and said that they would like me to come to the convention. They gave me a sheet of paper with details and instructions and the name of a photographer in Chicago to call in order to get some professional pictures taken to show to the agents. I'm not going to lie, it was pretty exciting to get invited to the convention, but because they invited quite a few people from that evening, I was a bit skeptical as to how legitimate this was. There was a $200 fee to go to the convention and another $200 to shoot with the photographer, but because it didn't seem like an astronomical amount of money, I decided that I'd give it a chance and see if it was for real. Why not?

A few days after that night, I called the photographer Paula had given me the number for and set up a test shoot with him in Chicago, where he lived. On a weekend that March, I drove to Chicago, to the photographer's studio, which turned out to be this cool industrial loft in the South Loop. I was a bit nervous, but a twinge of excitement made me want to at least see what the experience would be like. The photographer's name was Jeff. He reminded me a lot of the artists who I shared classes with in school and there was no pretense about him. We immediately hit it off, and he guided me through a series of different set ups and outfits which went surprisingly well.

Standing there in front of the bright lights, initially, I didn't really know what to do, but Jeff was great at giving direction. He described how he wanted me to pose in front of the camera in a way that felt collaborative and natural. It didn't feel like he was just some guy who I had paid $200 to take my picture

Not only did I have fun that day, I felt like I had met a kindred spirit. Shooting with Jeff opened my eyes to how fulfilling collaborating with another artist can be. Since then, having worked with hundreds of other photographers, directors, stylists, makeup artists and the like, I believe I have experienced the success that I have because whenever I have been hired to work with other creative professionals, it has been a true collaboration of artists

After the shoot, I went back to Iowa and continued on with my regular life, going to the library at night with my sixty-four-ounce Big Gulp of Mountain Dew and giant bag of Twizzlers, attending my last few fraternity parties, sporting my fabulous polyester tuxedo at the UIAC, and planning for my upcoming MCAT test to get into medical school. Of all the things that were going on, however, the convention was what I was most looking forward to.

A few weeks later, it was time for the convention. I had gotten my pictures back from Jeff and had them bound in a small, four-bysix-inch photo book, and I was ready. The convention was at one of the big hotels near O'Hare International Airport, so I drove back to Chicago for that weekend. When I arrived, I was shocked to see over four hundred people there. I walked into a large ballroom and was greeted at a table where I saw Paula and the woman I had met in Davenport a few months prior. I was given a sticker with a number on it and then was told to take a seat in front of a stage that had a couple of microphones and a video screen. There was definitely a buzz in the air, and you could tell people were excited and nervous, as was I. There were kids and adults and family members, and everyone was dressed to the nines. Some had dressed casually like I did, in jeans and a polo shirt, while others looked like they had broken out their prom outfits.

The convention started with Paula coming on stage and welcoming everyone. She introduced the agents who had come from New York, Los Angeles, Chicago, Miami, Seattle, and Atlanta. There were about fifteen agents there, and as they introduced themselves and told us about the industry, the excitement in the room continued to grow. We were shown a few videos of photo shoots and some of the campaigns and covers of working models who had been discovered at the Paula Palm Model Search, just like this one. The presentation was followed by a runway show, which was one of the most entertaining things I have ever seen. Watching all these kids, teenagers, and young adults doing their best Naomi Campbell or Cindy Crawford impersonations was quite entertaining.

When it was my turn, I was ushered up to the stage. As the person in front of me came back from doing the best rendition of her Kate Moss, I was sent out to walk in front all these random people. It was more of an out-of-body experience, to be honest, than anything else. To have four hundred people watching you walk is not something anyone can prepare you for until you experience it for yourself. It was a mix of excitement but also of self-consciousness because I started questioning my *walk*! Seriously? Was it the right rhythm or gait or tempo, should I strut, should I sway? I have a feeling I looked like a jackass, but regardless, it was over in all of fifteen seconds.

When the fashion show was done, they announced they were going to have the agencies that would like to meet with the participants that they felt had potential by calling the number associated with each participant. Agent by agent, they would call out numbers, and when it was all said and told, there were five agents that wanted to meet me. As I met with each one, they seemed nice enough, asked me how tall I was and a few other questions, and that was it. We were told the agencies would call us in the coming days if they were interested in working with us.

I left excited at the prospect of having one of these agents actually interested in representing me and drove back to Iowa the following day. I went to bed that night thinking about how crazy and random the weekend had been. The next day, Monday, I went back to my daily routine of classes and college life wondering if my phone would ring. Until finally, it did.

The call was from a gentleman named Sebastian McWilliams at the Aria Model Agency in Chicago. He said he wanted me to come to his office to talk about possibly representing me. I mentioned I was graduating in a couple of weeks and that I would come into his office when I got back to Chicago, right afterward. Sebastian was the only agent from the event to express interest. Even though I had received only one callback, it was still an opportunity, and I was pretty excited.

It finally came time to graduate. I was thrilled to be finishing college after years of hard work, angst, frustration, and dealing with that dreaded question: "What do I want to do for the rest of my life?" After my graduation ceremony, I took the MCAT, said my goodbyes to all my college friends, made my peace and hightailed it out of Iowa City back to Chi Town.

A few days later, I showed up at the Aria agency office in Chicago's West Loop, ironically, right down the street from where I currently live. When I walked in and came up the elevator to the second floor, I saw the Aria sign on the glass doors and proceeded to walk in. There was a receptionist who welcomed me, silhouetted by beautiful images of models on magazine covers and campaign photo shoots, including Cindy Crawford. It turns out the woman who started Aria was the woman who discovered Cindy, who is from a northern town of Chicago. That being said, I knew this place was legit.

Soon thereafter, I was brought back to Sebastian's office, where he invited me to sit down. He told me that he thought I might have some potential, and that he wanted to do a test shoot with me, but that I needed to lose some weight first. I wasn't necessarily surprised, considering I played rugby at Iowa, lifted weights regularly, and had pretty much existed on a college diet of ramen noodles, Wendy's bacon double cheeseburgers, baked beans, Kraft macaroni and cheese, chicken nuggets, Twizzlers, Mountain Dew, and Keystone Light for the past few years. I told him I was about to go on a European backpacking trip with a couple of friends for two months, and that I'd focus on dropping some weight during my trip. I thanked him for the opportunity and left with a little pep to head back home and begin packing.

At the time, I was twenty-three years old. I had been to Ireland a couple of times because my mom is from Dublin and we had gone to visit her family, but this was the first time I was striking out on my own to explore new adventure before committing to years of intense medical school study. At this point, I didn't think the modeling thing was going to amount to much because it still seemed a bit farfetched and unrealistic, but exciting enough to at least give it a shot when I got back. I was in a great position because I knew that I had medical school waiting to fall back on.

My two months in Europe were amazing! I got to visit with my relatives in Dublin, get reacquainted with my heritage and Guinness beer, learn all about English history by visiting Big Ben, Westminster Abbey, London Tower, and Windsor Castle. I saw the Eiffel Tower, the Place de la Concorde, the Bastille, and, of course, met

Mona Lisa at the Louvre. I got to experience the siestas in Madrid and witness how dinner starts at 10 pm where people don't go out until after noon and regularly like to party till 8 am the next day. I witnessed Flamenco dancers in Seville and the Alhambra Palace in Granada. I got to stay at the Vatican for three days because my college pastor happened to be in Rome at the same time that I was there. I was able to take in Michelangelo's incredible work at the Sistine Chapel and visit the Spanish Steps, the Colosseum, and numerous piazzas, and I stuffed my face with the best pasta on the planet. I then made my way up to Munich, where I swiped a beer stein from the Hofbrauhaus, hung out at a summer festival in Karlsruhe, headed up to Dusseldorf to eat wiener schnitzel and spaetzle, and finally round it off with an amazing visit to see Van Gogh's work in Amsterdam. I wrapped it all up with a friendly visit to the redlight district, just out of curiosity, of course.

Visiting so many amazing places opened my eyes to the vast differences there are in people and cultures around the world. But what I also realized was how similar people are no matter where they're from. As varied as the food, the culture, the way of dress, and the overall personalities of the people I met, I discovered they had more in common than not. One thing that did strike me as a major difference, however, was the overall attitude toward work and money. I noticed a stark contrast in how people in Europe seemed to work to live, compared to the States, where our culture is more work-centric. It started to become evident to me that we, here in the States, seem more focused on making as much money as possible so we can buy the latest and greatest iPhone and the biggest and newest SUV. I'm reminded of this daily, when I walk into the entryway of my building, here in Chicago. More often than not, it looks reminiscent of a Christmas morning, with piles of boxes and packages from Amazon, FedEx and UPS all stacked up.

The emphasis on being the best, having the most, and keeping up with the Joneses seemed to have less of an influence there as it does here. For good or bad, it made me start to appreciate how there is more to life than getting good grades to get a good job to then be able to afford what we have been accustomed to living with. People's houses and cars were a bit more modest, and for the most part, making time to be with family and extended family seemed the priority.

At any rate, for as long as I was gone walking around and sightseeing in the middle of the sweltering heat of the summer, I came back to Chicago having lost about ten pounds and sporting a pretty healthy tan. When I got back, I called Sebastian and went in to see him again. He immediately scheduled a couple of photo shoots and started preparing my portfolio and composite card to send out to clients.

Within a few days, Sebastian started sending me out on modeling casting calls. I enjoyed the excitement of not knowing if I was going to get cast or not, which played very well into my competitive nature. I also liked the social aspect of it, meeting new people and going all over the city to new places, meeting with casting directors for each job. Within a couple weeks, I booked my first gig for Kohl's department store. I was on my way.

The shoot was up in Milwaukee, so I drove the two hours and met the team on location at a beach. When I arrived and met the crew, my nerves subsided, and within no time I was busting out my best Zoolander poses and began my foray into the world of fashion. Even though I didn't really know what I was doing, it was fun to be working in this creative environment, and I immediately felt like this was something that I wanted to continue at.

A few weeks and a few jobs later, I got a call from Sebastian saying that one of the top photographers in the industry, Bruce Weber, wanted to shoot me for a Ralph Lauren campaign. Um, what?! I had no idea who Bruce was at the time, but being chosen to represent Ralph Lauren, one of the biggest fashion brands in the world, indicated to me that I could potentially work at the higher ranks in the industry.

Before you know it, a car service picked me up at my house and took me to the airport where I was flown to Miami. A limo then picked me up and drove me to this beautiful house in Islamorada, just outside of Miami Beach. Stepping out of that limo and onto the beach was the closest feeling to what I imagined a rockstar lifestyle would be like!

Bruce gave me a warm welcome when I arrived and after introducing himself, I got to watch him finish the shoot he was doing with Naomi Campbell and Tyson Beckford, Polo's campaign models at the time. The experience was the fashion equivalent of meeting Steven Spielberg on the set of a movie he was doing with Julia Roberts and Tom Cruise. That was essentially the modeling world I was entering.

Working with Bruce Weber and collaborating together to create beautiful images was nothing short of awe-inspiring. It was amazing just to be able to witness his creative process and to see firsthand how passionate he was when capturing an image he liked. It was a surreal experience, and I felt extremely privileged to have been chosen to work with one of the top photographers in the world. Strangely, though, I felt extremely comfortable and very much in my element.

After finishing the shoot, I went back to Chicago, and only a couple weeks later, I got another phone call saying Bruce wanted to shoot with me again, this time for the Versace campaign. Never in my wildest dreams would I have thought I'd be shooting not one, but two major fashion brand campaigns, back to back, with so prominent a photographer. That shoot was, easily, one of my favorites. Bruce and the art director designed the images with a special, almost indescribable artistry, and the pictures we created together came out beautifully. We captured some fantastic moments on film, not the least of which included the Versace Jeans campaign that ran, literally, all over the world.

At the completion of the shoot, Bruce asked me to stay an extra day to shoot the cover of L'Uomo Vogue, which to this day is one of the projects I'm most proud of. For whatever reason, working with Bruce just clicked. The experience made me recognize that being in that type of creative environment was something I wanted to continue doing. When I got back to Chicago from this shoot, Sebastian called me into his office to "have a talk". It was time to send me to the fashion capital of the world, Milan, for the men's fashion shows.

MILAN

"Twenty years from now you will be more disappointed by the things you didn't do than by the ones you did do. So throw off the bowlines.

Sail away from the safe harbor. Catch the trade winds in your sails.

Explore. Dream. Discover."

—Mark Twain

I landed in Milan the first week of January 1997 and was set up in an apartment/hotel by my agency, Beatrice Models. When I arrived, it felt as though I was living at the fashion U.N. There were models from all over the world and everyone was stunning. You name it: Germany, Russia, Brazil, Croatia, America, Canada, Iceland, Latvia, Korea, Australia. To be around all these gorgeous people was a bit intimidating at first, but once we got to know each other, we all realized that even though we hailed from extremely different places, we were very similar in many ways. We enjoyed playing cards, going out to the bars and clubs, and talking about our favorite movies and our dreams and aspirations. It was awesome being able to ask all these different people from all over the world what it was like to live in their respective countries. We had an incredible amount of fun drinking beers together while comparing our cultural differences. We talked about everything. Our topics ranged from the most random of subjects such as how different Big Mac's at McDonald's taste the world over, to more profound ones like politics and religion. I also enjoyed talking about and describing what the United States was like and being asked things such as if I had ever been to Disneyland or met Michael Jordan.

Every day, we would wake up and go to our agency, where our agents would print out the list of designers and showrooms we were to visit that day for castings. We would take the subway, buses and taxis, skateboards, bikes and scooters. For two weeks leading up to the fashion shows, it was madness. I showed up at castings with hundreds of other dudes and then waited in line to try on some clothes, show my model portfolio, and my runway walk. Not being the standard, requisite height of at least six feet, I had to rely more on my personality by trying to make conversation with the casting directors or designers I met. A lot of the time it didn't work, but sometimes it did, and those moments were the ones that made all the difference.

Once such instance was when I went in for the Giorgio Armani casting. I arrived at a nondescript address near the middle of Milan's city center where at least fifty other guys were standing outside. One by one, we were shuttled inside and down some stairs. Little did I know then that this was the mecca of the Armani brand. This is where Mr. Armani worked, lived, and held his runway shows. Coming from the Midwest where high fashion was Banana Republic or Ralph Lauren, and now being in Milan, the epicenter of men's fashion, at Giorgio Armani's place of residence and work no less, was starting to feel like a big deal. Before this moment, I hadn't really given the man nor the brand of Armani much thought. All I knew was that his suits were worn by high-power finance guys and movie stars, which was definitely not in my realm at twenty-three years old.

Making our way down the stairs, we got to a passageway that opened up into a decent-sized space with rows and rows of black seats. They were lined in a horseshoe shape around an elevated runway floor and made of semi-opaque plexiglass lit up from underneath. On the far end, at the beginning of the runway, was the Armani logo beautifully emblazoned on the back wall. As more and more guys started to fill in the seats, I noticed it was eerily quiet given how crowded the room was becoming. I think we were all just in awe of the Armani mystique. I know I was.

Before we knew it, Mr. Armani himself came onto the stage and began speaking to us in Italian. The first thing I noticed was how elegant he was in a tight black T-shirt and black tailored pants: understated, but definitely cool. He had a translator explain to us that we would all have an opportunity to walk on the runway for Mr. Armani so he could choose for himself which guys he wanted for his show. This is when the posturing began.

To see the most handsome men in the world starting to jockey and peacock was pretty amusing and quite intimidating. When it got to be my turn, I stepped up on the glowing runway with Mr. Armani at one end and about two hundred other guys watching from the seats. It was almost as if I had forgotten how to walk. I have never been so self-aware of putting one foot in front of the other. *Just don't trip, just don't trip*, I heard the voice in my head say. Was I walking straight? Were my feet crooked? Should I be strutting like George Jefferson? It would have been comical had it not been for the fact that it was almost completely silent in the room. You could pretty much hear a pin drop.

As I made my way to the other end of the runway, I passed by Mr. Armani and his assistants, which took all of about fifteen seconds. Mr. Armani's assistant said, "Thank you," and then I was told to sit back down. After all the guys had done their walk, Mr. Armani then thanked us in Italian and the translator then told us we were free to leave.

The next day, I called into my agency to check in for my daily castings. My agent, Rita, with excitement in her voice, relayed to me that I had a fitting back at Armani that day for the show. She mentioned I was one of roughly forty guys who was potentially doing the show. Holy shit! She said I had to go back to the Armani residence later that day at 5 pm and that if I fit the clothes, there was a good chance I would get confirmed for the show.

I excitedly took down the addresses of the other castings I had that day and proceeded to get ready and head out. Around 1 pm, I checked back in with Rita, who didn't sound as excited anymore. She now told me the Armani people had just called and released me, so there was no reason for me to go to the fitting later that day. She said they probably had already filled the allotted slots for the show. Before hanging up the phone, though, she said she had a plan.

There are many reasons why I loved Rita so much, one of the most important of which had to do with showing me how to create my own opportunities. Up until this point in my life, I was not as rebellious as many of my friends or my siblings, for that matter. I had more of a laid back personality, and I tried to be respectful of the rules, whether behaving at school or at home. I had only gotten one detention the whole time I was in high school. As such, I played by the rules and tried to make nice. It used to be that I let my goal to be liked and accepted more of a priority than what truly mattered to me. In doing so, I would regularly put the desires of others before my own.

Rita was a stubborn and passionate woman and taking no for an answer was not something she did much of. She hatched her idea over the phone with me. In her thick Italian accent she said that I should pretend I hadn't spoken to her all day and should just show up to the fitting at the time I was originally supposed to. The old me would have accepted the news that I was released, said something stupid like, "Ah, well, that's how it goes," and moved on. However, I was halfway around the world now, in a new environment, and since Mr. Armani and his production team had no idea who I was, I figured, *what did I have to lose?* Concurring, she added, "why not?"

She was right. Why not? Fuck it. Let's do this. When 5 pm rolled around, I strolled up the cobblestone street to the Armani compound, rang the doorbell, and waited. The door opened after a brief pause, and a man answered the door. He asked if he could help me, to which I replied, "I'm here for my fitting for the show." Without any hesitation, he said, "Right this way," and brought me back down the stairs to the runway theatre. This time it was nearly empty except for a few people scurrying around with random pieces of clothing as they were preparing for the show, now only a few days away.

And there he was, Mr. Armani, on the stage, fixing a bit of collar on a model who then turned, walked down the runway, and then back. Mr. Armani said something in Italian to his assistant, who then told the model he was free to leave. The assistant then turned to me and invited me to the back room to try on some clothes. So far the plan was working, and no one had said a thing. The assistant put me in a casual pant and shirt outfit that felt a bit too big. Shit. I was thinking that once I got out to the runway and Mr. Armani saw the clothes didn't fit, that he would ask me to leave. But I thought, *let's see what he says*. I walked out of the changing room and into the auditorium. Then I stepped up onto the runway and found myself face-to-face with Giorgio himself.

He looked at me and with a warm smile, said, "Ciao," which I responded to in kind. Holy shit, I thought, I'm face-to-face with The Giorgio Armani right now. He smelled of a sophisticated cologne, and his white hair was meticulously manicured, contrasted against a nice tan. He started to put his hands on my outfit and tucked some fabric over and under. He asked for some safety pins from his assistant and started to pin some fabric to make it fit better. He then took a step back, eyeing his work. Seeming pleased, he said, "Please, walk."

I got to the end of the runway, which felt twice as long now than it did before, spun around, and came back. I guess he was liked what he saw because he asked me to go change into another outfit. I did this two more times, different outfits, and each time, Giorgio said things in Italian like *fuori o dentro?* and *bello cosi*. He had a quiet but confident demeanor, and I was enthralled simply watching this master artist at work. With each change, he would carefully study my outfit, almost as if he were rearranging it in his head. His facial expressions would vacillate between curiosity and discovery as he made adjustments and relayed his thoughts to his assistants.

As an artist myself, I could identify - he seemed to be doing what I had done so many times before when going through the creative process. You could tell he was working from his instincts and experimenting until what he saw was to his liking. When it was, you could see it in his face, the look of certainty and contentment from having transformed his vision into a real form. I have to say, that experience has been one of the highlights of my life—having the privilege of witnessing the creative process of one of the most respected and inspiring artists in the world.

As it turned out, I got the call the next morning from Rita saying I booked the show! I was elated and excited beyond words. This was becoming less about trying clothes on and looking fabulous as it was becoming was my entree into a new world of art, fashion, creativity, and self-expression such as I had never before experienced. The artist within me seemed to be coming more and more alive. Working with Mr. Armani helped me recognize that creating was not something he "did". It was who he was. His influence helped me to realize the very same thing about myself.

HELL YEAH!

"Truth is like the sun. You can shut it out for a time, but it ain't goin' away."
– Elvis Presley

After spending three months in Milan and walking in shows for Armani, Versace, Dolce Gabbana, Ferré, and D-Squared, to name a few, I ended up moving to New York City. There was an agency there that wanted to represent me, as some of the editorial work I had done was starting to appear in magazines, including the cover of *L'Uomo Vogue*. Some heat began being generated around my name, and the agencies in New York were anxious to see what they could do. I ended up signing with a boutique agency called Company, which represented a lot of the top girls in the business and was now beginning to represent men.

After a week of go-sees and castings, I ended up in Calvin Klein's office, in front of him and about eight other people, trying on ten different pairs of underwear. A few days afterwards, bam! I was shooting the underwear box campaign for Calvin Klein. It was hard to believe that all of this was happening in such a short amount of time. I was just going along with the flow, following the momentum of what was happening and enjoying the ride. Each week was a new adventure. Before I knew it, I was working in Hawaii, Switzerland, Germany, Paris, London, Italy, Tokyo,

Turkey, and Brazil. Every six months, it was then back to London, Milan, and Paris for the fashion shows. I was truly living a rockstar life.

As much as I relished jumping on planes to new and distant locales, I also loved having my home base in New York. It was, and still is, one of the most richly creative environments in the world, and I loved having this vast culture right outside my doorstep. When it came to the denizens of NYC, I found their directness a bit abrasive at first. After a short while though, I came to appreciate the authenticity with which they would hurl an insult or beckon someone to get the hell out of the way. Because there are about 16 million people, 840 miles of subway track, and roughly 15,000 taxi cabs in Greater NYC, the pace can get pretty frenetic. It's not uncommon to get swept up in a wave of people, if you're not paying attention. More out of necessity than anything else, folks in the Big Apple are much more liberal with their self-expression and opinions.

I found this refreshing compared to the people I grew up with in the Midwest. For the first time in my life, I was exposed to a variety of different opinions, ideologies, and beliefs, which made me start to critically think about what mine were. Were the things I was raised to believe truly what resonated with me or were they simply ideas and beliefs that I adopted because of where I grew up? Everything from religion to putting ketchup on my eggs was open to debate, much like my first experience in Milan, living in the model's apartment. I was learning more and more about so many different cultures, and what their beliefs were, and I found it incredibly interesting and inspiring.

Being able to openly talk about faith, politics, sex, sports, etc. in such an authentic and honest forum, enabled me to gain a deeper understanding and appreciation for other people's ideas, beliefs, and traditions. People asked me what religion I practiced and why, what I thought about politics in the United States compared to other countries, and what the benefits and drawbacks of each were. I had amazing conversations about the Cold War with Russians while sipping flavored, infused vodkas at the Russian Vodka Room. I regularly discussed the state of Middle Eastern tensions, geopolitics, and the real-life effects of US foreign policy with friends from Syria and Iran while inhaling hookahs at a popular Turkish restaurant in Soho. I'd find myself at Swedish Midsummer parties, dancing with throngs of statuesque, blond Vikings, singing songs about frogs and learning about Scandinavian healthcare. On some nights, my friends and I would end up at *Bardo*, a popular drag bar in the West Village, talking about gay rights and the latest collection by Moschino. This was my world education, and it was open, honest, and real.

I found it so freeing and inspiring! Growing up in the Midwest, I had never been encouraged to think so critically and to explore as much as I found myself doing in New York. The more I learned, the more I started to recognize how much of my personality I had shrunk and conformed to Midwestern aesthetics and perspectives just to "fit in". Walking down the streets of Manhattan, now, by contrast, seeing people wear yellow pants with purple hair, sashaying along, would make me smile with my newly realized appreciation: when people feel free to express themselves, the world can be a much more interesting and beautiful place.

Because of all this new exposure and my interactions with so many different people from all over the world, I began feeling more and more confident and increasingly open to expressing myself. I began dressing differently and wearing more vintage clothes and some higher-end designer stuff that fit a lot better than the oversized GAP shirts I was used to wearing back home. I began to venture out to restaurants that served delicacies such as escargot and oysters, happy and excited to try new things. All of this exploration and discovery began to fuse into my work as an actor as well. I became more open to expressing myself and taking bigger risks in my acting classes and at the television commercial auditions my agent was starting to send me on.

The exciting thing was that I started to book some of the auditions I was going on! I think a big reason I was successful, early on, was mainly because I knew I didn't have much experience, and so I decided to focus primarily on enjoying the process with no attachment to the outcome. This served me well enough until my agent asked if I would like to start going on some legitimate television auditions for shows such as *Sex and the City* and *Law & Order*. Knowing I had no formal acting training, my agent suggested I start taking an acting class to see if it was something I liked.

Finally, I had found my "hell yeah!" Derek Sivers, in his book *Anything You Want,* writes about recognizing your passion and how to decide something. He says, "If you're not saying "hell yeah!" about something, say 'no.'" Following my experience at the World Trade Center, I realized that life is too short for it not to be a "hell yeah!". When I read this in Sivers' book, his approach really resonated with me. He continues on to say that when you say *no* to most things that do not light you up or do not excite you, especially with regard to a job or a relationship, "you leave room in your life to really throw yourself completely into that rare thing that makes you say, "Hell yeah!" Acting was just that for me.

With acting, I felt like I had found my true purpose. I had to go through the motions of self-doubt, frustration, and confusion to discover it, but I was grateful and excited for the opportunity to finally explore this new path. The pressure that I had placed on myself since my freshman year of college to make a decision about what it was I was supposed to do with my life had finally lifted.

Expecting someone to know, at eighteen, what they want to do for the rest of their life is kind of crazy. I've come to realize from speaking with other people as well, about how they found their calling that often, it happens because of a chance opportunity. The theme that keeps surfacing is that if you're seeking the answer to a problem or simply looking to enrich your life, it's important to get out of the same patterns and to keep an open mind. My brother, Sean, is the perfect example of this. He's now a captain for Southwest Airlines, but before that, he was my snot-nosed, red-headed, "Dennis the Menace," kid brother who approached life with passion and enthusiasm in everything he did.

Sean attended Western Michigan University, where he played football and studied pre-med. Little did he know that Western has one of the top aviation programs in the country. On a random weekend, one of his fraternity brothers, who needed to accumulate more flight time hours, asked Sean if he'd like to join him for a flight in a Cessna. Sean, being the open-minded, full-of-life person that he is, took him up on the offer. As Sean says, the minute that he got up into the air, he realized that this was what he wanted to do for the rest of his life. He just "knew." He had found his passion, his "hell yeah!" We never know when that moment is going to find us, but it is out there! It doesn't matter how old you are, either. It didn't happen to me until I was twenty-four. It takes some people much longer, but if you keep searching and keeping an open mind, you will find it!

Samuel L. Jackson didn't get his big break until he was forty-one years old in *Jungle Fever*. Stan Lee, who created everything Marvel, didn't create his first comic until he was thirty-nine. Vera Wang, after her dream of being an Olympic figure skater was crushed, performed various jobs until she entered the fashion industry at age forty, eventually becoming one of the most respected names in fashion. Ray Kroc, played brilliantly by Michael Keaton in *The Founder*, at fifty-two, turned McDonald's from a one restaurant burger joint in San Bernardino, California, to the global empire that it is now. Colonel Sanders, who we can thank for creating KFC, didn't open his first restaurant until he was sixty-two.

The moral of the story? It's never too late to find your "hell yeah!"

DARE TO SUCK

"Take chances, make mistakes. That's how you grow. Pain nourishes your courage. You have to fail in order to practice being brave." – Mary Tyler Moore

When you give yourself permission to fall down, you open the possibility to learn something from the experience. You keep getting better and better. As we get older, we're so afraid to make mistakes or to look stupid that we're not willing to put ourselves in a situation where we might fail. For that reason, we run the risk of living our lives operating from a very narrow lens, which can prevent us from seeing some amazing things.

As I began to study acting in earnest, I realized it can be both freeing and cathartic, but it also requires a hell of a lot of vulnerability and the courage to put yourself out there in front of people, knowing that you might fail. For me, personally, this is one of the reasons that makes acting so appealing. I find great enjoyment and fulfillment through the growth process of overcoming challenges, and acting is one of the most challenging things I've ever done.

Through the process of becoming a better actor, I have discovered so much about myself—what lights me up, what my limits and boundaries are, and how to push past them. I've learned how to be a better communicator and storyteller. I've learned what I'm willing to stand up for and what I'm willing to let go. It has been an incredible journey and one that never ceases to teach me new lessons and expose further truths and wisdom. This never would have happened, however, if I hadn't heeded the advice of one of my acting teachers in LA named Lesly Kahn whose mantra was "Dare to suck!"

Growing up, it was easier and safer for me to follow the rules. I always tried to understand what the boundaries were so I wouldn't cross them, or at least make sure I wouldn't get caught. In school, math was my favorite subject because there was a definitive answer. One plus one equals two. I understood that because it made sense. When it came to reading a book and doing a report describing its theme and what metaphors and personifications were at play, it was overwhelming because it seemed like there were a million different ways to analyze it. Couple this with my lack of vocabulary and skills to formulate a critical analysis of something that was written by someone light years ahead of me in talent and experience...it's understandable why I was completely intimidated by good literature.

Reading works by authors such as F. Scott Fitzgerald, Shakespeare, and Harper Lee and then being asked to give a critique felt much akin to being told to tell Michael Jordan how to shoot free throws.

I felt woefully inadequate when it came to literature. I remember a time when I was in seventh grade, and our first assignment for the year was to read a short story and do an analysis of it. I was paralyzed. I felt stupid and afraid that if I told anyone I couldn't do it, they would think there was something wrong with me. I was so ashamed and started to cry alone on my back porch, thinking that I was a failure.

After reading and rereading the story several times, I managed to piece something together. I usually had to force myself to read over and over until the material made sense. As a teenager with a normal hyper-aversion for looking stupid, I would usually try to disguise my insecurities by preventing anyone from getting too close to me. I was afraid of them finding out that maybe I wasn't as smart as I wanted them to think I was. Because of this, I now realize I was insulating myself from allowing people to see the real me, and it wasn't until I started to study acting that I genuinely began to understand this. Acting forced me to strip away the layers of emotional body armor that I had erected over the years.

I began to practice letting my guard down, not only in acting class but in real life. For better or worse, I was incorporating more of Lesly's mantra "Dare to suck!" into my life. Lesly had this moniker printed on pens, pads of paper, and on plastic bottles. She was great at luring us out of our shells to let our authentic selves be seen and teaching us to laugh at ourselves even when we did suck. Because failure is inevitable, what I also learned from Lesly is that the sooner you become comfortable with your failures and not make them mean anything other than being one step closer to success, the sooner you are going to be able to embrace your "Hell yeah!" and pursue the things that really matter to you.

In an interview on CBS's *60 Minutes*, Elon Musk was asked about the possibility of failure for SpaceX, which is one of his companies that builds rockets for space exploration.

"I'd have to be insane if I thought the odds were in my favor," he replied.

The interviewer follows up with, "Why even begin?"

Elon without hesitation then said, "When something is important enough, you do it even though the odds are not in your favor."

Musk has mentioned in other interviews that even if he dies before seeing the work they are doing become a reality, his hope is that if he is able to provide the ability for someone else to take the baton and keep moving it forward, then, he says, he and his company will have been a success. Elon is the perfect example of someone giving themselves permission to suck every day. Because of this mindset, he has been able to create some of the most innovative and aspirational technology companies in the world. "Even if you're the best of the best," he continues, "there is the chance for failure. It's important that you really like what you do. If you don't like it, life is too short."

What aren't you doing because you're afraid to fail? Life is too precious to do anything but that which provides you the utmost happiness and fulfillment. This definitely takes practice because it can feel uncomfortable and vulnerable at first, but by daring to suck and making failing not mean anything, you'll start to discover a sense of confidence as you become more proficient with whatever it is you're practicing.

The more scripts I read, scenes I rehearsed, and auditions I went on, the more proficient I became as an actor to simply show up, be in the moment, and play.

After I began truly living this mantra, "Dare to suck!" I began to find myself in bigger auditions, with fancier studio executives, working on bigger and better sets. This mantra has truly changed my life. I'm confident it will change yours, too, if you simply stop being so hard on yourself.

Give yourself the permission and space to "suck." This is the only way we can consistently, progressively live the life we know in our hearts is our "hell yeah! "

BARK LIKE A DOG

"To escape fear, you have to go through it, not around it."
— Richie Norton

I would argue that most guys in the world aren't normally encouraged to express their inner vulnerabilities, and frequently, when we do, it can be viewed as a sign of weakness. Acting class was the first place where I felt permission and was truly encouraged to push the boundaries of self-expression and vulnerability. As I mentioned previously, it can take some getting used to at first. One of the ways an acting teacher of mine in LA would help get us over our nerves and the fear of looking stupid in front of fellow classmates was to have new students prepare a song to sing for their first day of class.

Upon hearing this request from the teacher of this new class I was about to join, I immediately told him most people would pay me not to sing. I followed it up by telling him that it would be in everyone's best interest if I was spared this task of my massacring of the song. He insisted, explaining it was a prerequisite to join the class. So I hastily prepared "Fly Me to the Moon," made popular by Frank Sinatra.

The next day when I showed up, sure enough, before I even had the chance to sit down, the teacher called me up to the stage in front of about twenty-five complete strangers. He introduced me and proceeded to give me the floor to debut my song. I started out a bit slowly and awkwardly and ended up forgetting the second verse, having to start over again before finally butchering my way through. When I finished, I thankfully started to walk off the stage when he asked me to return to the stage. He then asked me to sing the same song, but this time to pretend I was a dog and bark the song. I wasn't quite sure if I heard him correctly, so he repeated himself, after which I could feel the sweat glands under my arms unleash a torrent.

I started again slowly, but this time with a bit less volume. He bellowed out, "louder!" At this point, I figured *what the hell*, the faster I get through this, the sooner I could end this charade. I proceeded to bark enthusiastically for the rest of the song, which I'm quite certain would have made Sinatra, himself, turn in his grave. Afterward, my new teacher came over and said, "Thank you very much, Colin. Now that you've made an ass of yourself in front of everyone, you're free to do anything in front of them."

He was right. I didn't get anything thrown at me, no one said anything cruel, and I didn't die. Some of the other students may have thought it was awful, but there were some giggles and chuckles as well. Because of my teacher's bold request that day, I realized that we are mostly in our heads about how we are going to look, or how silly we may appear. Those fears can limit us and shut us down, preventing us from achieving the things most important to us.

As I continued on with that class, our teacher would constantly remind us to focus on the present and what our intention was for the scene. This is where I started to realize that by putting 100 percent of my attention on what I wanted to accomplish in a scene that my fear of looking stupid and the barriers to accomplishing things would disappear. I could finally be free in front of a group of strangers to simply enjoy the process of moment-to-moment creation by focusing on my task of accomplishing what my character needed for the scene.

Watching new students do this same thing was really interesting, because having to get up in a room full of strangers and perform is very similar to the audition process. This experience opened my eyes up to what the casting director looks for when an actor comes into the room. Is the actor confident or nervous? Is the actor in the moment and enjoying themselves or are they self-conscious? I started to recognize that the actors who would commit 1000% to barking their songs and were actually enjoying it, would inevitably be the most enjoyable to watch. You couldn't help but fall in love with some of these people because of their commitment and vulnerability.

It began to sink in that when you love what you do, it allows people around you to enjoy themselves and subconsciously makes them feel bolder and empowered as well. This leads me to something interesting I read.

In *Scientific American,* author and researcher Jonah Lehrer interviewed Marco Iacoboni, a neuroscientist at the University of California at Los Angeles who is best known for his work on mirror neurons, a small circuit of cells in the premotor cortex and inferior parietal cortex. Lehrer writes from speaking with Iacoboni, "What makes these cells so interesting is that they are activated both when we perform a certain action such as smiling and when we observe someone else performing that same action. In other words, they collapse the distinction between seeing and doing."

Susan Perry, a contributing writer to the Society for Neuroscience for the past twenty years, confers, "Before the discovery of mirror neurons, scientists generally believed that our brains use logical thought processes to interpret and predict other people's actions. Now, however, many have come to believe that we understand others not by thinking, but by feeling. For mirror neurons appear to let us 'simulate' not just other people's actions, but the intentions and emotions behind those actions. When you see someone smile, for example, your mirror neurons for smiling fire up, too, creating a sensation in your own mind of the feeling associated with smiling. You don't have to think about what the other person intends by smiling. You experience the meaning immediately and effortlessly."

Thus, when we see someone having an emotional reaction, such as when they wince from stubbing their toe or their face lights up with excitement after they score the game winning basket, our mirror neurons kick in and allow for us to have the same experience. This is why we find watching others so compelling because, almost voyeuristically, we are able to feel what it feels like to be Tom Cruise flying Mach 3 in a fighter jet or to tear up when Rose tells Jack she loves him while he shivers to death in the ice cold waters of the Atlantic. When we see people committed to what they are doing, we can become enthralled with it if we allow ourselves to be taken on the same journey.

As actors, our job is to entertain. By getting out of our own way we provide a medium to feel the appropriate emotions in a scene. This enables an audience to be transported into the story and feel the same experiences, and thus, the same emotions as the super hero, the villain, and everyone in between.

One of my acting coaches reiterated to me that our job is to go into the room and be the answer to people's problems. The casting director has to answer to the director, who has to answer to the producers, who have to answer to the studio heads, who have to answer to the board of the media company, who has to answer to the shareholders.

Everyone is stressed out and nervous about making the wrong casting choice, especially when millions of dollars are on the line. Margie Haber, one of acting coaches I mentioned earlier, would always tell us, "live the life" and "enjoy it!" She told me, the best thing you can do is to go into your work, whether it be an audition or on set, and afford the people watching the opportunity to be transported to another realm through your commitment and joy in your work.

"When you're nervous, they get nervous. When you convey strength and vulnerability, they are able to experience in kind and live your "slice of life" with you! "

Being cognizant of this and removing our self-consciousness allows us to get out of our own way and go on a magical journey all the while providing the opportunity for others to join in.

As soon as I started going to my auditions with this mindset and committing completely to my work, in order to be of true service to the author, the producers, the director, and most importantly the audience, I soon found myself filming projects in Australia, Cape Town, and Thailand. It was amazing!

By committing to what you love and making the present moment the priority, your need to avoid looking stupid disappears and you are open to a whole new world of possibilities!

THE 30/30/40 RULE

"Some people will not think I'm funny and that's okay."
—Will Ferrell

My first acting teacher, Jacqueline Siegel, was very instrumental to me and my acting career. She was in her sixties when I began studying with her, and her life had been dedicated to theatre. Jacqueline was the link between the Golden Age of Hollywood and Broadway and we twenty-something-year-old aspiring actors who would pepper her with questions like, "what was New York like in the 60s?" and "what did Marlon Brando say when you met him?" When I first started working with Jackie, I was incredibly "green." I feel like I had good natural instincts, but it took time for me to remember and organically incorporate the myriad techniques and tools she shared with us into my work.

I learned a lot from her, not just about acting, but about life in general, and through our work together, a better understanding of myself. Before each class, she would read an excerpt from a play or a book that would spark a discussion about philosophy, love, dreams, and more. I absolutely loved going to class every week because it was such a great place to be immersed in this cocoon of creativity and growth. We would discuss acting theory and principles and then a few minutes later, she had us on the ground acting out various characters we had seen in Central Park or exotic wild animals, just to get out of our heads and into our bodies.

On Wednesday mornings, there were a few of us who would all meet at her apartment on 27th Street and read plays, including my some of my favorites, *Miss Julie*, *The Glass Menagerie*, and *Death of a Salesman*. As my appreciation for great writing and authors grew, the residual feelings of junior high angst and frustration regarding literature began to fall away. Instead of feeling intimidated, my imagination and creativity was sparked to bring these stories and characters to life in our next class.

One of the most important things I remember her saying came when a student in my class was having a particularly difficult time with a scene. Everyone in class could tell this student was selfconscious and it was preventing her from being able to fully inhabit the character and be present. Sensing this too, Jackie mentioned a little anecdote that I'll never forget.

She said, "When it comes to the people that you encounter in life, including those who pay to watch your performances, thirty percent of them are going to like you. Another thirty percent are NOT going to like you. The final forty percent ARE NOT GOING TO CARE, so you might as well do what fulfills you and gives you joy, and stop worrying so much about what other people think." In other words, *stop trying to please everyone because you're not going to*. It's simply not possible. When you try to please everyone, not only can it can come across as inauthentic, but it can be both exhausting and unfulfilling.

This coincided with my feeling more comfortable to share my authentic self with others and my desire to be more honest with people. Embracing this mindset felt right. I started to honor my feelings and needs more and not worry so much about doing things to please others, not only at work, but also in my relationships. As such, I definitely noticed a shift. My work became more grounded, I became less concerned with what people thought, and I began focusing more on the things that I felt were important to me instead of worrying so much about trying to be amenable and make everyone else around me happy at the expense of my own happiness. As a result, some people naturally fell out of my life, but my relationships became deeper, more fulfilling, and less shallow with the people who ended up sticking around.

It took me some time to navigate and to feel okay with not always telling people what I thought they wanted to hear. What helped were the daily and weekly exercises of rehearsing and performing scenes where I was on stage, saying dialogue I wouldn't have normally found myself saying. Being on stage, bringing to life master writers' works such as Tennessee Williams's *Cat on a Hot Tin Roof,* where Brick is drunkenly, regretfully, and angrily clashing with his wife as a result of broken dreams and heartache, and inhabiting the damaged psyche of Jamie in Eugene O'Neill's seminal *Long Day's Journey into Night,* nudged me to be more open about my own feelings. Playing these incredibly flawed and sensitive characters forced me to tap into the inner depths of who I am to discover my truths— what triggers me, what inspires me, and where my demons lie.

Getting in touch with my feelings and emotions at this level of depth enabled me to become more comfortable expressing anger and voicing my desires from a primal place, which was new to me. This, in turn, began to fuse my personal character with confidence and self-awareness. It was a very freeing experience. Focusing more on what fulfills me rather than trying to please others freed up a lot of my energy so I could better commit to doing what I love, to create. When I am creatively fulfilled, I am able to be present and available for others, further increasing my sense of purpose and overall happiness. When you honor your needs you are able to give more to others. It starts from within.

As I became immersed in watching films with Brando, Streep, Pacino, and De Niro, I began to recognize and appreciate their intense commitment to their craft and how honest and seemingly effortless their performances were. I, too, became obsessed with honoring the characters I portrayed on stage with the same type of honesty, and by doing so, I began to rely less on the opinions of others about my performance and more on my own personal feelings.

We actors go on hundreds upon hundreds of auditions throughout our careers, and most of the time we don't end up booking the job, so loving the process has to be a huge part of the reason why we do anything at all. By focusing on the enjoyment of the process, the need for validation from others will not factor in less. When you love what you do, despite the hardship and possible heartache it can cause, you keep doing it because it's simply who you are. Do you think Cézanne, Van Gogh, and Monet became painters to become rich and famous? We may never know, but my feeling is that they created simply because they needed to. It was in their DNA to do so. Looking at their works, it appears that the spirit of each artist is actually infused in their art. They painted because it was a true expression of themselves. *Find what you love and let it kill you!*

Take action, practice, be vulnerable and honest, show up on time, and share yourself with the world fully. In doing so, you'll get the feedback necessary to guide you along the way. When you find something you love to do, and pursue it with passion, regardless of what people think, then you have truly discovered the Agile Artist within you.

Three Takeaway Action Tips:

1. Get out, explore and show up! Don't judge something until you've experienced it for yourself.

2. Take risks and be vulnerable. The more you share of your true self, the more you give others the opportunity to genuinely connect with you.

3. Take constant action, be authentic and commit 1000%. This is your life. By honoring yourself, you'll teach others to honor you.

04 FREE BALLIN'

"When life gets you down, you know what you gotta do? Just keep swimming."
— Dory, Finding Nemo

There are few experiences that can test your courage and will as much as when faced with a life-threatening situation. Growing up, I was quite healthy and always very active, generally taking for granted my health until one of those rare days when I got sick. Whether it was the flu, chicken pox or mono, I always knew that with a few days of rest, I'd be healthy again. With the everincreasing diagnosis of serious disease these days, however, few of us seem to be spared from knowing someone we know and love being confronted with a serious health issue. Sometimes, in fact, we're confronted by such challenges ourselves.

Six months after booking my role on *All My Children* and feeling like I was on top of the world, having secured my first real, full-time acting gig where I could honestly tell people, "I act for a living," I was forced to deal with the words that no one ever wants to hear from their doctor: "You have cancer."

"What? You've got to be kidding me. I'm thirty-three and in the prime of my life. This is a joke, right?" I was living in my favorite city in the world, and I was doing what I loved. I had a great place in the West Village, and I finally felt like the past eight years of struggle and hustle had paid off. This was my time to enjoy life and reap the rewards of all the sacrifices I had made to get to where I was.

JUST WHEN YOU THINK YOU HAVE IT ALL

"When adversity strikes, that's when you have
to be the most calm.
Take a step back, stay strong, stay grounded,
and press on."
– LL Cool J

I have never before spoken about my experience with cancer publicly. I think it's important to include it here, however, because of the profound effect it's had on me. Because it was the honest and supportive sharing of others that helped me get through it, I'd like to "pay it forward" and share what I've learned from such a scary, uncertain time in my life.

For the first few months that I was working on *All My Children*, I felt like I was exactly where I was supposed to be in my life. Things felt right for the first time in a very long while. One day, however, I noticed my left testicle had swollen to about twice its normal size. It stayed that way for about four weeks, and I figured that this was one of the weird, random bodily things that happen and that it would just go away. But it didn't. Instead, it got bigger.

After a few more weeks, I mentioned this situation to my brother, and he encouraged me to go to the doctor and have it checked out. Reluctantly, I went. I didn't want to, of course, because I was afraid of hearing the worst, but the uncertainty was really starting to worry me. I finally decided to go and made an appointment to see my doctor early in the week. He confirmed that what was happening down there didn't look normal, so he scheduled for me to meet with a urologist a few days later.

When I got to the urologist's clinic in the East Village, a nurse drew some blood, and then I saw the doctor, Dr. Berman. From his physical examination he couldn't quite determine what was causing the swelling, so he had me then go to an ultrasound clinic, later that day, to see if they could identify the culprit. At this point, the dull ache of worry I'd been living with for the past few weeks became an intense bout of anxiousness that I could feel taking hold of my body.

After the ultrasound, I went home and tried to stay positive, worked out, ate some dinner, and went to bed. I went to work the next morning, and while I was at the studio, got a call from the urologist saying he needed to see me right away. Fuuuu.....what does that mean? When I finished my last scene, I removed the pound of makeup from my face and shot down to his office.

The receptionist greeted me and asked me to sit in the waiting room. It might have been only a few minutes, but it felt like an eternity until I was called into his office.

"How are you?" he asked.

"Eh, you tell me," I responded.

In a matter of fact way, he looked me in the eye and then proceeded to tell me I had a relatively progressed stage of testicular cancer, and that he was scheduling me for surgery the next day.

He followed with, "At this point, there's a chance that it may have spread through the veins and the arteries that lead up into your kidneys, so this needs to be removed immediately."

I told Dr. Berman I had to work the next day and asked him if we could do the surgery on Monday. When I think back on this, I see how idiotic it sounds, but in the moment, I think was probably just trying to maintain a sense of normalcy and control since I was terrified by having to face what was ahead.

I was just hoping to get this taken care of and then be able to return to my daily life and work routine. I naively thought I could do just that. I called my parents to let them know, and we decided that my dad was going to fly into New York from Chicago to be there with me for the surgery. I can't thank my parents enough for their unconditional love and support, which helped tremendously when my world was starting to be turned upside down. Even though there was nothing my dad could do other than be at my side, I've come to realize since, sometimes that's all you need.

On Monday, I went to work and put on the best face I could. Physically, I felt fine, but inside, the gnawing feelings of fear from not knowing what all this meant were beginning to consume me. I realized I needed to actively begin focusing my attention to implement whatever was necessary to prevent myself from being overwhelmed with this immense fear of uncertainty. I knew I had to take an intensely close look at my outlook on life and how I perceive things… While I've always been a believer in the power of positive thinking, dealing with such thoughts at that moment and trying to assure myself I was going to be okay couldn't match my fear, no matter how hard I tried.

I didn't want to be paralyzed by my thoughts and feelings, so I decided I needed to do something proactive. I Googled what fear really is, where it comes from, and what I could do to lessen its hold and influence on me mentally, physically, and spiritually. Already having a rudimentary understanding from my college biology classes about the fight or flight response our bodies maintain, I needed to find out if there was a way to gain more control over these natural physiological effects. What I discovered is that "fear" is the term humans have created to describe the nervous feelings that our bodies generate as a mechanism for survival. Feelings of anxiety that manifest in our bodies as the fight or flight response to danger is an essential component for keeping us safe. What I also discovered is that whether it's a real or perceived threat makes no difference—the reaction our bodies have in response to it is the same.

According to the University of Minnesota's website *Taking Charge of Your Health and Well Being,* fear prepares us to react to potential danger by releasing hormones in our bodies that slow or shut down functions not needed for survival. Blood is shunted away from our digestive systems, and our outer extremities and functions that help us survive (such as eyesight) are sharpened. Our heart rate increases, and blood flows to muscles so we can run faster. The flow of hormones to a part of our brain called the amygdala increases to help us focus on the presenting danger and store it in our memory to avoid the same potential danger in the future. This is why traumatic experiences get seared into our brain: so that we know to avoid the same situation in the future.

Once I started examining this process more deeply, I discovered that the brain reacts in predictable ways. To further what *Taking Charge of Your Health and Well Being* states, "Once the fear pathways are ramped up, the brain short-circuits more rational processing paths and begins reacting immediately to signals from the amygdala, instead of more rational processing. When in this overactive state sometimes called the "amygdala hijack," the brain perceives events as negative and remembers them that way."

When left unchecked and we subject ourselves to a constant state of fear, this can have disastrous effects on our bodies. "Fear weakens our immune system, can cause cardiovascular damage, ulcers, decreased fertility, and accelerated aging. It can cause memory lapses and interrupt processes in our brains that allow us to regulate emotions, reflect before acting, and act ethically. This impacts our thinking and decision making in negative ways, leaving us susceptible to intense emotions and impulsive reactions. All of these effects can leave us unable to act appropriately."

Since this is the normal way our brains respond, and we can't change how our amygdala or other parts of our bodies function in response to fear, I realized the only thing I could change was the perceived threat part. So, much like in the film *The Matrix*, where Morpheus tells Neo that life is actually not what we know it to be, I realized I needed to, in effect, use my mental capacity to pull myself out of this Matrix of perception, if you will, to remove myself from feeling trapped in my own mind. I decided to look at the physiological process of fear, from the outside, in order to objectively examine what I could do to prevent being controlled by this evolutionary response. By doing this, I believed I would have a better grasp on how "I" wanted to feel through this experience.

I'm sure you've heard the analogy that our brain is essentially a supercomputer that simply processes the information fed into it.

Our brains will automatically give us answers and, accordingly, will manifest emotions within our bodies based on the thoughts we focus on and the perception and associated paradigms we create. I started to think about the specific thoughts and viewpoints that I needed to program my brain with in order to deal with what I was facing rather than to allow the fear of the unknown to remain a perceived threat.

When we are young, life mostly happens to us. As an eight year old, we have neither the mental capacity nor the knowledge to deal with life in a mature and objective way when, say, we get punished for doing something wrong or our parents get divorced. With instances we don't understand or are traumatized by, our brains are programmed with the software based on an eight year old's way of thinking instead of from an adult's perspective. As we get older, though, a lot of the time we still operate from this "software" that was programmed by an upset eight year old who didn't have the wherewithal to discern the reality of a situation. As we get older and develop critical thinking abilities, we actually have the ability to reprogram the software in our brains toward a more empowered viewpoint. Sadly, more often than not, we don't even realize this is possible. It took for me to get cancer to be able to discover this.

Not knowing how my diagnosis was going to play out, I started thinking about who I needed to become in the face of a cancer diagnosis in order to prevent the perceived threat from hijacking my brain. I had two choices. I could focus on the fear and unknown and continue to perpetuate my anxiety or I could focus on feeding my brain wisdom and knowledge that would manifest feelings of strength, courage, and positivity. I chose to feed it with these more positive and bold thoughts and with those of the future and what I still wanted to accomplish in life. I focused on thoughts of becoming a movie star and things that inspired me with energy and passion. I created thoughts of having a family and making amazing memories together. I knew that if I didn't fill my brain with the things I wanted to manifest, the negative thoughts of fear and anxiety of the unknown would creep in. I recognized that the choice about what to focus on was fairly easy. I knew the last thing that was going to help me was to dwell on the unknown future. Instead, I chose to create a future that I could live into, a future in which I got through all this and was healthy again.

After work on Monday, I met my dad at the radiology clinic to get a CT scan so the doctors could determine if the cancer had spread to any other places in my body. Like most cancers, If left unchecked, testicular cancer can spread, and the most susceptible place for secondary tumors to grow is in the lungs. When the nurses inserted the IV and released the iodine contrast dye into my arm, a feeling of heat began flowing through me quickly, making me feel uncomfortable. I began to have trouble breathing and my skin became itchy. Soon red blotches formed on my skin and my face turned bright red. My airway began to close up and it became increasingly difficult to breathe. I was having an allergic reaction to the iodine.

The doctors immediately administered Benadryl, which took a few minutes to kick in. Until it did I was trying to focus on trying to stay calm so as not to exacerbate the problem. Within a few minutes, I could sense more oxygen flowing into my lungs—just another bump in the road moving forward. While I lay there with my dad at my side, the doctors came in after about twenty minutes and let us know they hadn't found any signs of other tumor growths, thankfully. The next step was the surgery.

To give some context of what the procedure is like, the surgery is similar to having other abdominal surgeries such as a C-section birth. The surgical procedure for treating testicular cancer is called an orchiectomy, which involves removing the testical and subsequent veins and arteries leading to the kidneys, as this is how the cancer is most likely to spread. A three-inch incision is made through the abdominal wall. I was told the recovery time would be about 2-3 weeks. I didn't care, I just wanted to get it taken care of immediately.

The following day my dad and I went to St. Vincent's Hospital on 7th Avenue and 11th Street. I was ushered into the surgical changing room, put on the light blue garment and hair net thing, and after a bit was wheeled into surgery. They put an IV into my arm and asked me to count back from ten. I think I got to eight, and then I was out.

I woke to a foggy blur of fluorescent lighting and the murmurs of nurses nearby. I felt pretty groggy and numb, but it was nice to see my dad next to me when I started to come to. We stayed in the recovery room for about three or four hours, and after they determined that I was stabilized, I was cleared to go home. It wasn't until I had to move that I noticed the pain from the incision, but for the most part, I was fairly well medicated enough to be able to get into a taxi and head back to my place.

Fortunately, with my schedule on *All My Children*, I had a whole week off, so, thankfully I didn't have to let anyone know at work or ask for time off. I was pretty much bedridden for about four to five days and simply getting up to go to the bathroom was a painful challenge. After staying with me for the rest of the week and seeing that I was on the mend, my dad headed back to Chicago. Quite a few of my friends came by, bringing books, food, and their company, which definitely helped with my recovery. A few days later, I was back on set at *AMC*, albeit still sore and bandaged.

Luckily I didn't have any scenes that involved exposing my pecs in the bedroom, so I was able to show up and appear relatively normal.

Things went fine with my recovery for the next couple months, and once I was healed up, the next phase of treatment was the radiation. Tests of the blood vessels leading to my kidneys indicated the presence of cancer cells, so the protocol was for me to receive radiation treatment for three weeks, Monday through Friday.

I didn't really know what to expect with radiation other than that my doctor told me it can cause some nausea, but I was soon to learn that nothing can truly prepare one for actually experiencing it. At my pretreatment appointment, I had to change into another hospital gown and was led into a room with a big machine that took up most of the space and was told to lie down on this flat hard slab. The radiologist began to line up a big contraption above me that projected red laser lines on my stomach in the shape of a grid pattern. After she lined up the laser lines, which indicated where the radiation was going to be targeting a specific part of my abdomen, she then poked me with a needle in various places, three places on my chest and one place on either side of me.

It felt exactly what you would think being stuck with a needle would feel like, which was confusing to me. When I asked what she was doing, she explained she needed to mark me so that when I came in every day for my treatment, they could line up the lasers to the exact same spots. Because these were needles she was using, I asked her to clarify what the mark was. She mentioned that it was like a tattoo. Incredulously I asked, "Tattoo? As in these are permanent?" She casually replied, "Yes."

Even though they are five small dots, they're still permanent on my body today and a reminder to me of the fragility of life. At the time, however, I was a bit frustrated that someone was permanently marking my body without letting me know. It was as if my body no longer belonged to me: that this nurse was simply doing her job and was completely devoid of any compassion. It felt as if I was being treated as an object instead of as a human being having my body forever marked. Regardless, I just wanted the treatment over with and arguing with her after the fact was not going to do any good. I only wanted to focus on getting better.

A few days later, I went in for my first round of therapy. It seemed simple enough. I changed into my hospital gown, came back into the same room where I got my new tattoos, and lay down on the slab. The technician lined up the laser to the five dots, which took all of a minute or two. They told me to lie perfectly still and then left the room and went into an adjoining smaller room with a window in it. This room had the controls and monitors and was shielded from the radiation. Through a speaker, they told me to lay perfectly still.

A craggly scratchy noise revved up and buzzed for about five seconds, and I was told to keep laying there. As the machine rotated below me, the radiation was then shot up from beneath, so that both sides of my body received the treatment. The whole process took about eight minutes, and then I was done. I put on my street clothes, felt fine, and left. I thought to myself, "that wasn't so bad." Until I got home, that is.

About an hour and a half later, back in my apartment in the West Village, I began to feel sick. A fever took over me, and I felt the urge to throw up. I became extremely tired and decided to go to bed even though it was only about 7 pm, I woke up the next morning feeling better, but noticed my stomach was a bit red. Other than that, I felt well enough to go to work. I had arranged my radiation therapy around my shooting schedule at work so that no one would know what I was going through. At the time, I didn't feel comfortable telling anyone at *AMC* about something as personal as this. I wanted to be better, and sharing my diagnosis and treatment with others would only make me have to keep talking about it, which was not something I wanted to focus on.

Each day, Monday through Friday, the same thing—go in, get zapped, and an hour later, crawl up into a ball under my covers and sleep as sweat dripped off my face and my stomach felt like it was on fire. My plan of not telling anyone at *AMC* was working until the third week of treatment. Because I had to work in the afternoon one particular day, I went to get my treatment in the morning and then headed to the studio. When I got there, the nausea set in and all I wanted to do was lay down. I was so tired and light headed, but I had to power through. When I was called to set, we ended up shooting the first two of five scenes which took about 30 minutes.

After the second scene we took a normal ten-minute break, and I sat down and put my head down to rest because I was so exhausted. Our director, Casey, came over and asked if I was okay. The weight of trying to hold all of this in for weeks finally made me cave. I looked up at Casey, struggled to contain my feelings of fear and desperation and simply said, "No, I'm not okay." No longer could I do this by myself.

Casey looked concerned and asked me what was wrong. I briefly explained to him about my surgery and the treatment I was receiving. He asked me if I had told anyone, especially our executive producer, Julie, to which I replied I hadn't. I told him I was okay to finish the scenes we had left and that I would go tell her afterward.

When I went up to Julie's office and told her, she responded with nothing but kindness and support. She told me that I could take all the time off I needed and that first and foremost I should take care of myself. I told her I only had a couple of more days of treatment left and asked if my scenes could be moved to the mornings from now on. This way, I could come to work, then go to the hospital afterward to get my treatment and then go home to sleep it off. She graciously and caringly agreed, which was a huge relief, knowing that now I had the support of the people I worked with and didn't have to hide anything anymore.

Up until this point, having worked at *AMC* now for about nine months, I felt I had a great relationship with quite a few of the actors as well as the makeup, hair stylists, and the wardrobe folks, but my relationship with Julie was not the most open. She could appear to be icy and not very friendly, but after I shared with her my experience and authentically communicated my real feelings about it all, Julie responded in kind.

The entertainment industry can be tricky because its foundation is based on acting truthfully on screen as well as the stage. Actors are applauded and rewarded for their honesty to bare their souls, but when it comes to real life, sharing who we truly are and what we care about can feel as if we are making ourselves too vulnerable and are putting ourselves at risk for getting hurt. At a lot of the Hollywood parties I've been to, there are pleasantries abound and plenty of admiration that can easily be attributed to how famous or successful someone is at that given moment. Meeting people who genuinely care, not only in the entertainment industry, but in most other places of business may not always feel easy, but from this experience, I began to realize that by opening up on a personal level, it seemed to make people look at me in a different light, if you will. No longer was I the Calvin Klein model and son of Erika Kaine with the six-pack abs, but it felt like in the eyes of some of the people who I didn't have the best connection or relationship with, I became more authentic and therefore more able to connect honestly with.

In turn, I came to realize that hiding my feelings prevented me from truly connecting with people. After telling my executive producer about my cancer and treatment, she shared with me that her husband had passed away from a heart attack and how overwhelming and scary it had been for her. I spent more time in her office that day, genuinely connecting with her over real life experiences, than I had in the whole nine months I had been working at *AMC* altogether. It was one of the most open and authentic conversations I've ever had, something I hadn't considered possible up until right then. It felt great to know, now, I wasn't alone anymore and that I had support. I started to recognize that opening up to others conveys the opposite of weakness.

It shows strength and vulnerability that gives others permission to be and share their authentic selves which provides amazing opportunity to connect.

After my radiation treatment was completed, the follow-up protocol required me to get checkups every three months. These consisted of chest X-rays and a blood test including a CT scan at the six-month mark. The CT scan was to detect any secondary cancers or tumors not only from the original cancer, but from the radiation treatment. Since the doctors knew I was allergic to the iodine dye for the CT scan, the alternative was to drink this thick barium liquid that tastes like liquid chalk. After drinking three large containers of this, I had my CT scan and thankfully, again, there were no signs of the cancer having spread. It looked like the radiation had worked. Fortunately, my tests for the first two checkups came back clean, and I continued to go on with my normal life, trying to put this experience behind me—that is, until my third checkup, shortly after New Years Eve, not even a year from my first diagnosis.

It was January 2007 when I went in for this third post-treatment appointment. As my doctor was doing his normal physical examination, asking me how my celebrations had been, I told him I had gone to Miami with my girlfriend and that we'd had a great time. About to ask another question, he stopped and hesitated. He followed with, "Colin, I think I feel another tumor."

I just remember standing there, speechless, with my pants down at my knees. Dr. Berman then told me I would have to get another ultrasound and a CT scan to confirm what he suspected. Statistics say that once someone gets testicular cancer, there is only a 5 percent chance of it happening again. For whatever reason, I happened to be one of the "lucky" 5 percent.

STARING DEATH IN THE FACE

Neo: "I thought it wasn't real."
Morpheus: "Your mind makes it real."
– The Matrix

Dr. Berman said we'd need to do another battery of tests to confirm his suspicions. I don't like to jump to negative assumptions right away, but I admit I was pretty scared. I was thinking, primarily, if it were indeed a tumor, then *why and how was it happening again?* I had been taking good care of myself, eating well and exercising, so what was wrong? Was it me? My environment? Was my body trying to tell me something? Dr. Berman mentioned to me that there were no conclusive studies to prove any causal links to testicular cancer, so there simply were no answers. I found this very hard to believe and had to keep directing my focus away from the unknown and lack of understanding, otherwise it would have driven me crazy.

"Here we go again," I thought, as I was sent to get another ultrasound and CT scan. I went for the ultrasound first, where after changing into another hospital gown, I found myself standing in front of the technician. He applied a cold, wet gel onto the flat metal head of the device and then onto my testicle. As he rubbed it around, the technician stared at the monitor in silence. After a couple minutes he said, "Okay, we're done." I asked if he was able to see anything that looked abnormal, to which he replied, "Yes, I can see something that looks like a tumor." Then he cleaned off the device head, turned, and just walked out of the room.

Doctors and medical personnel aren't necessarily supposed to be counselors or therapists, but I was surprised by his lack of compassion and how despite the opportunity, he offered no support. I remember how emotionally shaken I was - I'm not sure how anyone couldn't have noticed. As soon as the door shut when he left, I broke down. I don't think I've ever felt so terrified or alone as I did in that moment.

After I collected myself and put my clothes back on, I left to get the CT scan done. On my way, I called home and my mom answered. I told her what was going on and remember sharing with her how scared and alone I felt. She told me something that helped immensely. She said, "Honey, I know you're scared and you have every right to be, but in this moment, what you need to do now is put your armor on. You have to be a soldier and do what is necessary to get ready for battle." That's all I needed to hear to remind me that I had to focus on who I needed to be to get through this with strength and confidence. In that moment, I needed to create myself to be a warrior.

Thankfully, the CT clinic was able to squeeze me in at the end of the day, and after wading through NYC traffic, I finally arrived around 5:30 p.m. Since it was the middle of January, it was already dark out and frigid, and when I arrived, the clinic was empty save for a couple of receptionists. I checked in, they gave me the tubs of barium liquid chalk to drink, and then I changed into the cotton gown. CT scans take about twenty minutes, and when it was over, I asked the technicians if they were able to detect anything abnormal, hoping to contradict what the ultrasound tech had told me. Unfortunately, the technician said the radiologist had already left for the day, so I would have to wait until the morning for him to look at it and let me know.

I remember walking out of the clinic by myself, into that cold winter night, realizing how alone I felt and that I needed some support. As I stood there on the street waiting for a taxi, I recall how, as I tried not to be overwhelmed, feelings of helplessness permeated my brain. This is one of the few times in my life where my mental constitution had been pushed to its absolute breaking point. It's as if there is a constant tug of war between what our brains react to emotionally and how we try to rationalize what is taking place all while seeking to find some semblance of comfort and security. In that moment, I knew I had to stop focusing on what was happening if I was going to be able to get through it. The only thing I could think to do was call someone to be with, for that support I knew I needed. I reached out to one of my really good friends, Katrin, and she agreed to have dinner with me.

———

I met Katrin at a restaurant called El Quijote on 23rd Street in Chelsea, and when I saw her, she gave me the biggest hug. After we sat down, I told her how afraid and sad I was because I was only thirty-four years old and felt like I had so much more life to live. I told her I was terrified that I wasn't going to have that opportunity. I didn't come right out and say it, but inside I was beyond frightened, that because the cancer had come back, there might be a more serious reason as to why. My fear was that the cause could be one from which I might not recover a second time. She listened intently. Instead of offering empty platitudes like "it's okay, you'll get through it" or "keep thinking positively," she just let me talk and acknowledged how I felt, which made me feel less alone.

Something I've noticed not only about myself, but about others as well, is that when things have gone badly, the simple act of listening to and acknowledging what someone is feeling is usually all that they need in order to feel supported. One of the most significant pieces of wisdom I have gained from attending seminars, listening to spiritual advisors and TED talks, and learning from my own experiences, is that the answer to most problems lie within us. More often than not, we know, deep down, what the best answers or decisions are, we just need someone to ask the right questions for us to be able to discover them. Oftentimes I find a problem when I share something I'm dealing with that most people want to jump in with their own solution on how to fix it, which may or may not work. However well meaning, their offer to solve my problems for me doesn't make me feel recognized and understood, so my anxiety and loneliness persist. Most of the time, it's not the answer to the problem that we are seeking, but rather, we hope to having our immediate fears and frustrations to be alleviated by someone we trust.

What I have found works for me, and what I think is the best gift someone can give, is to actively listen and acknowledge the state someone is in without judgement or trying to fix it. Most people fail to realize that offering solutions to solve someone's problem can make them feel even more upset. When offering your opinion for a solution or an answer to someone else's problems, you're subconsciously saying to them, "there is something wrong with you, and I will now fix you because you don't know how to."

The more effective approach when someone is upset and dealing with a problem is to ask them how they feel and why. If your wife had a bad day at work, ask her why and refrain from offering a solution or trying to figure out how you can fix it. Instead, say something like, "Wow, that sounds frustrating, how did that make you feel?" Asking someone if they would like to hear your thoughts or insight about their concern makes them feel recognized and empowered. In doing so, you are offering them a choice, not simply telling them who they need to be or what they need to do. Following up with something that will make them feel supported in the moment like, "Can I make you dinner?" usually goes a long way too.

By recognizing someone for exactly where they are, without trying to change them or how they are feeling, their emotions will likely dissipate. In doing so, you alleviate the emotional hijack from the mammalian brain, and a clearing is thus created for the person to listen with a more receptive and level head to what their true self is telling them. It's also likely they will lean toward the insight you feel might help.

With Katrin recognizing and acknowledging my fear and anxiety without trying to tell me how to fix them, I started to feel better and was able to be more present. As the noise dissipated from my mind, I was able just to sit with her. Finally, I was able to muster the strength to begin to focus on what I needed to do in order to remain calm and strong. After a couple hours, I left, went home, and tried to sleep.

In the morning, Dr. Berman called to inform me that it was, indeed, a tumor, with a high probability of being cancerous. Hearing this, I knew that I needed to keep telling myself that I was going to be okay. I asked myself over and over, "What do I need to do to get through this? What do I need to focus on?" Within a couple of days, this time, my mom flew out to be with me for the surgery.

TOUR DE FORCE

"Never tell me the odds! "
— Han Solo

One of the most important and inspirational touchpoints for me during all of this was a book about Lance Armstrong called *It's Not About the Bike*. My sister bought it for me, and it detailed his experience with testicular cancer and specifically how he got through it all. This was before his doping scandal broke, and at the time, he was an inspiration to millions and was raising a substantial amount of money for cancer research. Before reading about him, I didn't know much about Lance other than he had overcome cancer to win the Tour de France several times. The yellow bracelets that read "Livestrong" were everywhere, only adding to his prominence. Reading his book was the biggest source of support while I was going through my treatment this second time.

Years later, his improprieties, which I don't condone, were revealed, but reading about how he overcame cancer and the mindset and practices that he adopted to get through it, helped give me strength and hope. Knowing that if he could get through his cancer experience, which was worse than mine, his having spread to his brain, gave me the encouragement I needed to believe I could do the same and beat my cancer.

Reading about Armstrong made me feel empowered. I was inspired to overcome whatever I needed to in order to become 100 percent healthy again. I meditated and did visualizations of my body being healed on a cellular level. One big takeaway from *It's Not About the Bike* was that Lance's doctor didn't tell him the chances for his survival. He knew the statistics regarding the survival rates of Lance's particular stage of cancer, but instead of relaying this data, he cemented in Lance's mind, confidence that he was going to overcome his cancer.

Before Lance received treatment, he went to see two doctors who were considered at the top of their field. One was in Houston and the other, at IU. The first doctor told him the chemotherapy was going to be extremely caustic and cause serious side effects, including damage to his lungs, which would preclude him from ever racing competitively again. The second doctor at IU told him that he would be back to racing after his treatment. Lance asked the doctor at IU why his prognosis was so different from the doctor's in Houston, to which the doctor at IU replied that they were using some new experimental drugs that had shown promise, and that he felt Lance would respond well to them.

When Lance asked the IU doctor how he could trust him, the doctor replied, "As good as you are on your bike, I'm even better as a doctor." That was all Lance needed to hear in order for him to decide to be treated by him. A year later when Lance was healed and cancer-free, he went back to IU to visit the team of physicians that cured him. When Lance asked the doctor what he thought his chances of survival were a year prior, the doctor said, "At the time, realistically, I would have given you a 15 percent chance. If I had told you that, however, you probably wouldn't be here right now."

The placebo effect has demonstrated that our brains can be highly suggestible to outside influences. There was a study done with a group of cancer patients where half were told that the drug they would be taking would make their hair fall out and the other half were told nothing about hair loss. The group that was told they would lose their hair exhibited significantly more loss than the other group, even though they were taking the same drug.

There are many similar examples of experiments like this, which is why I don't place a huge emphasis on statistics for specific outcomes. Statistics can help predict and determine generalities, but when it comes to health, I am not an advocate of knowing all the specifics. I know that if I hear a certain number, then it's easy for my brain to latch onto it and potentially result in a self-fulfilling prophecy regarding the outcome.

For example, if you hear or read a statistic stating that 85 percent of people who get diagnosed with a particular disease die and only 15 percent live, then most likely your brain is going to perceive this low survival rate as a threat. This can then initiate the fight or flight response processes I previously mentioned, which perpetuates fear and other feelings of stress and discomfort. Even though you very well may be in that 15 percent who will respond favorably to the treatment and be cured, the negative thoughts and feelings you have allowed your brain to cause may make you think you're actually the 85 percent who are not going to survive. For this reason, I knew not to ask my doctor too many specific questions about survival rates or anything of that nature.

To be clear, I'm not a physician or a scientist. I'm simply conveying theories and experimental results that I have read about, not only from clinical trials but also from other's experiences, such as Lance Armstrong's. When it comes to medicine and actual diagnoses, each person is different, and each ailment has varying degrees of severity and prognosis. I'm only sharing with you my personal thoughts on the matter in that I chose to focus on feeding my brain with positivity and thoughts of certainty about being healthy. I had no way of knowing what my outcome was going to be, but what I knew I could control was how I thought about it. For me, there was no other option.

I knew I had to focus on what was going to make me healthy. I didn't want to introduce any negative outside influences that might affect my recovery. Instead of looking at this from a negative place, I decided to look at this as an opportunity to practice discipline and feel what it meant to empower a commitment I had made—my commitment to becoming healthy again.

I knew this second go-around was going to require a ton of discipline. It was like walking on a tightrope. If I let in any thoughts beyond my complete focus on recovery and the steps I needed to take in order to stay calm and empowered, the negative thoughts and anxiety might take over, overwhelm me, and make my immune system weak. My body, I thought, would not be in its optimal state to heal itself.

The main thing I needed to contend with now, having this second surgery was the fact that both of my testes were going to be gone. This meant having to face two life-altering realities. The first was that I would have no way to naturally have children, so now I had to go to a sperm bank and store my dudes on ice. The second was that since testosterone is made by the testicles and my remaining one was about to be removed, I would have to go on hormone replacement therapy for the rest of my life.

Knowing that my body was going to be significantly altered forever and that I was now going to be dependent on an outside source in the hope of maintaining a "normal" life was something I was very anxious and to be honest, angry, about. I kept having all these random thoughts emerge in my mind. Was I going to live, considering the cancer had come back? Was I predisposed for more recurrences? Even if I did survive, would hormone replacement therapy change who I am? Was I going to start growing hair in weird places? Would my mood change? Would I ever be able to have an erection again? Would

I ever be able have sex after this? With only a certain amount of sperm stored, would I ever be able to have children of my own if the in vitro process didn't work? These are all questions I didn't know the answers to and was too afraid to even ask at the time. In that moment, my main concern was my survival and making it through the surgery and eradicating this fucking cancer.

YOU'RE NOT ALONE

"Courage is being scared to death and saddling up anyway."
—John Wayne

Before my next surgery, I met with the head urology oncologist at Sloan Kettering for a couple of consultations to discuss my options. It was determined that I did, indeed, need to have my entire right testicle removed, which would now prevent me from having children naturally. As I walked out of the hospital and hailed a cab to head home I was having so many thoughts racing through my head, none the least of which was, *could this possibly be real?*

As I walked to the curb, I bundled my scarf around my neck to protect myself from the frigid January cold. I hailed a taxi and jumped in as soon as it pulled up to the curb. Alone in the backseat with my thoughts and emotions starting to get the best of me, I put my head down so the cab driver wouldn't see the tears welling up in my eyes. The next thing I heard was a voice in a thick Russian accent asking, "How are you?"

I looked up and met his eyes in the rearview mirror. Normally, I don't share much about who I am, let alone my personal well-being, with random strangers. Even when I go to places such as the barber, I'm not the biggest chitchatter, nor am I into small talk. Some people find it entertaining, but for introverts like myself, we can find it a bit overwhelming and draining. I try to be polite and oblige when people do initiate conversation, but in this instance, as vulnerable as I was feeling, I didn't have it in me to pretend that I was fine.

I did what I wouldn't have normally done with a perfect stranger. I told him how I was really feeling. For some reason, looking into his eyes, it just felt right in that moment to be honest with him. I got the sense that he wasn't just asking me how I was doing to make idle conversation. It felt like he was asking from a genuine place.

"I'm not doing very well." I heard the words come out of my mouth, almost surprising myself.

Without any reaction, without any sympathy or inflection in his voice, he simply inquired, "Why?"

I wasn't expecting him to be so direct, but in this moment I welcomed his honesty. I looked up again at him in the rearview mirror. This time his gaze was set on the street ahead. I studied his features for a couple seconds and noticed he was probably in his mid-to-late fifties and had a strong, thick face. "I just found out I have to have surgery," I said.

I don't know how or from where this man came. Perhaps the universe or some higher power had put him in my life at this very moment because of what I was going through. But from other experiences like this in my life, I knew that the more in tune I have become with myself, mentally, physically, and spiritually, people have come into my life in ways that seem too purposeful to write off as random, chance experiences.

After I answered him, without hesitating, he asked, "For what?"

"For cancer." I responded almost as if to test him for being so straightforward with me.

"What kind of cancer you have?" he continued.

"Testicular," I responded.

We came to a red light. As we slowly nudged to a stop, he glanced up at the rear view mirror and stared at me for a few seconds without saying anything. It almost felt like he could see straight into my soul. With his thick, Russian accent, he delivered the following words, "You are going to be okay."

I was speechless for a few seconds. How did this complete stranger have such conviction? I followed with, "How do you know that?"

He nodded, "Trust me. I *know* it. I have cancer too and you are young. You will get through this."

There was such certainty and confidence in his voice that it literally bolstered me from the inside out, and, in that moment, imparted much needed support. The fact that he had told me that he had cancer too immediately made me feel less alone knowing that we shared something I knew he truly understood. Here we were, two perfect strangers, from opposite ends of the world, sitting in a taxi cab in the middle of Manhattan, sharing one of the most open and honest conversations. It was nice to share that moment with someone with whom I felt a kindred connection. "What kind of cancer do you have?" I asked.

Without hesitation, he responded, "Prostate."

"How are you? Are you getting treatment for it right now?"

He replied, "No, I can't afford it." "What do you mean?" I asked.

"I have family that I have to take care of, and I can't afford."

His response almost didn't seem real. Here he was driving a taxi to make money for his family, all the while not being able to afford paying for the treatment he needed. This man made me realize what true selflessness really is and how no matter how bad you think you may have it in life, most likely there is always someone out there who has it worse. The fact that this man could not receive treatment because he couldn't afford it tells me that there is something seriously wrong with the way our society has structured access to healthcare. Regardless of whatever your beliefs are about the healthcare system, on a basic, fundamental, human level, something needs to be done to fix this.

I rode with this man for all of about fifteen minutes, but the effect he has had on my life is profound. There's no way for me to know if he's alive anymore, but I do know that his kindness, his honesty, and his spirit live on in me. Whenever I think about him, it's with utmost gratitude. This man is one of the reasons I'm writing this book, to honor him and so many other people like him who selflessly remind us about the important things in life, how regardless of what we are going through, being with each other in intimate and honest moments are what truly matter. This kind stranger made me realize, once again, that it's okay to be vulnerable.

It's okay to be afraid, and it's okay to communicate how you honestly feel. He made me feel, in that short cab ride, that I could be genuinely open and by doing so, feel less alone. He gave me a little bit more courage and strength to keep believing that I was going to be "okay." I will forever remember this amazing man.

This is one of the reasons why I'm very active with charity work and try to make a difference in other people's lives who are going through similar challenges. It's why I have volunteered at children's hospitals where kids are going through treatments and have worked at youth centers where kids just need some encouragement and for someone to tell them that they are not alone. It's why I also get involved in St. Jude charity events. Giving back matters. The money that we raise matters greatly. It saves lives. It really does. I'm living proof that science and medicine and all the research that doctors, scientists, and other medical professionals are doing can pay off. I'm so very grateful for all the people who have supported me and so many others in our efforts. Thank you!

BADASS MOFO

"We are stronger in the places we have been broken."
– Earnest Hemingway

After my second surgery, I had to go up to Sloan Kettering Hospital every month for a chest X-Ray and blood test to monitor my health and progress. Every time I walked into the hospital, however, I literally felt like a ticking time bomb, wondering if this was the day that they were going to find another tumor. This was one of the hardest things I have ever had to do. There was no way around it though, I knew this was the only way that I was going to ultimately be able to put my mind at ease. The only solace this provided was the fact that if the cancer did come back, it would hopefully be discovered and dealt with quickly, which would allow for the best prognosis.

So as not to dread going to the hospital for these checkups every month, I framed them in a positive context. Each time I was scheduled to go in, I would write in my calendar "Good Health Appointment" to confirm my good health in my mind and create the certainty that I was going to be okay in the face of something that terrified me.

I would tell myself, "I'm just going in to see my doctor to confirm what I already know to be true. I'm healthy and my cancer is gone!" Because I had read that our brains can't distinguish between what's real and what's not with regard to what we focus on, I decided that I needed to look at my situation from an empowered perspective. While we can't control everything in life, what we can do is frame our mindset in a way that allows us to feel that we have more control in certain situations. By creating this empowered context, I was able to pick up the phone and actually make my appointments, get in a taxi ,and head up to the hospital to sit in the waiting room, have needles poked in me, have radiation sprayed on me, and to pick up the phone the next day to listen to my doctor tell me what the results were. I did this every month for twelve months.

Each month's visit reminded of my mortality and of just how precious life is. I learned to appreciate the simple joy of being able to walk down the street on a nice day and to always be present. I did this, because each month, there was the underlying possibility that I would be told my cancer had returned. The experience emboldened me to become more daring and to take more risks in life, like being more open and honest about the things that matter to me. I no longer let myself care as much about what others thought, because the fear of judgment from them paled in comparison to the anxiety I was dealing with now. Ironically, in a way, this was one of the most freeing situations I've ever experienced. I literally didn't care what others thought because I knew in my heart what mattered was what I truly wanted to do. I was living a fine line between overwhelming, terrifying anxiousness and resolved, confident calm, hoping that at any moment I wouldn't slip into that dark and negative place of uncertainty.

The alternative to all this was to just skip my appointments and ignore the whole situation. I knew this would only prolong my anxiety and worry. A quote by author Richie Norton sums this up nicely by saying, "To escape fear, you have to go through it, not around it." Avoiding doing anything you don't like only prolongs the inevitable and usually makes a situation worse the longer you wait. Whether it's going to the doctor, doing that term paper, or having that difficult conversation with a coworker or spouse that you've been avoiding, ignoring it doesn't make it go away.

I knew if I didn't keep to the schedule and actually write the appointments into my calendar to make them real, then it would have been easier to avoid them. Sometimes you just have to suck it up and do what you need to do. The fear of the cancer spreading would always be in the back of my mind, so I knew I had to just go. One of the biggest motivators for me to go to my appointments was from Lance Armstrong's book.

Once Lance realized his testicle had swollen up, he was reluctant to go to the doctor to have it looked at, partly out of fear and partly out of the same "I'm invincible" mindset I used to identify with. Because Lance waited for a very long time before seeking treatment, his cancer had spread to his lungs and his brain, a much worse situation than the one I was going through. Reading about this made me realize that if I truly wanted to be the strong and courageous man I had always wanted to be, this was my opportunity to become just that.

It's amazing how life presents us with so many opportunities to decide how to react to our experiences. My cancer taught me that being a victim is a choice and I realized that the last thing I wanted was to choose to be one. No matter how unfair life may seem, how others may seem to have more or better opportunities or a better life in general, we all have the power to decide how we want to react to any situation. I myself, knew that by complaining about my situation, wallowing in self-pity and playing the victim I would be giving up my power and in effect lose before even having gotten started. Regardless of how bad a situation is and even if it feels as if you can't do anything about it, at the very least you can always choose who you want to be.

I'm not saying I never complain, but what I don't do is let a situation perpetuate and act like I can't do anything about it or how I react to it. Instead, I just ask myself, "Do I want to remain helpless and perpetuate the problem?" or "Do I want to be someone who manifests empowerment despite this adversity?" When it came to going to my "good health appointments," I asked whether I wanted to be weak and immature or did I want to be an adult who deals with my reality? The only way I could have done this was to watch others have similar experiences and to try to emulate them, like the taxi driver who took me home from the hospital before my surgery. Another hero of mine is Jim Valvano.

In 1983, Jim Valvano was the coach of the improbable North Carolina State Wolfpack basketball team that stunned the college basketball world when they won the NCAA tournament, one of the most prized victories in all of sports. Ten years later, Jim was diagnosed with terminal cancer that had metastasized throughout his body. Knowing full well that he had only a limited amount of time left to live, on March 4, 1993, he spoke at ESPN's first *ESPY Awards* at Madison Square Garden. It was a speech that inspired me and brought me to tears.

While accepting the inaugural *Arthur Ashe Courage and Humanitarian Award,* he announced the creation of The V Foundation for Cancer Research, an organization dedicated to finding a cure for cancer, and announced that the foundation's motto would be "Don't Give Up . . . Don't Ever Give Up." His whole speech is incredibly moving for its bravery and inspiration; I recommend you watch it on YouTube. What really hit home for me was at the end of the speech, he said, "Cancer can take away all of my physical abilities. It cannot touch my mind, it cannot touch my heart, and it cannot touch my soul. And those three things are going to carry on forever. I thank you and God bless you all."

Jim passed away only two weeks later, but his legacy lives on because of his decision to be empowered in the face of what he was dealing with. With my cancer diagnosis, when I truly started to do some soul-searching, instead of remaining in a place of fear and disempowerment and focusing my thoughts on all the negative things that could happen, I looked at what I could control. I chose to focus my thoughts on having a positive mindset, on reading books, dieting, exercising, and making sure I went to all of my doctor's appointments. What I knew I couldn't control were the actual surgeries and the radiation treatment, which was obviously not something I was trained to do. Therefore, I chose to put my trust in my doctors.

Next, I decided to figure out who I needed to be in the face of all of this adversity. Did I want to remain fearful, anxious, and a victim, which, in my mind, meant lessening my chances of survival? Or did I want to keep focusing on deciding to be someone who was going to beat this setback? No one can decide these things for you - I had to decide for myself if I wanted to have the best outcome possible or not. I decided that I was going to commit to doing and being whatever I needed to do and to be whomever I needed to in order to beat the cancer. I decided I wanted to remain empowered and certain that regardless of what was going on with the things I could not control, that, on the inside, I would be certain that I was going to be okay.

In making this decision I derived a sense of security and control. I found my ability to move through this change with power, dignity, and grace. I'm not saying I didn't have my breakdowns and my rages of yelling, crying, and complaining, but after I let these emotions out, I would remind myself of what I could control and then regain my focus on those things.

I understand that this may sound simpler than it actually was, and in reality, it was one of the hardest things I have ever experienced. But to give up and remain in a place of fear and victimhood was, in my mind, not an option for me. When presented with change or challenges such as disease or job loss or break-ups, it's very easy to justify our right to be a victim. The danger with this is that no matter how bad things are, by deciding to be a victim, one has the opportunity to gain a lot of attention as one and therefore have no reason to decide to take any action to do anything solve the problem.

Because I decided that I never want anyone to feel sorry for me, I've also chosen never to let myself be a victim. That choice is there for you too. This is exactly what Jim Valvano touched on when he said cancer could take some of his abilities, but that it couldn't take away who he truly was. We are always still in control. We still are empowered because we choose to be.

This is neither arrogance or entitlement. This is looking at a cancer diagnosis, listening to doctors say, "Your body will be altered forever. You will never be able to have a child by natural means. There is the possibility that the cancer may have spread to other parts of your body," and instead of letting my brain react from a place of unbridled fear of the unknown, recognizing that I had the power to decide what my outlook was going to be. To do so dictates how influences our related actions and empowers us to be our true selves.

What I discovered after exploring these thoughts was that the most empowering question one can ask when faced with adversity, or anything for that matter is:

"WHO DO YOU WANT TO BE IN THE FACE OF WHAT YOU ARE DEALING WITH?"

When I posed this question to myself during my experience with cancer, I honestly decided and declared myself to be:

"GRATEFUL FOR MY PERFECT HEALTH AND A BADASS MOFO WHO RELENTLESSLY DOES WHATEVER I NEED TO DO TO BE HEALTHY."

By deciding who we want to be, with power and conviction, we are exercising our ability to decide. This is coming from a place of personal power and control instead of helplessness. By deciding who I was going to be, I was sending a signal to the universe that I was going to make this happen on my terms. There was a great deal of strength and comfort in this for me. Did I know for sure if I was going to survive? No. But what I did know for certain was that I could decide who I was going to be in the face of it, which enabled me to confidently keep moving forward.

As I write this, it's hard not to feel conflicted about why and how what happened, did, in fact, happen. Cancer and so many other diseases and other tragic events happen to people every day, to good people. Why did I survive, yet why did Jim, and so many other great people like he and my father and my friend Erik did not? These are harsh realities we must face and deal with. The only way I know how to move through experiences like this is to keep focusing on purposeful, actionable things within my control to begin the healing process and to move forward.

To do so takes a great deal of support from others. This is why I'm inviting us to come together as a community to offer each other support, so that regardless of what you might be going through, you'll know that you are not alone. My cancer experience was incredibly humbling and brought me to my knees. I am so grateful for all the people in my life who extended their love and encouragement to me. That went a long way toward giving me the strength to keep fighting and renewing my commitment to always staying empowered. By participating in this community of Agile Artists, my hope, is that you too, will feel the same.

IT'S NOT ABOUT THE ABS

"To thine own self be true."
– Shakespeare

I have always taken pride in how I take care of my health. I have been an athlete my whole life; I played baseball, ran track, and played football in high school, played a year of college football, and played rugby my remaining few years of college. Up until this point, I had run three marathons and I worked out almost everyday, so the idea of having to be dependent on hormones for my well-being was not something that I took lightly, mainly because, as I have touched on before, I did not like the idea of having to rely on anything but myself. In my mind, this was a form of weakness. A big part of my modus operandi was that I didn't want people to think I wasn't capable or strong, so I never wanted to let anyone see that I needed anyone or anything for my survival.

Having to have my family take care of me and telling people at work that I was dealing with these health issues made me have to face the reality that my belief that "I don't need anybody" was a fallacy. My experience with cancer has taught me we cannot get through life on our own. Like it or not, we are dependent on others.

I'm incredibly grateful for my family, friends, and doctors for taking such good care of me, and I also immensely appreciate the scientists and drug companies that have created the treatments necessary to keep people like me alive. In my opinion, this is nothing short of a miracle. By welcoming this and allowing all these sources to take care of me, my life has become more enriched, and my relationships with people have grown immensely. As a result, I am able to relate to people on a much more personal, human level.

This whole experience helped me realize I was placing a lot of emphasis on trying to appear "perfect" to the world for fear of people not liking or accepting me for who I truly am. I think it's inevitable for those of us who grew up in Western culture to compare ourselves to pictures of movie stars and models who are plastered all over Instagram, magazines, and billboards. We see athletes and singers and entrepreneurs making ridiculous money, walking on red carpets, and launching huge IPOs.

With the mainstream media blasting this in our faces on a daily basis, it's easy to get wrapped up in the desire to go the best Oscar parties, Leo's house in the hills where all the Victoria's Secret models hung out, or St. Maarten for Jay-Z and Beyonce's New Year's Eve party. It's even easier to feel slighted when you're not invited. Years ago, a friend of mine and I tried to sneak into the Playboy Mansion without invites or tickets. We rented a limo to make it look like we were invited to Hef's annual Halloween Party, but, regretfully, we got out of the limo (which we had only rented to drop us off) and were shot down by the door staff in front of a bunch of people. Since we didn't have any transportation back, we had to walk about a mile down the road before we were able to call a taxi. Looking back at this now, it's amusing, but at the time when I was a budding actor trying to network and meet Hollywood executives it made me feel like a loser.

Before being diagnosed with cancer, I can easily say I let superficial experiences like these influence the value I placed on myself, which, I noticed, was leading to my unhappiness and to frustration with who I was. I don't wish a disease or health issues on anyone, but when I was trying to find something positive from this experience, I began to see that I've learned there were more important things in life to identify myself worth with that were both healthier and more authentic. All I had to do was look down at my scars and the blue dots tattooed on my stomach to remind me that life is short and that I was grateful to simply be on this planet for another day to have the gift to pursue the things I truly love.

Something else I recognized from my experience with cancer is that it's been harder for me to tolerate superficiality. I realized in my darkest hours, it didn't matter how defined my abs were, how many covers of magazines I had been on, or what actress I was going to meet at the next Emmy party. What really matters, I've come to understand, are the people who show up to help you go to the bathroom when you can't get up on your own, those who come over to make you dinner when you're not feeling well, and those who get on an airplane to be with you when you need them most. I've been fortunate to have had quite a few people be there for me over the years, especially my family, which has made me a better man for so many reasons.

These experiences have motivated me to want to give back in many ways. Choosing to be more involved with charities and focusing on how I can make a substantial difference in other people's lives as a result has been incredibly rewarding. My experiences have humbled me and reminded me that it's truly important in life to share yourself authentically with others and accept them for who they are. By doing so, I have gained love, support, and a more well-rounded and genuine sense of self-worth.

DECIDE IT IS SO

"I figure life's a gift and I don't intend on wasting it. You don't know what hand you're gonna get dealt next. You learn to take life as it comes at you...to make each day count." – Jack Dawson, Titanic

After a year of observation at Sloan Kettering, my monthly appointments were moved to every other month. We were now hopeful that I was on the path to full recovery. I was feeling good about where I was with my health, but at *All My Children*, new writers didn't seem too receptive to my character as the transplanted, unaborted, fetus of Erika Kane, and my story line started to decrease.

After three years of working intensely with this great group of people, I was looking forward to the security of continued work with a renewed contract. When it didn't happen, I was concerned about the prospect of getting another steady acting gig, considering it took eight years for me to secure one with *AMC*. When I talked about it with some of my friends, however, I recognized that working on a soap opera was not why I got into the entertainment business. When I looked at the situation, the universe was giving me what I was subconsciously asking for. As much as I loved working on *AMC* and the people I worked with, truthfully, I had aspirations of working on primetime television and in films.

When I really looked at it, I could have been pissed off at the writers and producers for writing my character off, but what I ultimately realized was that I was the one who was responsible for not being there anymore. The more I honestly looked at it, the more clearly I saw that the only reason I wanted to stay on *AMC* was for the comfort and security. From a creative and artistic standpoint, I was not fulfilled. Subconsciously I was sending those signals out to the universe. Sure enough, as the universe does, it answered with the frequency and messaging that I was subconsciously giving off.

I know several people personally who have been fired from jobs who were first devastated, only to then find an even better and higher paying job. After Steve Jobs was pushed out of the company he created, he is quoted as saying, "Getting fired from Apple was the best thing that could have ever happened to me. The heaviness of being successful was replaced by the lightness of being a beginner again. It freed me to enter one of the most creative periods of my life."

What people don't always recognize is the energy they are giving off. If you are unhappy at a job and are only there for security, you are not likely to be fully committed to doing your best. The people you work with are going to notice this, not just by your performance, but from your thoughts, which manifest themselves as energy and are thus perceptible to others around you.

This is what I realized when I was let go from *AMC*. As sad and as afraid as I was to have been let go from a good-paying, secure job, I knew in my heart it wasn't the career path I truly wanted to be on. It was time to start focusing on the future instead of dwelling on the past.

So, I jumped back into an acting class in NYC and started to devote my time and energy into getting better at my craft to get my next acting gig. Because of the speed at which soap operas are filmed, there are certain bad habits actors can get into. These techniques serve the purpose of delivering lines in a serviceable way for soaps, but they don't always translate to film and primetime TV, which require a deeper understanding and analysis because the characters tend to be more complex and multi-dimensional.

I committed to becoming better and more confident in my craft. In the process, not only did I become a better actor, but I could tell I was growing as a person intellectually, mentally, and spiritually. I liked who I was becoming. I was putting a lot of energy into creating the space for my next acting job to appear and making sure I was ready for it when it did. I went to see plays on Broadway to be inspired by my favorite actors, and I began to audition again for new roles. As it were, I auditioned for a TV pilot where I'd be playing a doctor in a family of doctors for a new show on CBS. I really resonated with the script and my character, and after auditioning in New York, the producers flew me to Los Angeles for the test audition. If this studio test went well, then I'd audition for the network.

I was incredibly excited and feeling like *this* was more in line with what I wanted to be doing with my acting career. I did all my prep, got ready, and was flown out on a Thursday for the audition.

I'm always nervous before I go in to audition, but once I'm in the room and connect with the casting director and go for the ride with what the scene is, it is the best and most fulfilling experience ever! This was just that. I went in for the studio test and felt like I nailed it. Everything just flowed and it felt great. There were about ten people in the room, and it seemed they felt very receptive to my performance.

I wasn't surprised when my manager called me a few hours later to tell me that I was heading to the network test the next morning. While not entirely taken aback, nonetheless, I was excited and feeling confident. He also mentioned that after that network test, there was another audition my agent had booked me on for the reboot of the hit show *Melrose Place*. I didn't think much of it because I was feeling good about the network test, but I briefly looked at the audition and worked on it for a bit.

The next day, I was feeling good and went to the CBS Studio Center on Radford Avenue in Studio City. I went in, signed the contract in triplicate, which outlays how much I'd be making per episode, how many episodes per year, where my title card would be, what size trailer and other stipulations that are normal in these contracts that the lawyers go back and forth on. There were three other guys there, one of whom I knew. It's kind of an awkward experience sitting there in a room with other actors, knowing that most likely one of us is going to get the role and the rest are S.O.L.

The casting director came out and told us what order we would be going in, which I don't even remember. Because what I do remember was the horrible experience of going in there and forgetting my lines halfway through one of the scenes. It wasn't so much my forgetting the line as much as it was that for some reason, I didn't feel as comfortable in that room as I had the day before. This network test now had about twenty people in it, and we were in a bigger auditorium, which has less of an intimate feel than most auditions.

This is the reason the audition process and booking an acting job can be incredibly frustrating because you may have four great auditions leading up to the final one, and if that last audition is not as good as the first four and someone else is able to deliver in that last audition, most likely, they will get the job over you. These are incredibly stressful situations which can "make you or break you" so to speak. I tend to thrive in these kinds of environments, when there is a lot on the line, but sometimes the pressure can amplify the smallest mistakes or the smallest of insecurities. That's why it's so important to do the work necessary, so that when I walk in the room, I can be confident, relaxed and able to perform at a very high level. I equate nailing a network audition to nailing a double layout pike in the Olympics. No matter how much and how hard you have practiced, it's that one moment in the room that counts. For some reason, the stars in the room did not align for me, and I was not feeling grounded in that auditorium.

I can sometimes fake certain moments, but in a final audition like this, I've realized every moment needs to be truthful and authentic. Because there are so many people watching and everyone in the room needs to feel comfortable and secure that you are capable of handling the responsibilities that come with the job, you need to demonstrate you can succeed at the audition. On this particular day, I let my nerves get the best of me and I wasn't completely connected with my heart and gut in that room. I was distracted from being in the moment, I became too concerned with what the people in the room thought of me and instead of being in the moment, I was trying to show them my choices for the scene. The result? I forgot one of my lines. I attempted to continue, but the rhythm and the magic in the room evaporated and all that was left was an actor who was saying lines he wasn't connected to.

I walked out of there pissed because I knew I could have booked that job, as I had done several times before, and unfortunately, in that situation, I didn't stick the landing, so to speak. I couldn't dwell on it too long though, because I had this other audition for *Melrose Place* coming up. I quickly looked at the scenes for it in my car again, which I had printed out, and went to the location where it was at.

I had just come from an incredibly pressure-filled auditorium, and when I walked into the room for *Melrose Place*, there were about eight really friendly people who made me feel at home. When I finished my audition, they asked where I was from and some questions about what I thought of my character and the storyline. I was surprised with how well this audition went and the feeling I had with everyone in the room. I headed back to New York that weekend and the following week got a call from my agent saying that the CW Network wanted to test me for the show, and that they were going to fly me back out the following day to LA.

"Here we go again," I thought. Except this time, I made sure I knew my lines inside and out so I wouldn't forget them like the week prior. I knew the material very well and because I really connected with my character, Auggie, a bit of a loner and outcast, struggling with his inner demons, I was excited to tap into his angst and use it in the audition. Sometimes I connect better with certain characters, and as the stars would align, this was one of them. I flew back to LA and as it turned out, the audition test was in the same auditorium where I had recently crashed and burned.

Before I went into the room, I took a deep breath and made it up in my mind that the part was mine, and that nothing was going to take it from me. I have discovered, there are certain factors that come into play to manifest something. Being certain about the outcome is one of them. Having just gone through my whole cancer experience, I recognized I had to decide what the outcome was going to be, despite my uncertainty. I decided to adopt the same mentality going into that audition and made up my mind that I was going to book it. As soon as I started the audition, I felt grounded and connected. I could feel the energy in the room building and as I hit the climax of the scene, where I'm passionately telling the girl I like why I think what she did was wrong, I was able to bring the perfect combination of anger, frustration, compassion and love. It felt amazing. I could tell when I finished my last line that the casting director thought I did good job because he had a big grin on his face indicating I had, indeed, nailed it. This is what makes the business so exciting… moments just like that.

The next day, I flew back to New York, and the day after that, I got the call that I had booked the show. I was ecstatic. But on a deeper level, I wasn't surprised because I knew deep down I had done all I needed to in order to earn it. You can't control whether anyone is going to say "yes" to you, but when you do your part to make their decision easy, then you have done your job. With this audition, I had done just that.

It was time to pack up and move my life back to LA after four years of being away. Moving back to LA also meant I had to find a new oncologist to see for my checkups. I was now entering my third year removed from my surgeries and was only required to go for my "good health appointments" every three months at this point. Once I found a new doctor at UCLA, I continued to focus on being one hundred percent healthy, and simply trying to live a normal life (albeit on a TV show), doing what I love to do.

Two more years went by where I was going in for checkups every six months until I reached the five-year mark with no detectable signs of cancer. A couple of days after going in for my final chest Xray and blood tests, I received the results, confirming that I was now officially cancer-free. I think I instinctively knew I was, but receiving the official results allowed me to finally take off the metaphorical armor I had been wearing for six long years and permit myself to breathe a deep sigh of relief.

I felt both grateful and proud that I had finally gotten through it all. More than anything, it an affirmation of something I already knew to be true. At the risk of sounding arrogant, I felt as if I had transcended the possibility of being trapped by the reactive tendencies of my mind. I also felt that I had grown to become better at handling my emotions and not letting that voice in my head dictate how I was going to feel. More than anything, I felt peace. It was time to move on, take what I had learned from the whole experience, and let it infuse my life with more compassion, drive, and creativity.

Three Takeaway Action Tips:

1. Decide who you need to be in the face of adversity to overcome it.

2. Be authentic. This is about sharing enough personal things about you that will help those you meet get to know the real you.

3. Listen. By offering to simply listen, you provide the space for others to discover the best solutions to problems they are facin

Poster for "Beautiful Dreamer"

Calvin Klein Underwear Box

Clinique Happy Fragrance Campaign

Donatella and Allegra Versace

before he was killed Gianni Versace two weeks

**Giorgio Armani at his Fashion Show
Hilary Swank at the pre-party for
*Something Borrowed***

Melrose Place Campaign Poster

**My mom and I in NYC with my Calvin Klein Ad
on a Phone Booth**

The inside of my studio apartment across the street from the World Trade Center

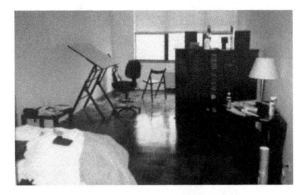

World Trade Center in proximity to my old apartment in NYC

People Magazine piece 3 months before
I was diagnosed with Cancer

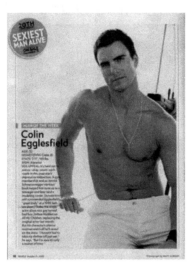

Red Carpet pic from the Premiere of *Something Borrowed*

Something Borrowed Movie Poster

Susan Lucci and I at the *Daytime Emmy's*

Sylvester Stallone and I on the set of Backtrace

Star Magazine piece with Kate Hudson

Tom Cruise and Me on the set of "The View" on my last day of "All My Children"

Versace World Wide Jeans Campaign

Vogue Italia Cover

Wallpaper Magazine Cover

05
EVERY BREATH YOU TAKE

"I've got to keep breathing. It'll be my worst
business mistake if I don't."
—*Steve Martin*

From trying to avoid road rage on the 405 on my way to auditions, to performing in front of complete strangers in the hopes of being booked on a television show watched by millions around the world, to be able to fulfill my life's passion while creating some semblance of financial and personal stability, I've discovered that one of the single most profound, yet easily overlooked acts in our life is the art of breathing. Haaaaaa.

According to *John Hopkins Medicine*, on average, a person breathes 12 to 16 breaths per minute. This converts to an average of 840 breaths per hour, 14,1120 breaths per week, and 7,363,289 breaths per year. For someone who lives to be eighty years old, that's approximately half a billion breaths. For as much breathing as we do, I would argue most of us (especially in the Western world) don't fully utilize our potential to intentionally breathe to heal, relax, and calm. I know I didn't.

I grew up as an athlete, and still to this day, I love how I feel after rigorous training. To date I have completed six marathons, seven triathlons, and several shorter distance races. I don't always enjoy the training, but I love how it makes me feel and how it contributes to my overall well-being. Whenever I get stressed out or worried about something, physical activity has always been my go-to for relieving stress and anxiety.

For as long as I can remember, I've always had a bit of social anxiety. Whenever I would get up in front of the class in school to answer a question or give a presentation, my body would immediately respond by going into fight or flight mode. My body temperature would surge, my sweat glands unleashed Niagara Falls, and my chest would tighten, making it difficult to speak, let alone breathe. This is just one of the reasons why I would normally keep to myself and avoid drawing too much attention for fear of having one of these small panic episodes.

When I was about twelve years old, my brother and I acted in a local production of *Tom Sawyer* by Mark Twain at the Illinois Theatre Center, where I was cast as Huckleberry Finn and my brother played Tom. I remember walking out on stage for the first time in our first performance, and when I opened my mouth to say my first line, I literally choked on my own words. My throat buckled with nerves, and though I was able to quickly collect myself and continue, that was one of the first times I remember actually having stage fright and recognizing that it was a real phenomenon. As such, I shied away from theatre growing up except for doing one more play as an understudy for the lead actor in a play at the ITC when I was a sophomore in high school.

As I grew older, I slowly gained more confidence and became more accepting of my faults. Even so, I noticed that sometimes these paralyzing physical effects would rear their ugly head and sabotage me. In most social situations, I feel totally comfortable around people, but as I began to go on more and more auditions and put myself in situations where I'm scrutinized by the likes of casting directors, directors, and producers, I noticed that I would become nervous and begin having anxiety-inducing, mini panic attacks before I even walked into the room. For this reason, I knew that I had to actively address my subconscious and learn how to mitigate these debilitating effects so I could audition and perform without being paralyzed by the tightness in my chest and shortness of breath.

As I got older and started to realize it was my subconscious need not only to be "perfect" but probably, more importantly, to avoid being made fun of, I began seeking out therapists and books to help me gain a better understanding of where these thoughts came from. I wanted to see if there was something I could do to mitigate the stranglehold over my ability to be comfortable in front of people and allow myself to be vulnerable. I also went to seminars and initiated discussions about my experiences in my acting classes. More often than not, I discovered that many of my friends and colleagues experienced the same feelings.

The more we talked about the root of these insecurities and identified the triggers that manifested them, the less debilitating they were. Knowing I wasn't the only one experiencing these same things also made me relax a bit and realize that we're all dealing with our own demons and insecurities. An important conclusion I came to was that I had allowed the criticism and judgment I experienced mostly from classmates to affect me because I didn't have the resources to feel confident about who I was.

Because I was really skinny growing up, I would sometimes get picked on by some of the other kids in my class who thought it was funny. I remember in seventh grade getting hit in the head with an umbrella by the class bully, who burst out laughing with some other kids when he nearly knocked me out of my chair. Because he was bigger than me and would have kicked my ass if I had tried to retaliate, I ran out of the classroom, frustrated and humiliated. More than anything, I was angry that I couldn't stand up to him. I internalized that I was simply weak and therefore needed to hide in a sense so as not to become a target again.

When I look back to when I was younger, I can now easily say that I was insecure with who I was. As such, I was defensive and sensitive to criticism and attacks. The older I've become, however, and the more comfortable I've gotten in my own skin, the less I care what others say or think. This is because I have become better at accepting myself for my faults and shortcomings. What I've also come to realize, as I've gotten older, is that no matter how great someone's life might appear on the outside, everyone's dealing with something. Sharing my cancer experience with others has opened my eyes to the myriad issues people contend with. It surprises me how similar we all are in trying to hide things.

As I've mentioned earlier, however, the more I began to open up and share my experience with others, the more I began to feel supported and accepted for who I am, authentically. This orientation has empowered me to take bigger risks in and go after the aspirations I have created for myself that excite and fulfill me. This includes working on major motion picture projects such as the movie I did with Kate Hudson and Ginnifer Goodwyn called *Something Borrowed*. To this day, it's the project I'm most proud of and the one I was most fulfilled with shooting. It was, by no means, easy though. Before we started shooting, in order to make sure I was fully prepared to perform at this level, I was offered the opportunity to work with one the most prominent acting coaches in the business, Larry Moss. Everyone needs assistance at certain points in their life and for me, a week away from starting to shoot the most important job of my life, I knew I could use some good help to prepare.

SOMETHING BORROWED FOR SOMETHING DORROWED

"Life is not measured by how many breaths we take, but by the moments that take our breath away." —Maya Angelou

This Maya Angelou quote is such a beautiful way to describe the profound moments in our lives that truly make life worth living. We've all heard sayings such as "breath is life," "breath is healing," and "breath is the key to relaxation." Nothing could be more accurate or more profound, yet few of us practice it consciously and truly reap the restorative and calming benefits that intentional breathing can have on our well-being.

There are a few exercises I've learned in some of my acting classes that have helped calm my nerves before an audition or big performance, and I have to say the central tenet to each one has been to simply breathe. I remember being so nervous before shooting *Something Borrowed* that it literally felt like I had a fortypound weight on my chest. No matter what I did, I couldn't seem to get enough air into my lungs. We were only a few days away from starting to shoot, and I was beginning to freak out because this was the biggest acting job in my life, and the last thing I wanted to do was show up on set and hyperventilate all over Kate Hudson.

I tried going to the gym, I tried running, I tried mediation. This all helped a little bit, but the tightness in my chest wouldn't subside. I had heard of Larry Moss from acting circles and his reputation preceded him. Larry has prepared the likes of Leonardo DiCaprio, Jim Carrey and Hilary Swank for their films and when the producers offered me to coach with him, I jumped at it. Ironically, Hilary Swank is one of the producers of *Something Borrowed*.

When I first walked into his apartment on the Upper West Side of New York City, Larry warmly greeted me and asked me how I as doing. I was anxious, struggled to breathe, and began word vomiting in front of him before he kindly but intentionally said, "Stop."

It felt as if he could see right into my soul. He stared at me for a few moments and then simply said, "Breathe." It felt as if my body was given permission to relax for the first time in weeks. Being in the presence of someone with whom I was able to connect right away on a deep level, who I felt understood exactly where I was at and why I was so nervous, made my anxiety start to dissipate. His ability to recognize my true state of nervousness made me feel that I didn't have to hide it anymore. I recognized that I had been trying to disguise these feelings in front of everyone, including the producers and the director, for fear of being fired. This only made the situation worse.

We just sat there, and he had me breathe for about five minutes. It was incredible. It was almost as if the oxygen-starved cells in the whole of my body were finally nourished again. I began to relax and my voice even started to drop down, closer into the power center of my belly. I rehearsed with him for four days before the start of the film. We dissected every part of that script, forwards and backwards. We psychoanalyzed my character Dex, and honed in on some incredibly rich aspects of his personality for me to bring to my performance. What truly made the difference, however, was Larry's ability to have me reach deep inside myself to identify the aspects of myself that were similar to Dex.

What I discovered about Dex, and what I felt was important to bring to the role, was his frustration with being misunderstood. Much like me, Dex grew up in an environment where to express one's true feelings was not nurtured, but rather, stifled. Similarly, there was a lot of pressure placed on Dex to succeed and live up to certain expectations. This all coincided with how I was actually feeling in my real life. What Larry helped me do, instead of hiding these feelings, was the exact opposite, to put them on full display in my performance.

This concept is not something that was new to me. In fact, it's what most acting teachers encourage their students to do, to use whatever real-life angst, frustration or emotion you're feeling and put it into in your performance. The problem was that I wasn't truly in touch with my emotions and feelings at the time. Much like what had happened with my World Trade Center experience, what I hadn't realized was that I was suppressing all my real feelings, including my anxiety and fear, with regard to the possibility of failing at this job and getting fired. It's not uncommon for actors to get fired from jobs and because I was trying to suppress this fear, I was also inhibiting all of my other emotions as well, which were manifesting now in my body as stress, anxiety and tightness. What Larry had me do was get me back in touch with all of these feelings and then let them out.

I remember him having me recreate a scene where I had to yell at my father. This is something that I would have been incredibly uncomfortable doing in real life, but in the safety of Larry's apartment, I was encouraged to let loose. It was incredibly powerful and unlocked all my pent up feelings and emotions. They were now free to be accessed by my conscious mind to be used in my performance. It was one of the most empowering exercises I've ever done and it reminded me how necessary it is to reconnect with our authentic emotions and feelings.

On the last day of coaching with Larry, as we closed the last page of the script and completed our rehearsal, he asked me how I felt. I told him I felt our work had been a tremendous help and that I believed I was able to now tap into all of the necessary feelings and emotions of Dex – that I could combine them with the choices I had created. (This is the true artistry of acting and a part of the process that I absolutely relish.) I also took the time to mention that I was still a bit nervous since again, this was the biggest project I'd been cast on to date.

He looked at me with stern, kind eyes and said with absolute certainty, "You're going to be great."

It was weird, and I'm not sure how to describe it other than it was as if the vibration and energy of the words themselves moved through the ether and into my body where they permeated every cell of my body with a shot of belief and confidence. I instantly felt it, but still didn't necessarily trust it. Before I knew it, I responded with, "How do you know?"

Again, he squared his gaze right at me and said, "Because Leonardo DiCaprio was sitting right where you are now, a few years ago, and I told him the very same thing."

Knowing that Larry coaches some of the top actors in the world instilled in me the final piece of confidence I needed in order to venture off and fulfill my life's dream of doing a major motion picture on the highest level. When I showed up on set for our first day of filming to shoot the bar scene with Ginny before we kiss in the cab, instead of being overwhelmed with anxiety, I was lit up with excitement. I will always be grateful for Larry's time, generosity, and wisdom and allowing me to borrow from him what I needed to help make my dreams actually come true.

SWEAT THE SMALL STUFF

"Don't think. Thinking is the enemy of creativity. It's self-conscious, and anything self-conscious is lousy. You can't try to do things. You simply must do things." – Ray Bradbury

I studied biology back in my early college days when I was planning to become a doctor. The miracle that is the human body was not lost on me. The way it adapts and protects itself, working in tandem with the mind—especially in stressful situations—is absolutely amazing. Our bodies are obviously sensitive to a multitude of influences, and one of the biggest influencers is stress. In order to be able to grow and become better at anything, we need a certain amount of stress in our lives, much like when you go to the gym and lift weights to get stronger. By contrast, when our bodies and minds are overloaded by stress, this can cause harmful and deleterious health consequences and at the very least get in the way of our fulfilling what it is we want to accomplish.

According to a recent Chapman University survey on American fears, public speaking ranked number one. The weird and geeky name for the fear of public speaking is glossophobia. A study was reviewed in a 2013 article written by Kaya Burgess and published in London's

The Times, showed that people fear public speaking more than they fear death.

To get up in front of people and confidently speak on a subject or to deliver the lines of a script in front of an audience for many people, including me, can induce varying degrees of anxiety and physical symptoms, such as heart palpitations, sweating, shortness of breath, and lightheadedness. I have had it so bad in the past that I literally had to wear a different shirt on my way to an audition because by the time I got there, I had already sweated through that shirt. My recurring nightmare is of me waiting in the wings about to go on stage to deliver a *Hamlet* soliloquy and not remembering my lines. I literally wake up in a cold sweat only to realize it's not real.

Your mind and body, however, can't tell the difference between perception and reality, so it's important not only to be able to alleviate the symptoms but also to get in touch on a deeper psychological level of where the perceived stress comes from. Because stress can be incredibly debilitating and make your body tense up, it's exceptionally important for actors and anyone else who must appear in front of people to be in tune with what these stressors are as well as certain techniques that help relieve this stress.

For an actor performing up on stage or in front of the camera, stress can be a career killer, so a lot of attention is paid in acting classes to help deal with and alleviate stress so we can be in the moment, remember our lines, and not throw up. Not everyone is affected by this kind of stress, but many people, especially actors, including me, who go through up to six auditions in front of thirty different people just to get a role, stress and nervous energy can get in the way of our ability to be at our best.

I've seen actors drop down on the floor of waiting rooms before going into audition to do push-ups. I've worked with an actor who drank a whole bottle of vodka before he went on set (which ended up getting him fired). I've seen a couple of actors literally yell at people to shut up on set because they were about to go on camera. I've read about Tobey Maguire saying Leonardo DiCaprio used to do cartwheels in the hallways before auditions to get rid of nervous energy, and I've seen a sportscaster on ESPN during a live interview completely freeze up and apologize that he couldn't continue.

I also remember reading an interview with Peter Sarsgaard (*Dead Man Walking, Shattered Glass*) who was doing a play on Broadway. When asked about whether or not he got nervous before each performance, he summed it up by saying that if there were a gun on a table right near the curtain before he went out on stage, he would rather take it and blow his brains out than walk out on stage. He followed it up however, by saying that once he got out on stage and started to say his lines and connect with the other actors and the story itself, he was in his element and was able to create.

Stress can make us do a lot of crazy things and make our bodies do things we wish they wouldn't. I can totally relate to some anecdotes that I've heard and read about other actors. One of the things it has made me realize is that I'm not alone. We all have our insecurities and doubts because at the end of the day, we are all human.

During my earlier years of acting study, I was in class with another one of Hollywood's premier coaches named Susan Batson. Susan has coached and works with several of the industry's best, including Juliette Binoche, Oprah Winfrey, and Nicole Kidman. In one of our classes, Susan was describing one of her recent experiences on set with Nicole working on the film *The Interpreter* with Sean Penn. After Susan described some of the scenes and the work they did together to get ready, I asked her what Nicole's approach to her scene work was like when she's on set and actually filming.

I'm a firm believer in modeling the actions and behaviors of successful people, so I was just curious about learning something from Nicole that I could perhaps use in my work. Susan proceeded to explain how Nicole is meticulous with her preparation and rehearsal, which wasn't surprising to hear, but what was surprising was that Susan mentioned that when Nicole is in her process, she is in a world of stressed-out creativity. She mentioned that because Nicole cares deeply about her work, she wants to make sure she is bringing to the role everything required to fully and truthfully portray her character. Susan also said that sometimes Nicole becomes frustrated with her own analysis of not having quite hit her own high expectations. She further went on to say that Nicole is hardly ever satisfied with a performance and holds herself to such a high standard that she has even expressed to Susan how she thought she would never work in Hollywood again. Mind you, this was after winning her Academy Award and before being nominated two more times!

What I've come to realize is that everyone has their doubts, fears, and insecurities and that even people at the top of their field have the same feelings as everyone else. What Susan said she would do is remind Nicole to refocus her energy away from her negative thoughts back onto the character she had created and the intention that she had decided on for the scene. You can either let your fears and insecurities paralyze you, or you can take action regardless of their presence. For Nicole, focusing on her love for acting, selfexpression, and portraying a character truthfully is the fuel for overcoming everything that could stop her.

Susan made me realize that in order to be able to fulfill the task at hand, we must focus on the things that are within our ability to control and let go of the rest. Hearing how experienced actors face the same stress I was starting to encounter in my auditions and performances, and then learning how to deal with and mitigate it, has been invaluable for my growth both as an actor and a person.

A great exercise that another of my acting teachers, Sheila Gray, would have us do was a guided meditation before each class. She would burn incense, play ambient music, and guide us through a series of breathing exercises. After practicing this for a few months, I began doing the same thing in my apartment before my auditions, which would calm my nerves and allow me to focus on my lines and character instead of my anxiety. I learned that such techniques are called "anchors," and when practiced the proper way, they can be incredibly helpful in establishing a different physiological response to the triggers that can prevent us from being effective.

Mediation has been incredibly helpful to me throughout my acting career. When I got back to LA in 2009 to film *Melrose Place,* I took a transcendental meditation course as a way to deal with the anxiety and excitement that was starting to build around the show. Meditation has helped ground me when I have felt scattered and has helped calm my nerves when auditioning. Sometimes after the audition, the waiting part can be even more stressful than the audition itself, especially when it's something as exciting as a major studio film. Mediation has made me practice being more in the moment, and have less attachment to the outcome.

The meditation course I took was incredibly grounding and very relaxing. What I was taught is that by meditating two times a day for at least twenty minutes at a time, or whenever you feel like you need it, you can reduce stress and anxiety to better deal with the rigors of life. One of the important distinctions I learned from mediation is that your emotions *are not who you are* and they can cause us to take actions that we wouldn't otherwise. Therefore, it's never wise to make decisions or take action when we are in an emotionally charged state, especially when angry or frustrated. Emotions have a way of clouding and influencing our better judgment and often can result in our taking actions that we end up regretting. But with twenty minutes of meditation before taking any sort of action or with decision-making, you will more likely not regret the decision.

Margie Haber, the acting teacher who helped me book my role as Dex on *Something Borrowed,* has taught me several other ways to alleviate tension. She wrote a great book on acting called *How to Get the Part without Falling Apart,* and as soon as I saw the cover of her book in the Drama Book Shop in Manhattan, I knew I had to buy it. I would recommend it to any actor who is looking to get started in the business or up their game when it comes to auditioning.

In class, she would have us do all sorts of mouth- and jawrelaxing exercises that involved tongue twisters, such as "chicken kitchen, chicken kitchen, chicken kitchen" and "red leather, yellow leather, red leather, yellow leather." I always thought that if some random person had walked into one of my acting classes during certain exercises, they would have thought they had accidentally walked into an insane asylum. We were constantly doing exercises that forced us to get out of our heads and into our bodies to shift our way of being from a thinking perspective and into a feeling and instinctual realm. That is where the magic happens.

Sheila Gray would have us do all sorts of exercises that would allow for us to connect with our inner feelings and break down the barriers so these feelings could be expressed. She taught us tactics that enabled us to tap into the appropriate emotional state for whatever scene we were working on and fully express those feelings. I remember she had me do an exercise where I was running around the theatre singing at the top of my lungs as if I were the lead singer of Motley Crue on tour in front of forty thousand fans in Cincinnati. Talk about getting out of your shell. In acting class there is no place to hide. It is both an uncomfortable and exhilarating place where you learn an immense amount about who you are on many levels. It shows you what your limits are, and by learning how to overcome them, you learn how to deal better with stress how to connect and communicate better as well. In a nutshell, acting classes are laboratories for human experimentation, self expression, and growth. This is exactly what I have always loved about them. I have learned how to let go of fears and insecurities, and by doing so, I am free then to create from a blank slate. Without my personal barriers getting in the way, I have learned to connect more wholeheartedly to something that I find to be sacred and incredibly fulfilling.

You may be asking if getting up in front of people is this anxietyinducing, this stressful, this scary, why in the hell do actors do it? We do it because once we move past the fear and anxiety and are able to be in the moment to create, nothing is more magical, more fulfilling, or inspiring.

As a performer, I deal with judgment on a daily basis. Getting hung up by the anxiety this can cause has, at times, prevented me from being able to do my best work. I've had to work hard to become a better actor as well as practice quite a bit of self-care in order to overcome it. That's why working out, eating right, and meditating are crucial given the benefits they offer for dealing with stress and anxiety.

CREATE A CREATIVE SPACE

"Creativity takes courage."
– Henri Matisse

You can't force a moment to happen or magic to appear on screen with another actor. You have to do the preparation to let the moment breathe and to cultivate the optimal conditions for creativity to be nurtured and to live. In the acting realm, by analyzing a character, putting on the costume, and memorizing your lines, you begin to invite the necessary subconscious elements into the space. Whatever it is you're doing, you must work to create the environment so you are open and free to receive inspiration or the cues from whom you're working with to be able to exchange the flow of energy back and forth.

If outside judgment or self-criticism are present, it can be very difficult for this process to begin, especially when you're first starting to do something new. *You must be fiercely protective about maintaining a safe space when you are initiating anything new.* Beginning something new can be scary and uncomfortable, and it's important to maintain the space to be able to fall down and not feel like you're being kicked while you are down.

Margie Haber calls this the "protective parent" looking after the "playful child." To bring creativity into your life takes courage and resolve because in the beginning you're probably not going to like what you first create. Whether it's writing or learning to play an instrument, in the beginning, whatever you produce will only get better with practice. It's important to be gentle with yourself until you begin to see the results you're looking for.

An artist can also only truly create if he knows his medium well enough to be able to use it without thinking about it. Making mistakes, getting feedback, and using this feedback to learn from is something you can't rush. For example, when learning to play the piano, you need to practice exercises to develop dexterity and skill. You need to push the wrong keys in order to hear the wrong sounds to then be able to correct it for your next attempt. It's the same in learning how to use whatever medium you love. You must first do the drills, practice, and develop the skills in order to then be proficient enough to let whatever impulses come up to be expressed.

A mistake many people make is that they get so frustrated with not being good enough right away that they give up. Much like riding a bike, you have to pedal and hold the handlebars, which all feels weird in the beginning because you've never done it before. When you fall down, you pick yourself up and try again. Before you know it, you will discover a new distinction. In the case of learning to ride a bike, the distinction is called "balance."

It can be frustrating to watch all the older kids who are more proficient than you at riding, doing jumps and wheelies and tricks in a half-pipe. If I were to ask these kids, though, to teach me balance, they wouldn't be able to because certain distinctions in life such as balance need to be learned through personal trial and error. The trick is to be motivated to keep getting back up, even after you fall down and skin your knees. By being consistent and focusing on what you need to, not worrying about what other people are doing or how you compare to them, eventually you will discover whatever distinction associated with what you're trying to learn.

Distinctions cannot be unlearned. They allow you a transcendent vantage point and can open up and expose you to completely new worlds. Before knowing how to ride a bike, my world consisted of Aspen Avenue and about ten houses in either direction of my house. After I learned the distinction of balance, I was able to use my bike to ride around the block, into town to the hobby store, and to the park.

I was no longer dependent on my parents to take me places which allowed me, then, to experience the new distinction of freedom. Point being, putting in work to learn how to do something new can open up new worlds to us that we never even knew existed.

It would be very easy to give up trying to learn how to ride a bike after falling a few times, scraping your knees and having people laugh and question what you were doing. But if we have a strong enough vision and determination, we can make it happen.

For me, I was so determined to learn how to ride a bike that at eight years old I found my dad's tool box in the garage, grabbed a wrench, and removed the training wheels by myself. My mom was aghast when she came outside to see me trying to learn without my training wheels, but she could tell how determined I was. Soon, I was riding down the street and doing jumps in the park. That's the beauty of being in that creative space—it can transform your world in so many exciting ways!

I talk about this because I meet so many people who talk about wanting to try something new or wanting to bring more fulfillment into their lives. To do so requires stepping out of your comfort zone and putting yourself in new situations that are most likely are going to feel strange at first.

The key is to give yourself the space to not be good at it in the beginning. Whether it's signing up for an art class to get back in touch with your creativity or a writing class to write the book you've always wanted to, don't let the little voice in your head or anyone else talk you out of it.

Take a risk and try something that you've always wanted to. It can be insanely rewarding and if you stick with it, can open up completely new worlds you never knew existed.

TRAFFIC JAM IN YOUR BRAIN

"Life moves pretty fast. If you don't stop and look around once in a while, you could miss it." – Ferris Bueller

According to research done by Nobel Prize–winning psychobiologist, Roger W. Sperry, our left brain is more verbal, analytical, and orderly than our right brain. The left side is better at things like reading, writing, and computations. Functions that involve logic, sequencing, mathematics, and facts are primarily processed there. The right hemisphere of the brain, according to Sperry, is more visual and intuitive and has more creative ways of processing information. His research suggests that the right brain is also connected with imagination, holistic thinking, intuition, arts, feelings, daydreaming, and rhythm.

An article on Healthline.com states, "Whether you're performing a logical or creative function, you're receiving input from both sides of your brain. For example, the left brain is credited with language, but the right brain helps you understand context and tone. The left brain handles mathematical equations, but the right brain helps out with comparisons and rough estimates."

Our brain is constantly reorganizing itself and adapts to change very well depending on what tasks are required of it. New neural pathways are created when learning a new task, such as learning a language or learning how to play an instrument, and similarly, if a certain task or function is not used for a while, those same neural pathways can atrophy. That's why if you learn a language or an instrument and stop using it or playing for a while, your neural pathways will atrophy until you dust off that French dictionary or the flute you played in high school and consistently use them again and re-initiate those connections. Creativity and the use of your imagination are similar. If the areas in any part of the brain are underutilized, they will not have as many connections to fully take advantage of the creative potential that our brains maintain.

According to market research group Neilson, Americans spend on average more than eleven hours a day watching, reading, and interacting with media, either on their smartphones, iPads, computers, or TVs. Eleven hours! Furthermore, a study by global tech protection and support company Asurion found that "the average person struggles to go little more than ten minutes without checking their phone." This equates to approximately eighty times a day, with some checking it as much as three hundred times per day. I'd say thanks to Instagram, I'm guilty of being somewhere in the middle.

The reason we are so addicted to snoop on our phones so much is because every new notification, every ding, every new email or Facebook or IG 'like' causes a neurotransmitter in our brains called dopamine to be released. Dopamine is associated with the pleasure centers in our brains. Whether from food, alcohol, drugs, or sex, dopamine's release only perpetuates this cycle of craving and addiction. Every ten minutes we are literally giving ourselves hits of dopamine, similar to a drug addict.

Chris Bailey, in his book called *Hyperfocus,* says that our biggest problem in today's day and age is constant stimulation from our devices and focusing too intently on projects without taking time off. With constant engagement we prevent the right side or the creative side of our brains to have the space to do what it does best, which is to create new ideas and ways of addressing and solving problems.

Because there are so many things competing for our attention throughout the day, we need to give our brains a break. We may feel the need to hustle and do more, but this cannot only cause stress and burnout, it can prevent you from being able to solve problems utilizing the key problem-solving areas of your brain. What we need to try to do more of is unplug, detach, and recharge, even if it's only for a few minutes.

It may seem counterintuitive, but it's similar to the concept of working smarter, not harder. We don't need to do more. What we need is *more space*. We tend to think that by working harder and longer that our problems will be solved. Bailey describes how when you look at traffic, what allows it to move forward is not how fast cars are moving, but rather how much space is in between the cars. Space is what allows traffic to flow and move faster.

It's the same with our work and our lives. When we allow our brains to wonder, ideas come to us. Our minds are overstimulated; by setting limits on your phone usage and general attention to devices and active problem-solving, you allow the creative side of your brain to subconsciously process your day and experiences. Give your mind the space to allow it to do what it does best. By being the protective parent for your creative side, you will be able to approach and handle the things in your life from a more balanced and fulfilling perspective.

I remember a time in acting class when I was doing a scene from Chekhov's *The Seagull*. I was playing Trigorin, a well-known writer who is seducing the character of Nina in this particular scene. To get me out of my head and out of the left side of my brain, my teacher, Martha Graeff, asked me if I could imagine my character as an animal, what would I be? I thought about it for a few seconds and thought that because Trigorin was being predatory and dangerous with Nina, a wolf was the perfect animal to personify him. Martha then told me to get down on all fours, on the stage, and stalk Nina like a wolf would, using my instincts and imagination to play the scene the way a wolf would. By getting me out of the analytical part of my brain, I was able to fully inhabit the character of Trigorin and play him, not just from inside my head, but from my whole body in a similar manner to how Larry had me reconnect with my suppressed feelings and emotions. To be fully actualized human beings in life, it's important that we stay connected with all aspects of who we are so we are able to fully embrace life and all it has to offer. All of these exercises have taught me that, much like therapy, when we are out of touch with our true selves, it's easy to become shells of who we know ourselves to be. Instead of human beings, we become "human thinkings."

I suggest watching Marlon Brando in *A Streetcar Named Desire* to get an idea of what I'm talking about. Watch the scene where Stanley, played by Brando, meets Blanche, his sister-in-law, for the first time when she comes to visit. Brando slithers around oozing danger, sexual masculinity, and unpredictability. You can barely even understand the words coming out of his mouth, but it doesn't matter because his energy and body communicate everything you need to understand about who he is and what he wants. If you want to connect to people on an authentic and primal level, get out of your left brain and ask them creative questions. Tap into your imagination and your gut and communicate from there. I promise, people will respond differently to you than if you are stuck in and trying to connect from your left brain. It doesn't happen except on a superficial level.

People respond instinctively to right brain energy. When we are too in our heads and in the left side of our brain, we are only half a person. By taking our focus off of our devices and letting our brains wonder and daydream, we let the right side of our brains activate to bring a whole different perspective to what we are dealing with. Next time you are in a fight with your spouse, you're dealing with a problem at work, or you're frustrated with writer's block, go for a walk. Go for a drive. Make some food.

Give your mind a break and do not look at your device! Give the creative side of your brain a chance to work its magic and provide you the solutions that are all within us, waiting to be discovered. We simply must be vigilant enough to allow for this. Before going to bed tonight, instead of checking your phone, write in a journal. Think about the three great things you are thankful for today and write them down. Think of three things you'd like to accomplish tomorrow and write those down. Write about your day in descriptive and colorful language. Then put your journal down and for five to twenty minutes, sit in the quiet, and do nothing. By allowing your brain this space, you create an environment for it to process the things you are dealing with. You'll be surprised what your own mind will produce for you and how you will feel.

VULNERABILITY IS THE KEY

> *"It's tougher to be vulnerable than to be tough."*
> *— Rihanna*

From the first moment I got up on stage and did a scene in my first acting class, I knew it was something I had to do for the rest of my life. The first time I booked a role and got to be on set with all the different crew members rushing around, adjusting lighting, moving cameras, positioning props, getting everything ready was absolutely exhilarating. The problem for me and so many of my colleagues frequently has been the audition. By its very nature, the audition creates an environment in which you're judged. The fate of whether or not you are going to be doing a project is in the hands of a select group of people who have been charged with finding the right person for a role.

In the beginning of my acting career, my mindset walking into these rooms was essentially that *I have no idea what I'm really doing, so let's just explore this and see where it goes.* Looking back, I didn't have any expectation of getting the roles, so I went in to these first auditions with an adventurous, curious, and open mind. I knew that I didn't have the credits or the experience, so most of the time I would just wing it. I'd think to myself, I don't know what the hell I'm doing, so I might as well show up and try to be in the moment. As a result, I started to book some roles.

After booking a couple of roles and auditioning for a part on *Sex and the City* (which I didn't get), I started to understand how the process worked, and how to break down a scene quickly to make strong choices that felt right for the parts I was going in on. I began to take studying acting more seriously and watching actors on *Inside the Actors Studio* talk about their craft and listen to how intellectual they were as they elaborated how they prepared for a role. As such, I began to become "heady" about my craft. I read all the books, soaked up all the techniques, and spent hours at a little boutique bookstore on Crosby Street in SoHo reading Shakespeare.

Much like when my mom showed up at the end of my gymnastics practices, I found myself trying to show that I understood acting in my auditions instead of just being in the moment and acting. The more I learned and crammed into my brain how to show up on set and be the best actor I could be, the more I experienced the opposite effect of what I was working toward. My goal, naturally, was to walk into auditions with as much confidence as I could muster, but overthinking and incorporating too many techniques created an inability for me to stay in the moment. I wasn't necessarily listening as closely as possible to the casting director or my scene partners. As a result, my responses became less authentic and genuine.

This has always been something I have struggled with. Finding that balance between putting in the work so I'm confident knowing my material and what my character needs to do in a scene, but also, not being so married to what I have worked on so I can be in the moment, actively listen, and be able to respond authentically. The more I have worked, the more I have recognized the importance of bringing as much play and creativity to my roles as possible to keep my performances fresh and in the moment. As Jude Law says, "My only obligation is to keep myself and other people guessing." This is what makes for not only a captivating performance, but a captivating life.

Through years of study in my acting classes and having lived through the tragedy of the World Trade Center and my experience with cancer, I have realized that to get through life, whether it's on set, at work, with family, or in a relationship, with any sort of meaning or connection, requires laying our sword on the ground, lowering our well-fortified defenses, and allowing people into our hearts. Put simply, vulnerability is the key.

It was a Monday morning on the set of *Melrose Place* when Michael Radey, who played Jonah, came and sat next to me on our folding actors' chairs while we were waiting to shoot our next scene. He seemed to be more energetic than normal and explained to me that he had gone to a seminar that weekend with his wife. It was essentially a group lecture about personal growth, communication, and connection. He described it as doing quite a bit of self-exploration and delving into your psyche to better understand how your beliefs and opinions about things in life influence who you are, how you act, and where these ideas had come from.

I've always been curious about why people do the things they do and what motivates them, one of the biggest reasons I became an actor. I've always been intrigued, too, with my personality traits and specifically why I, as Margie Haber would say, "fall apart while trying to get the part." Even after working for several years and experiencing a modicum of success, having booked several guest starring roles on shows such as *Charmed, Gilmore Girls,* and *Nip/Tuck,* several films, *AMC,* and now *Melrose Place,* I still hadn't fully exposed what was deep inside of me that would cause me to shut down whenever I felt judged or was perceived as less than perfect.

After talking with Michael about the seminar, being the inquisitive person I am, I decided to check it out myself. I've been to therapy before, and it has helped, but this seminar was different. There, I explored the issues that I grew up with, such as feeling like I had to succeed in order to be accepted and all the other normal growing-up angst we deal with. It wasn't until I went to this seminar, however, that I learned an important quality about myself. I discovered that I will do everything in my power not to be vulnerable. Growing up, somewhere I picked up the idea that to be vulnerable meant weakness, and to my psyche, weakness meant being invisible. Because of this I have always attempted to come across as independent, strong, capable, and someone who could do it all on their own. This is, of course, why I didn't want to tell anyone at *AMC* that I had cancer, because I didn't want anyone to see that I was weak and vulnerable. As much as I could intellectually appreciate this, it wasn't until my audition for *Something Borrowed* that this truly resonated for me.

As I've touched on already, when it comes to auditioning and actually booking the role, you literally have to be Olympic-performance good to be considered to move on to the next round of auditions. Even then, there is no guarantee that the gatekeepers will think you're right for the role regardless of how brilliant your audition is. This is one of the aspects of having an acting career that can make you want to pull your hair out. No matter how good you are or how well you nailed the audition, quite a bit of the time, there are factors outside of your control that determine who gets the role. These include, among other things, how popular an actor is at that given time, which now includes more and more the size of someone's social media following, as well as whether or not the actor simply has the essence and physical traits that producers feel are right for the role.

You may look too much like one of the other lead actors, you may be too short, or your nose may be too big (Peter Gallagher lost a role because a producer thought this), you may have brown hair and they want blonde. Why don't the producers just ask you to dye your hair, you ask? Because a lot of the time, producers, casting directors, and directors don't know what they are looking for until someone walks into the room who simply has that 'it' quality that best fits that role.

One of my acting teachers described how the character in the story is searching for the right actor to play him or her as much as we as actors are searching to play the role of that character. When the essence of both are in sync, it's like catching lightning in a bottle. Think Jon Hamm as Don Draper in *Mad Men,* Sarah Jessica Parker as Carrie Bradshaw in *Sex and the City,* Tom Cruise as Jerry Maguire, Al Pacino as Michael Corleone in *The Godfather,* Marlon Brando as Stanley Kowalski in *A Streetcar Named Desire,* and the whole cast of *Friends.* When you think about it, can you imagine any other actor playing these roles? Again, it's not necessarily the right actor finding the right role, it's the right role finding the right actor *and* being open and vulnerable enough for people to see the real you.

The producers had been auditioning hundreds of actors for the role of Dex, and they just couldn't seem to find him. When major studio films such as *Something Borrowed* are being cast, the producers and casting directors usually first offer the roles to the A-list actors who they think are right for the part. If the actors they have offered the roles to are not available or simply don't like the role and pass, then they start to open up the role to other actors, which is how I got to audition for Dex.

I had no idea that this movie was based on a popular book series by Emily Giffin, and I really didn't know much about the script other than it was a romantic comedy. I didn't know who was cast yet, so I really didn't think much of it when I got to the Warner Bros. lot to audition. I went in, did the audition much like I had hundreds of other times, and felt good about it. This doesn't mean much because I have felt great about auditions and then never heard anything about them again.

So, much like any other audition, after I left, I threw away my audition sides and didn't think much of it until my agent called a few days later saying that the producers wanted me to come back and audition again for a callback. I'd say about 50 percent of my auditions usually result in callbacks, so I wasn't too surprised. I did feel pretty good about my audition and my grasp of the character. For the callback, I was told that I'd actually be reading with the lead actress, Ginnifer Goodwin. This is called a chemistry read.

The producers had about five guys come in for this chemistry read to see who might be the best fit with Ginny. There are obviously plenty of films that have great actors in them, but when there is a lack of chemistry, especially between potential love interests, it can make or break a film. As a result, producers are very conscious of trying to cast actors where you can tell there's some magic or the potential for sparks to fly.

When I went back in for this second audition, I walked into the same casting office again on the Warner Bros. lot, signed in, and sat down, waiting for my turn at potential stardom. Before I knew it, the casting door opened up, and one of the casting directors led me into the room where I was introduced to Ginny, who was super cute and incredibly sweet. I instantly felt a connection with her and I could tell that she was very open and ready to create together and to bring the scenes to life at their fullest.

When you go in for auditions, it's hard to really remember everyone's faces. I'm more focused on remembering my lines and my choices for the scene. I did, however, realize that this time, there were more people crammed into the casting room than at my first audition.

Because this was the second audition, I had some more time to work on the scenes with my acting teacher, Margie Haber, where I did more character and scene analysis. I also made sure I knew the dialogue cold so that when I walked in the room, I was able to be present and not have to second-guess myself with the choices I had made for each scene.

When I started to do the scenes with Ginny, it felt fun, exciting, and incredibly natural, as if we had known each other for years. This truly is a testament to how giving an actress Ginny is and how present and open she is with those she acts with. It was quickly evident why she enjoys the success that she has earned. We had three scenes to do and the first two felt great. It felt like we were hitting the right beats and it was playful and connected, which was obviously important. When it came to the last scene, however, a scene where Ginny's character and I are sitting and listening to the band that I may be hiring for me and my fiancé's (Kate Hudson) wedding. After discovering that she had feelings for me but never told me about them, my character, Dex, confronts her about it and professes his love for her. For this scene, however, I simply felt like I was too much inside my head. I was too focused on remembering the right words and how I thought they should be said.

I also had a feeling that everyone else in the room could tell that the scene was simply falling flat. I was having difficulty making the words authentically mine. I was working hard to deliver them in the powerful way they were written in the scene, but the words weren't resonating with me the way I knew they could have. The words themselves weren't the words that I would have used personally. In other words, they didn't ring true for me, and everyone else could sense this. I had been acting long enough to know that those rare moments when you find yourself so immersed in a scene, where time and space disappear—those "magical" moments that reveal a unique connection between you and another actor, the inspiring *moments* that touch others, causing them to take notice. This, unfortunately, wasn't one of those moments when it absolutely needed to be.

As much as it felt like the other scenes went well, I could tell this one was on its way to the trash heap. There wasn't the *juice* or the *energy* that the scene needed. That's when the director, Luke Greenwald, whom I consider one of the best directors I've ever worked with, stepped in. His ability to have an actor see a scene in a way that brings it to life with inspiration, is what makes Luke so special. He could tell what was needed, got out of his chair, and approached me in front of everyone. He proceeded to kneel down in front of me and, with generosity and support, he gave me one of the greatest pieces of direction and advice I have ever received. He said quietly and simply, "Just be yourself."

As I sat there, latching on to his words for life support in a ship that I could tell was ready to sink, he continued, "Say the words however you would say them if this was you in real life." I can't thank him enough for that bit of direction because that's all I needed to hear. He was giving me permission to simply be me, to trust my instincts as the artist I had worked so hard to become, and to let my guard down so that the people in the room could be invited into the scene to share this authentic experience as well.

When we started the scene again, I looked over at Ginny and took a deep breath. I looked into her eyes and simply took her in with that one important breath. It felt as if I could see into her soul. I saw how beautiful she truly was. I saw her strength. I saw the things she was afraid of, the things that made her light up. I could also see her kindness, and the love that effortlessly inspired the words that started to fall out of my mouth.

It was as if Shakespeare, Nora Roberts, Nicholas Sparks, and all the great romance writers I knew were channeling their words through me. I centered all my focus on Ginny, allowing myself to be completely vulnerable and open to her and to fully focus on what she was saying.

I simply responded naturally to her. I said whatever I needed to say to let her know how much I cared about her, how much I loved her, and how much I still was in love with her. Everyone and everything else in that moment disappeared.

There were no other people, no cameras, no Warner Bros. lot, no pressure about needing to get a job so that my agents wouldn't fire me, no worrying about how to pay rent, no anything other than Ginny and I and our mutual desire to bring service to the story. Before I knew it, tears were flowing out of my eyes, tears of frustration, salty tears of joy, and cascading tears of love. I could tell Ginny felt it as well because soon tears began to well up in her eyes, and gently stream down her flushed cheeks. After we finished the last few words in the scene, we both just stared each other for a few more moments, not wanting the moment to end.

I didn't want to break the bond we had created, but I also suddenly became aware that there were eight other people in the room sharing that intimate moment. I slowly turned my head to look at them. It was one of the most gratifying moments in my acting career. The expressions on everyone's faces conveyed to me that they too had been taken in and had gone on the beautiful and amazing journey of the scene. We had all experienced it together.

I honestly don't remember what anyone said after that because I was on such a high that I pretty much floated out of there and into my car. I drove home knowing that regardless of what happened, I had given my all and, most importantly, I had delivered all of my authentic self without inhibition, without judgment and without worrying about how it was going to turn out. It was an incredibly liberating experience and again, one of which, we as actors, are in constant pursuit.

I immediately called my agent and told him how well I felt it went. He said he would find out what they thought and get back to me. A few days later, I got the call from him. I was sitting on my bed watching *Sports Center*, saw my phone ringing, picked it up, and heard him asking,

"Do you want to go to New York?" That's all I needed to hear to begin jumping up and down on my bed. I think everyone in my entire neighborhood heard that I had gotten the role.

It wasn't until a few weeks later that I was on set during the first week of filming and Hilary Swank, one of the producers, took me to lunch. There she shared with me the details as to why I had gotten the role. I'm a huge admirer of Hilary's work. I've watched all of her movies and have always admired that she went from a small role on *90210* to her two wonderful Academy Award wins. It was surreal to find myself sitting across from her in a restaurant in Manhattan's Upper East Side.

We chatted for a bit about the movie and other projects, and finally the subject of how I booked the role came up. Because Hilary was not in the room when I auditioned, she said that her producing partner, Molly Smith, had gone to her house with copies of the tapes of the handful of guys who they had auditioned for Dex. As they watched each of the auditions, Hilary said, as soon as I came on the screen, she saw how open, honest, and vulnerable I was, and that it was those qualities I exhibited that pulled her into the scene, convincing her that I truly was Dex.

To be having lunch with Hilary Swank, let alone having her compliment me on my acting, was one of the highlights of my life. It's special life moments like that one that make me humbled and grateful for the opportunities with which I have been blessed. I will forever be grateful to Hilary, Molly Smith, and Luke Greenfield, all who advocated for someone who didn't necessarily have the big credits often required to play such a prominent and incredible role. And thank you to everyone who has seen and supported the movie and helped to make it happen. I can confidently say it will always be my favorite acting role ever. All because I allowed myself to breathe and made myself vulnerable enough to share my truth and let people in.

Three Takeaway Action Tips:

1. Learn to meditate. This is the key to relaxation. If you have trouble meditating, check out the hundreds and hundreds of meditation pieces of music free on YouTube. They will help you relax and let go of the things that are stressful, allowing you to open up a door to creative thinking that can lead to new opportunities.

2. Take time off or take different paths from the ones you usually take to allow the creative right side of your brain to engage. Doing things differently or not doing some of the things you usually do, like watching TV, can really help you open up new, creative ways of thinking.

3. Get vulnerable. There is strength in vulnerability. Being vulnerable allows you to connect in an incredibly authentic way. Brene Brown, author and expert on vulnerability, has helped so many people tap into their creative power by allowing themselves to be vulnerable.

06 **SUCCESS**

"You just do it. You force yourself to get up. You force yourself to put one foot before the other, and God damn it, you refuse to let it get to you. You fight. You cry. You curse. Then you go about the business of living. That's how I've done it. There's no other way."
– Elizabeth Taylor

The humid summer early evening breeze blew on my face as an orchestra of cicadas buzzed in the tall grass beyond the outfield. Clapping and the occasional, "Come on Colin! You got this!" could be heard from behind our bench where the rest of my teammates sat with their rally caps on backwards. "All we need is a base hit, Colin!" It was bottom of the last inning. Bases loaded. We were down by a run, and I was up to bat for my eight-year-old little league team in Rochester, Michigan. The sun was hanging low above the batch of tree tops in left center, casting some broad shadows near short, tempting me to blast a home run toward it.

It was a full count, and even if it wasn't a dinger, all I had to do was make contact with the pitch, a little base hit. An easy knock and a run would score to tie and possibly another to win. My teammates would come running and screaming to congratulate me and hoist me on their shoulders as I'd look over at my parents to witness pride in their eyes because their son had won the game. From that day forth, I'd be the hero, a champion, and everyone could go to Dairy Queen to celebrate with cherry-dipped soft serve. Except, the pitch came in ...I swung and missed.

Life can absolutely suck sometimes. I've often found myself somewhere, wherever, staring off into the distance and wondering, how could this have happened? I've tried to do the right thing, I've played by the rules, I did what I was told, I ate my vegetables (except the time I tried to hide my green beans in my glass of milk and my dad found me out), I raise money for charities and I strive to treat people the way I want to be treated. I've committed to working hard, rolling up my sleeves, not being afraid to get dirty to pursue my dreams, all with the hope of making the world a little better because I was in it. So why, then, do shitty things happen?

Why have I been written off shows? Why have I not booked jobs when I had more experience and in my mind was way more qualified? Why did my dad have to die when he did? Why do people get cancer? Why do our hearts get broken, and why is there so much suffering in the world?

We can drive ourselves crazy asking questions like these because there really are no answers. As much as I'm a firm believer in our lives being a direct reflection of our self-image, how hard we work, and what we attract into our life, I think that sometimes, random bad shit just happens. Learning to deal with adversity and not letting it completely shut me down and become numb to the human experience is something that I have had to wrestle with through the ups and downs of my life experiences.

From sharing my experiences and talking with others, I'm very aware that most everyone is dealing with some sort of adversity in their life, whether it's happening to them personally or someone close to them. From meeting people all over the world and from all walks of life, I learned that no matter who you are, where you're from, what you do, what you look like, how much money you have, or how old you are, people the world over deal with all the same struggles and challenges and share similar triumphs and successes.

This raises the issue of success and achievement. From my perspective, I wouldn't say that success and achievement are the goal. In my observation, anyone who loves what they do is not doing it for the fame or recognition. They do it because it is innately who they are, and they derive immense pleasure and satisfaction from the pursuit of being their greatest self.

This is not to say that the seeking to be the best at what you do is a bad or selfish. As a competitive person myself, I love the challenge of facing off against an opponent because it motivates me to become better in order to find a way to win. For me, winning is not the end goal so much as it is that I enjoy the process or the game itself, knowing that in pursuit of winning, or in the case of auditioning, getting the job will provide me the opportunity to grow and create. Whether we are auditioning, meeting with a client to bid a job, seeking the lowest cost way to do business, or simply seeking ways to be a better spouse or parent, no matter how competitive we might be, we all seek success in some way or another.

Crappy auditions, being let go from agencies, friends and family members passing away, and having relationships fall apart have all forced me to take to look deep inside myself and nurture the internal strength to get through it all. For me, there is no other option. In my mind, life is not worth it if I'm not living up to what I feel my potential is and doing the things that allow me to know myself as who I am. Putting all of my heart, soul, creativity, and self on the line is the only way for me to fully experience life. Having come close to death has only made my desire to fully live that much more urgent and real. Pursuing the things in life that I know to be fulfilling and that I am passionate about have involved some amazing victories and crushing defeats. For me, the journey to achieve and attain success is worth the risk of falling down and getting hurt.

As someone whose livelihood has depended on consistently successful performances, I have worked incredibly hard to become proficient in my ability to book jobs. I've done this with the help of insights gained from acting teachers, agents, managers, casting directors and the actual experience of auditioning and working. All of this has made me grow as an actor and as a person. This has increased my competitive edge and, thus, my odds of booking the role. Whether you're looking to increase your productivity or effectiveness in the workplace or your desire is to be able to turn your personal goals and dreams into reality, it can be beneficial to have a basic understanding of competitive analytics.

In my twenty-year acting career, I have gone on over two thousand auditions. If you look at my IMDb page, you'll see that I have worked on approximately forty jobs. This equates to about a two percent success rate. In other words, I HAVE NOT been successful ninety-eight percent of the time. In any normal business or work setting, if someone was successful only two percent of the time, do you think they would stick around for long? Would you be happy and fulfilled only succeeding two percent of the time?

I can either look at my success rate as, "I failed ninety-eight percent of the time," or I could look at it and say, "ninety-eight percent of the time I learned something. I have grown in some way to overcome a challenge that has helped me become a more wellrounded, mature, better-skilled, and wiser person. This continues to make me better to acquire more work." Even though I have only been successful two percent of the time, it's this two percent that has paid for me to travel the world, work with Academy Award and Golden Globe–winning actors, meet foreign dignitaries and royalty, attend the Cannes Film Festival, produce my own projects, and be able to raise money for the charities I care about on a large scale.

Even though I haven't been successful most of the time, I've grown a lot from my "failures" and have learned more from these experiences so much more than if I'd simply been offered the job. This is the important thing to remember and to track. When you start anything new, it's important to measure your progress so that each week, month, and year, you can gauge your progress and adjust accordingly. If something is not working the way you feel it should, or if you notice that your effectiveness is decreasing, you can then measure what that is and take the necessary steps to correct the direction in which things are heading.

As an actor, one of the things I have become aware of, in the past twenty years of studying human behavior, is that our emotions can either be our best friend or just as easily, if not more so, our worst enemy. Emotions can serve as a trusted ally in helping us attain glorious victories and amazing fulfillment, or they can sabotage our dreams and desires in the blink of an eye. I'm naturally an introvert, but because I'm passionate about the things I want to accomplish, I've recognized the importance of mastering control of my emotions to be able to dial them up when needed and keep them at bay when necessary.

Having gone on thousands of auditions and having the proverbial door slammed in my face over and over again has taught me some important lessons about how to deal with crushing setbacks and adversity. I've also needed to cultivate persistence and the ability to pick myself back up when I've found myself on the ground. We see it time and time again when people are brought to their knees only to get back up and triumph again. So, what makes us get back up when we've been punched in the face? What allows us to dust ourselves off, pick up our cap, and keep moving forward?

WHY? 20 X

> *Luke Skywalker: "I can't believe it!"*
> *Yoda: "That is why you fail."*

In addition to acting, I also rehab houses and invest in real estate. Because I go anywhere between three and six months between acting jobs, I decided that I needed to do something not only to supplement my income, but also to keep from being bored out of my mind as I waited for my next acting opportunity. What I love about real estate is that I'm essentially acting the role of a producer on a film.

A producer doesn't act, direct, hang the lighting, operate the cameras, or dress the actors. But what a producer does do is hire all the people who do this work. He or she project manages to make sure everyone is working together synergistically and on budget. I don't hammer nails, hang drywall, paint, or install cabinets. What I do, however, is find a candidate house, run the budgets, hire the contractors and subcontractors, and then sell the house when it's all done. I also help pick out the aesthetic components of the houses such as the tile and cabinet combinations to be installed, what color paint for the rooms, and if we are going to rearrange the layout of the house. I love it because it satisfies my creative ambitions, and I'm fulfilled by the contribution I'm making to help the communities of Chicago thrive. I rehab and own properties in some of the city's most underserved areas, which has helped not only make some of these places nicer and more livable for families, but has also provided employment opportunities for some of the local residents struggling to find secure work.

Through working in the South Side, I've gotten to know quite a few residents and the people we employ. In doing so, it has given me great satisfaction to know that what I and so many other people are doing to help revitalize and support some of the city's most underserved communities is actually making a difference.

When I first started going to my real estate investment seminars and courses, the moderators and lecturers would always start by asking us why we were there. Most of the people in these courses were in their thirties, forties and fifties. As I got to know them, I learned everyone had full-time jobs. So why then would all these people, already working fifty to a hundred hours a week, be sitting in these lectures for entire weekends? Was it just to learn strategies to buy crappy, run-down houses full of mold and asbestos followed by how to put up backsplash and replace plumbing?

Why do we do anything? Is it for the money? Is it for glory? Is it for security? Or is it because we simply love to do it? The answers vary for each person, but when it comes down to it, we all do things based on a sliding scale best described by Maslow's Hierarchy of Needs. In 1943, Abraham Maslow proposed in his paper A Theory of Human Motivation that human beings are motivated by a certain set of "basic physiological needs" that gradually leads up to the highest form of human desire he later posited as "transcendence."

Maslow theorized that first and foremost we are compelled to take action to satisfy our basic physiological need for food, water, sleep, shelter, sex, and general homeostasis. Physiological needs must be met first. This means that if a human is struggling to meet their basic intrinsic needs, then they are unlikely to pursue safety, belongingness, esteem, and self-actualization.

Once these basic physiological needs are relatively satisfied, one's need for safety takes precedence and dominates behavior. This includes personal and environmental safety, economic and job safety, and assurance with regard to one's health. It's intrinsic in us to need to feel protected against accidents and illness and their adverse impacts on our well being. The pursuit of these first two groups of needs can be all-consuming, causing stress, anxiety, and depression. Indeed, such disorders like post-traumatic stress symptoms can cause people to make irrational decisions not based on logic or common good of the whole. Marketers and politicians both know this all too well and will play into these basic needs to convince us to buy their product or service or to vote for them based on promises that if we do so, these primal needs for survival will be met.

Social belonging is the next level of need. Humans need to love and be loved both sexually and non-sexually by others. When left unfulfilled, feelings of loneliness, social anxiety, and clinical depression are common. It can be difficult for unfulfilled people to maintain emotionally significant relationships. This is why people join clubs, sports teams, religious groups, online communities, and gangs. We like to feel we connect with people, even in the most trivial or obscure ways. We find comfort in knowing that there are other people out there that are just as unusual or different as ourselves.

The next level up is our self-esteem needs. Once we have french fries in our stomachs and clothes on our backs, a roof over our heads, health and car insurances, and a membership card to our local knitting club, Maslow says we have the need to satisfy our egos by way of recognition and a concern for status, importance, and respect from others. We desire to feel valued by others and to feel a sense of contribution, that we matter for what we have accomplished or who we are.

He goes on to explain that most people have a need for stable self-respect and self-esteem. However, low self-esteem or an inferiority complex may result from imbalances growing up where someone was neither acknowledged nor accepted for who they are. This can lead people to seek fame or glory to prove their self-worth not only to others but also themselves. This, Maslow says, is a fool's errand because fame and glory, he continues, will not help the person build their self-esteem until they accept themselves internally.

The next level on Maslow's hierarchy is that of self-actualization, or in words as described by Kurt Goldstein, "What a man can be, he must be." This need has to do with our full potential and the realization and experiencing of that potential. If we know ourselves to be an athlete, we have the need to play sports. If we have the desire to be a parent, we'll have kids. As an artist, I have the innate need to create. It is just who I am.

Whether I'm on set creating a character or in a house imagining how to redesign it, it's in those moments I feel fully connected to who

I am and fully fulfilled. Even the pursuit of self-actualization can be fulfilling. Recognize within yourself who you want to be, what you want to be doing, and go for it!

In his later years, Maslow explored a further dimension of motivation, a last and final level of need, transcendence. He theorized that one finds the fullest realization in giving oneself to something beyond oneself. In one of his later books The Farther Reaches of Human Nature, Maslow expounds, "Transcendence refers to the very highest and most inclusive or holistic levels of human consciousness, behaving and relating, as ends rather than means, to oneself, to significant others, to human beings in general, to other species, to nature, and to the cosmos."

The reason I bring this up is because through my years of pursuing different things, I have wanted to realize and create, and I've discovered the first step on the road to success is that it's crucial to know why you're doing it. If you don't have an insanely important "Why?" that motivates you to act, giving up before realizing your goal will be all too easy. It's inevitable you are going to get knocked down in pursuit of what you love. You have to have a strong enough reason "Why?" you're doing something to get back up time and time again. There is no way I would have been able to go on all the auditions I've been on, fail as much as I have, time and time again, and still be able to go on more unless deep down in my inner being, I loved to act. Creating allows me to be self-actualized, and as Maslow says, this connects us to the "cosmos."

In one of the real estate seminars I mentioned earlier, an instructor asked us to write down why we were in that room, learning how to rehab houses and purchase real estate investment properties. Most people's answer, including my own, was to make more money. The instructor then asked the question again: "Why?" Then we were told to write down the answer. I wrote, "So I would be able to afford the lifestyle that I want to have and to be able to help my mom make more money for her retirement." The instructor asked, "Why?" again. To which we were told to write the answer down again. This literally went on until the instructor asked us "why?" twenty times. Twenty times.

By the time we got down to answering "why?" to each of the prior questions, we all had a hyper specific idea of why we were there. More specifically, we had identified our motivation for being there. By asking us the why repeatedly, our instructor essentially was leading us through Maslow's hierarchy of needs until we ended up in transcendence. What this made me realize is that a lot of us struggle just to meet our basic everyday needs of survival. Perhaps there is some significance here in that we're not always present to our full potential as human beings. By having us drill down deep to discover what our motivation is for doing what we do, we started to get a bigger and grander notion of ourselves, which was both enlightening and empowering!

What I ultimately discovered through doing this exercise was that my "Why?" is firmly rooted in having the freedom to create my dream life to take care of all the people in it that I care about. This is what gets me up in the morning and keeps me motivated to go on audition after audition and look at house after house.

What was really cool about this exercise, too, was that after we were all done, we went around the room and shared with each other what our "Why?" was. This exercise also made me realize that at the end of the day people's "Whys?" were inevitably related to wanting to be able to provide for loved ones and to create more experiences of happiness. Hearing everyone's "Why?" reminded me how vulnerability truly bonds people on a deep and authentic level. By sharing what mattered to us, we were able to connect. As a result, we found out the specific desires of each and every one of us in the room and we were able to then offer support and assistance to those that needed help with their endeavors and projects. By creating community, we create a resource for us all to benefit from. Some of these people have become my closest friends and colleagues just because of this one exercise.

The instructor followed this exercise up with another where we had to write out our goals for the future. I'm sure most of you have written out goals for what you want to accomplish in life. Similar to how Wendy had me write out my goals, it's important to remember that the key is to write them out in the present tense, as if they are already happening. What was different with what our instructor asked us to do, however, which was unlike anything I had done up until that point in my life, was he asked us to think about our onehundred-year legacy.

He first asked us to write down what our goals were for this week, then by the end of the month, then three months, then six months, then one year, then three years, then five years. He continued until it was, "What are your goals you want to have accomplished by twenty-five years time?" This is where it got interesting. He then asked, "Think about what your one-hundred-year legacy looks like and write that down." Wow, I just thought to myself.

I never thought of that before. He continued on to say, "100 years from now, when you and all of your loved ones are gone from this earth, what do you want people to remember you by?"

I started to realize that I want to be remembered as someone who made a positive difference in as many people's lives as possible. Someone who shared his heart and vulnerability authentically, so that people from all walks of life would feel cared about and inspired to pursue self-actualization themselves.

We all have it in us to be great, to find happiness and fulfillment. As exciting as it is to walk on the red carpet and to work with some of the most creative and famous people in the world, nothing is more satisfying than knowing that I made a difference in someone's life.

Where do you find yourself on Maslow's scale and what is your "Why?" Ask this of yourself twenty times and see what you are able to narrow it down to. Write this down on a piece of paper and put it on the mirror in your bathroom at home or on a sticky pad on your monitor at work. Knowing exactly "Why?" you're doing something is the fuel to light your fire to make it happen. Then think about what you want your one-hundred-year legacy to be. Even if it's to be the best mom or husband you could possibly be. As long as it inspires you and lights you up to take action, that's all that matters.

GOOD TO GREAT

> *"Wanting to be a good actor is not good enough. You must want to be a great actor. You just have to have that." – Gary Oldman*

In the pursuit of building my acting and real estate careers, I've made the effort to attend as many seminars and lectures as possible, to listen to podcasts and TED talks, and read numerous books on performance and success. One of the more notable courses I attended that helped me create a framework to overcome adversity was given by Hollywood publicist Michael Levine. Over the past thirty years, he has written nineteen books on publicity and branding and is considered one of the world's experts on the subject matter. He has represented 58 Academy Award–winners, 34 Grammy Award–winners, 43 New York Times bestsellers, and consulted with three Presidents. He's also an incredibly generous and giving person and someone I consider one of the bigger influencers with regard to my success in life.

At Michael's seminar, he started off by saying he worked with "super successful" people. They ranged from Michael Jackson, Prince, Barbra Streisand, Sharon Stone, David Bowie, as well as U.S. Presidents Ronald Reagan, George Bush, and Bill Clinton. Michael says that he became curious about how these people were able to achieve the level of success and what differentiated them from people who weren't as successful. He differentiates the two by labeling "successful" people and "super successful" people.

Michael wanted to know if there were certain qualities that "super successful" people had that allowed them to reach the highest peaks compared to others who, on the surface, appeared to have similar talents and abilities, but didn't share the same high level of success. He also wanted to discover that if these people did indeed possess a certain set of qualities responsible for their super success, was it transferable to others like you or me? Or was it just some intangible 'it' quality that they were born with?

What Michael discovered after getting to know and working with the hundreds of clients he represented over the years is that the clients at the top of their field had four major qualities that less successful people neither possessed nor utilized. He describes these qualities as the "Four Os."

The first quality Michael described was "OBSESSION." This is not simply an interest or a love, but what he describes as a "burning, maniacal rage as if their life depended on it." He went on, stating that a lot of people have ambition, but the super successful maintain something "deeper, intense, and more primal" than mere desire. He used the analogy of the obsession a heroin addict has who will do anything necessary to get their next fix. It's an itch that cannot be scratched, that keeps them maniacally engaged trying to do so.

Michael went on to say that they have an URGENCY about what they want and will do what it takes to take massive action as soon as possible. He also noted they get incredibly CREATIVE when it comes to thinking outside the box in order to make things happen. Simply put, they have an idea in their head about where they want to be and they will not stop until they achieve it.

The second quality that super successful people possess is their eternal "OPTIMISM" with regard to possibilities. He describes how this optimism is born from a militant need to face the truth of what the reality of any situation is and that they usually view life or situations as games that can be won. 'SS' people have a clear understanding that whatever 'game' they are playing is A, not easy and B, not fair. They believe, however, that even though the game is neither easy nor fair, that with enough focus, drive and determination, the game is winnable. He mentioned that former Secretary of State Colin Powell once said, "Perpetual optimism is a force multiplier." Optimistic people are contagious to be around and inspire us to believe that anything is possible.

The third quality he describes the 'SS' have is their obsessive commitment to "OBLIGATION." Super successful people are very responsible. They are the type of people who come up with a plan and stick to it. They create goals and write them down with dates. Instead of saying, "I'm going to lose some weight," SS people will say "I'm going to lose eight pounds by June 1st." Michael said, "A damn fool with a written plan will beat a wandering genius 100 times out of 100." Something does not exist until it is created in reality by putting it in your calendar. How many New Year's resolutions have you made, only to forget about them come February 1st? If someone asked you what your resolutions were for this year right now, would you be able to rattle them off without having to think about them?

If you woke an SS person up in the middle of the night and asked them what they are up to in life and what they are committed to, without hesitation, they would be able to tell you. There is no confusion with SS people regarding their identity. They know who they are and have lived by the ideas that they have created themselves to be. I have decided that because I love to act, build businesses, and give back to others, I have created my identity to be that of an actor, an entrepreneur, and a philanthropist. By choosing to be each of these things, I choose to be used by the distinctions of each. In other words,

I let myself be defined by what it means to be an actor, an entrepreneur, and philanthropist. I am an actor, so I act. I go to auditions. I go to acting classes. I work on my voice exercises. I am an entrepreneur, so I buy real estate and create businesses. I go to business seminars. I create myself to be a philanthropist, so I participate in marathons and triathlons and work to give back to people in my community.

This is who I am. By creating and declaring yourself to be whatever you desire and allowing yourself to be used by the distinctions of what you have declared, you automatically begin to do whatever is required to be just that. It's actually quite simple and incredibly powerful because it has nothing to do with motivation, discipline, or being inspired. You take actions because you are what you have created yourself to be. If I say I'm an actor then I do what an actor does.

International bestselling author and multimillionaire entrepreneur Dan Lok describes how one of his business partners, with whom he has traveled for the past eleven years, wakes up every day at 6 am to go running. Dan said no matter where they were, what time zone they were in, how late they had gotten to their hotel the night before, or whether Mike is healthy or sick, he gets up in the morning and runs for an hour. When Dan finally asked him, "Mike, how did you develop such discipline? What gives you the motivation every day to wake up so early and run? What's your secret? Mike simply replied, "Dan, I'm a runner, so I run."

The source of Mike's motivation doesn't come from his selfdiscipline or his willpower. It comes from his self-image as a runner. We all behave in a manner consistent with whom we know ourselves to be. SS people have an intensely close relationship with who they know they are and because of it are very responsible when it comes to the obligations necessary to fulfill on creating this identity.

The last "O" in Michael's analysis of SS people is "ORGASM." Some may snicker at the word for its technical definition, but in this sense, Michael describes it as a metaphor for people who vibrate at a contagiously high frequency. SS people radiate confidence and exude that vibration because of what they passionately believe in. You can literally sense this energy from people who have committed themselves to greatness.

Michael went on to say SS people realize that no one is going to "save them." They know if they don't "save" themselves, no one else will. Mark Duplass, an actor, director, screenwriter, and producer who, with his brother Jay, has created countless television shows and movies, gave a great talk about this at the SXSW Festival in Austin, Texas a few years ago talking about this very subject. He described how his career didn't start taking off until he and his brother faced the reality that "the cavalry isn't coming." They realized the only way they were going to make it in the business was if they started to take action to create their own opportunities.

The brothers started making their own films, and in 2015, they made a feature length film called Tangerine entirely shot on an iPhone. Mark basically said that if you want something badly enough, there is no reason for you not to start TODAY working toward that goal. He went on to say that if you want to be an actor, you should be shooting scenes every weekend with your friends. The entire thrust of his keynote speech was that there is no excuse for you not to take action in order to get you closer to where you want to be. No one is going to hand you the keys to the kingdom. You have to be willing to take them on your own accord.

Another quote I like because it inspires me to keep taking action despite whatever concerns I may have is by Werner Erhard, which reads, "It is important that you get clear for yourself that your only access to impacting life is action. The world does not care what you intend, how committed you are, how you feel or what you think, and it certainly has no interest in what you want or don't want. Take a look at life as it is lived and see for yourself that the world only moves for you when you act." So, regardless of how big the audition is, how daunting the project, how scary it may to ask the person you want to go on a date with, or how frustrating the challenges in life are, I can't stress this enough, never stop taking action in the direction you want to go.

Michael went on to say that SS people have the passion and desire to make things happen. They will not let anything or anyone get in their way. He says, "an SS person will first ask you to please move, then tell you to move, then knock your ass down." They know where they are headed and they possess the self-awareness and drive to get there. He further explained that no matter what you want to do in life, that you and you alone have to set the tone and be the driving force.

Most working actors have an agent, a manger, a lawyer, and a publicist. Typically, an agent and manager will get 10 percent each in commission of whatever your salary is for a project. Your lawyer will usually will get 5 percent, and a publicist ranges between $2,000 and $10,000 a month, depending on how much they're doing and what projects you're working on.

That means, on average, 25 percent of your income is going to your team. However, the mistake that people, especially actors, make is to assume because they have engaged someone to get them work, act as if their representation should do all the work to get them jobs. Golden Globe–winning actor Anthony LaPaglia, best known for his award winning role on Without a Trace, elaborated on this quite succinctly when asked about reps in the business and their responsibilities. When talking to a group of young actors, one of them expressed to Anthony that he didn't feel his agent was getting him many auditions, which he was frustrated about. Anthony responded with a question. He asked the young actor, "How much does your agent charge you in commission? To which the actor replied, "Ten percent." Anthony retorted, "Then you should be doing ninety percent of the work to get your next job." Have you ever heard the quote, "If it is to be, it's up to me," by Lori Pratt? Obviously, if you don't take charge, most likely, no one will.

DON'T GIVE UP

"I'm convinced that about half of what separates successful entrepreneurs from the non-successful ones is pure perseverance."
— Steve jobs

When I was in college, I joined a social fraternity called Phi Gamma Delta. Movies like Animal House depict the debaucherous life of college kids drinking their faces off and performing shameless acts of idiocy, but for the most part, fraternity life was a great place for me. At the fraternity, I met new friends, had people to do homework with, go to football games with, and yes, party with. Our annual Fiji Island party was epic, complete with a ten foot tall papermache, smoking volcano and a waterfall coming out of the third floor bathroom that crescendoed into the makeshift three-foot lagoon, on the side of the fraternity house, and everyone adorned in grass skirts. Reggae music jammed all night and the evening usually culminated with a few of my inebriated frat brothers jumping into the lagoon naked. Ah, good times.

As much fun as we had partying together, however, my fraternity experience will always be remembered as one of bonding, support, charitable outreach, and a rich tradition of encouraging us young men to realize our full potential and do great things in the world. Many notable Phi Gams include authors Jack Kerouac, E. B. White, and Norman Vincent Peale, and golfers Jack Nickaus and Payne Stewart. Talk show hosts Johnny Carson and Seth Meyers and Nobel Prize winners Luis Alvarez and Frederick Robbins were also members.

The most prominent member of Phi Gamma Delta, however, is probably the thirtieth president of the United States, Calvin Coolidge. President Coolidge wrote one of my favorite sayings about not giving up. I have it posted on my wall in front of my desk to remind me every day of this sage advice. It reads, "Persistence: Nothing in the world can take the place of persistence. Talent will not. Nothing is more common than unsuccessful men with talent. Genius will not. Unrewarded genius is almost a proverb. Education will not. The world is full of educated derelicts. Persistence and determination alone are omnipotent. The slogan "press on" has sold and always will solve the problems of the human race.

I've been an actor now for over twenty years, and when I'm on set, it's still as new, fresh, and exciting as the first day I stepped into acting class. I've had many exhilarating successes and many crushing defeats when I didn't get the job I so wanted. What has kept me going is my love for what I do and my drive to want to aways learn and grow, despite the challenges and setbacks that have sometimes made me question myself. When it comes to any it's not always the best or most talented who works, it's the one who stuck around the longest and was able to keep his chips on the table that ends up getting the work. NHL hockey legend Wayne Gretzky said it best: "You miss 100 percent of the shots you don't take." The moment you stop or give up, you're giving up on the possibility to realize what you want to create.

Having booked my first roles on Law & Order SVU where I played a male escort named "Steven," and another show called The Street where I played, ironically enough, "The Artist" and had to jump into bed in my underwear with Jenny Garth from the original 90210 . I was beginning to feel a modicum of confidence about my acting and my ability to work in the business, even though I still knew I had a lot to learn. Much like when you're in your junior or senior year of high school, I was starting to see myself as a little more experienced and confident and not so much as a "fresh off the boat" actor who was still trying to figure things out.

As I started to feel more confidence in my acting abilities, I began noticing I seemed to be generating both serendipitous connections and meetings. When I arrived in Los Angeles for the first time, I went to the Budget rental car place on Wilshire Boulevard in Beverly Hills. The guy behind the counter seemed pleasant enough, and upon asking for my driver's license, noticed that it was from New York. "Welcome to LA," he said cheerfully. Still buzzing with excitement and nervous about my new adventure in a brand new city, I thanked him and asked him a couple questions about some of the different areas nearby.

I remember it was It was the second week of January, and it was probably about 73 degrees and gorgeous outside. This rental car guy continued on about how great the weather had been and asked me where I was going to be living. He told me I should check out Malibu, Santa Monica, and some other notable places. Then gave me the rental slip, told me my car was outside where another attendant would meet me to give me the keys and get me into the car. Before he let go of the papers though, he asked, "By the way, are you an actor?"

This caught me off guard a bit. I wasn't sure if he was about to play some sort of joke or ask me to help him get an agent or what not, but he seemed genuinely interested, so I simply responded, "I am. I haven't done much, but I'm here for pilot season."

He responded, "That's awesome." Then he looked up at me and zeroed in on my eyes much like the cab driver did years later back in NYC. Similarly, as if he were speaking directly to my soul, this complete stranger smiled and said, "Don't give up."

This was another of the unique moments in my life where I have felt a bizarre, but familiar connection to something grander than me guiding me forward in the direction of my dreams. I gazed at his name tag briefly. "Thank you, Joe." I said. He nodded his head and I walked out.

Even now, just thinking about this exchange reminds me that when we're connected to who we know we are, pursuing what truly fulfills us with joy and gratitude, there are certain celestial, miraculous signs that transcend our plane of perceived reality and appear to remind us when we are on the right path.

This isn't to say one's path will be easy. For me, however, whenever I have connected with my spiritual self, the universe has given me signals to either keep heading on my current course or to change directions. My career has been full of many zig zags and changes, of course. However, by sticking with what I know fulfills and inspires me, and listening to the signals that appear when I give them space and allow them to, I have always been steered in the direction that gives me confidence.

On the flip side, with ever more frequency, I now find myself extolling some of the same advice and encouragement that I received coming up through the ranks. As I look back at these experiences, I know deep down they are not merely by chance. Whether I've been on the receiving or giving end, either way, I believe we beckon people into our lives by our way of being and the energy we exude, consciously or not. These experiences remind us what we are meant to make our contribution to this world and that we can make it a better place for having been here. Fleeting as these instances may be, they have constituted some of the most important moments in my life. I hope they will for you too.

FAKE IT TILL YOU MAKE IT

"Sometimes you have to put on lipgloss and pretend to be psyched." – Mindy Kaling

Much as Wendy Spiller had me write down the things I wanted to manifest in my life and to write them in the present moment, like, "I am so thankful now that I'm working on a hit TV show watched by millions!!", we must continually nurture the feelings associated with what we want to manifest. Again, it's not just wishful or positive thinking. It must be felt and experienced on a cellular level even if the current reality is anything but true. Because our brains cannot distinguish between what is real and what is imagined, whatever we feed into it, is the fuel for what comes out. As Michael Levine says about super successful people, they "believe that it's the mandate of the heavens" and that what they want to create already exists.

Your belief must be rock solid and unshakable. Regardless of what hard evidence there is (or is not) to back up your mantra, you can literally manifest the results you seek into reality by believing them. This is a key component to how Olympic and professional athletes prepare for their routines, matches, and games. Jamie Foxx, after winning his Oscar for "Ray," was asked if he could ever believe something like this happening for him. He replied that he had dreamed of it since he was a little kid.

Everything starts first with a belief even when there is no evidence that something is possible. So what turns a belief into reality? What made me move out to Los Angeles with a few hundred bucks in my pocket to pursue my dream of being in TV and movies and to see my dreams, literally, become real? What allowed Jamie Foxx or, for that matter, anyone else to win an Academy Award?

Considered to be one of the top experts in the field of personal performance and life coaching, Tony Robbins says he has interviewed thousands of people to study how someone manifests a belief or dream into fruition. After all the research he has conducted, Tony posits that the number one characteristic that makes people take the action necessary toward manifesting their goal in the face of something not existing is CERTAINTY.

Robbins says that even if something does not exist, because your brain doesn't know the difference between reality and a belief, by DECIDING to have certainty, you will be propelled into the actions required to fulfill your dream and make it happen. You must decide for yourself that there is no alternative. There is no plan B. You must see it in your mind, first as happening, and then let that visualization elicit the feelings associated with it. This is exactly what Wendy Spiller did with me on her couch. She had me create a visual in which I became so enrolled that I could, literally, feel what the Parisian breeze felt like on my face. I am convinced this is what caused the reality of the film to literally materialize a few weeks later.

In 1996, Dr. Blaslotto from The University of Chicago conducted a study where he split people up into three groups and tested each on how many free throws they could make at a basketball gym. While having the three groups shoot for a while, he recorded their proficiency.

After this, he had the first group practice free throws every day for an hour. The second group he had visualize themselves making the free throws without stepping a foot in a gym or actually handling a ball. He had the third group do nothing. After thirty days, Dr. Blaslotto tested them all again. The first group who had actually gone to the gym and practiced making free throws improved by 24%. The second group, without touching an actual ball, improved by 23%, and the third group did not display any improvement, as expected. Tony Robbins says it's not just practice that produces results—it's "perfect practice" that produces results. Meaning, if we're using the basketball analogy, you have to visualize not just shooting basketballs, you must visualize the balls going through the hoop as well, then enjoying the feeling of success as you watch the ball go through.

Whenever I'm presented with a challenge or opportunity, I think of the quote by Audrey Hepburn, "Nothing is impossible, the word itself says I'm possible," and I start from there. Nothing can change unless you start to believe it can. Roger Bannister is a perfect example of this. Up until 1954 the idea of anyone running a mile in under four minutes was considered humanly impossible. Bannister, as well as least forty other runners around the world, had flirted with breaking the four-minute mile, but for nine years, the record of 4:01:4 held. What is truly remarkable is that after Bannister broke the barrier on that fateful day in Oxford, on May 6th, 1954, only 46 days later, his record was broken. Furthermore, within 2 years, 37 other runners ran sub-four-minute miles. Up until May 6th, 1954 no runner had ever run a mile under four minutes - for nine years, no one person was able to break this barrier. After it was proven to be possible, however, the certainty of knowing that it could, in fact, be done, has enabled hundreds of runners since to do the same.

As Bannister himself exclaimed, "It became a symbol of attempting a challenge in the physical world of something hitherto thought impossible." At the 50th anniversary of the run, Bannister added "I'd like to see it as a metaphor not only for sport, but for life and seeking challenges." It definitely has for me and so many others in fulfilling on dreams including Phil Knight, who credits Bannister as the person who inspired him to create Nike, according to Tom Ratcliffe, who directed a documentary about Bannister.

By believing in my dreams, letting them inspire me with feelings of excitement and gratitude, and making CERTAINTY a part of the equation, I have been able to make a lot of amazing things happen. When combined, these ingredients can create some incredible opportunities and experiences . Even when the exact outcome of what I was aiming for didn't work out, there has ALWAYS been something positive that has helped me to become more of the person I want to be.

CHANGE IS THE ONLY CONSTANT

"A man who views the world the same at fifty as he did at twenty has wasted thirty years of his life."
— Muhammad Ali

"Don't go riding in those dirt hills!" I heard my mom beckon from the kitchen. "I won't!" I yelled back as I ran out the front door to rendezvous with my neighborhood cohorts, Russell and Jimmy. I bounded into the garage past our 1986 Jeep Waggoneer with the simulated wood grain finish on the sides and hopped on my Schwinn BMX bike, complete with red mag wheels and matching iridescent paint job. I LOVED that bike. No destination was too far nor terrain too tough for me and my two-wheeled dueler. I had an insatiable desire to pedal into the farthest reaches of our neighborhood for new adventure, craving yet another moment to be airborne.

I had just gotten off the phone with Russell a few minutes prior, and we were planning to race to Rochester Park to risk life and limb. This was the very place my mom had warned me to avoid. What good were my alloy steel frame and fat, knobby tires if I couldn't use them to reenact Evel Knievel's latest death-defying jump over the Snake River Canyon?

Besides, a mother giving her daredevil eight-year-old son wellintentioned advice and expecting him to heed it is like telling a bird not to fly. Phooey! This kid and this bike were built to take on the best that Rochester Park had to offer and we weren't going to let my mom deprive us of chasing Russell to kick up some dirt on the snaked terrain of a path that disappeared into the forest bordering the park.

With Jimmy on our heels, we shot toward the mouth of the forest into the lion's den. We took each turn with reckless abandon, matching balance and weight ratios with the calculated flight trajectory of the next hill from which we would launch. One after another, we'd approach the soft earth berms, and with a burst of one more powerful pedal stroke, each of us created our own flight plan proportional to how daring we felt with each new bump. With a canopy of hazy summer leaves overhead, our race course was speckled with shade. This made the optics of each jump a bit more harrowing than normal, but no matter—just another challenge to overcome.

This is just one of my favorite memories from when I was a kid, so I'm fully aware and understand the need and the want to cling to what we remember as great. I loved my home in Rochester, Michigan and when my parents told my we were moving to Chicago, I distinctly remember saying, "Have a good time," because in my mind I wasn't going anywhere. I loved my friends, my soccer team, and especially my Schwinn BMX bike and being able to ride to the park to do jumps on the soft dirt hills. I didn't want anything to change.

I realize now, looking back, I was so resistant to change because my perspective on Chicago was very limited and I was basing my judgement on a small sample size. Because my mom grew up in the South Side of Chicago, having immigrated there from Dublin, she still had lots of family in Chicago, including my grandparents. As such, this is the only place in Chicago that I had really been to. As cool as it was to see the planes hang overhead as they came in for their landings at Midway Airport nearby and having fond memories of my Grandpa Sean taking me to Old Comiskey Park to watch the White Sox, every time we would visit this area of Chicago, I never felt quite at home as I did in Rochester.

It's no surprise then that at ten years old, I suggested to my parents that they leave me in Rochester after my dad accepted a job in Chicago's Hyde Park community. What I didn't know at the time of my staged protests was that Hyde Park was not where my grandparents had lived, so I just conflated the small area that I had visited as "Chicago," when in fact I wasn't even aware of the incredible things Hyde Park and the rest of the city had to offer. Home to the University of Chicago and the Museum of Science and Industry, Hyde Park is teaming with culture and things to do. I could literally walk to hundreds of shops, restaurants, parks, and Lake Michigan as well as a captured WWII German U-Boat, which were right in my backyard.

After making all new friends and starting to feel a bit settled in Hyde Park, we then moved to the suburbs of Chicago after only a year to a small farm town called Crete. More change. Another school and new friends. I'm not saying I didn't miss Rochester and everything that I loved about it but each of these two new places had some cool and unique things that I learned to appreciate. Because of these experiences, I had to deal with getting used to change and making the best of it, primarily because it was out of my control since I wasn't the one paying the mortgage. In other words, it wasn't my choice to change. Or so I thought.

Change can be incredibly overwhelming for some and a pleasant way to push the reset button for others. Change is great for creativity and stimulating energy and getting you out of a rut of the mundane such as when you take a vacation, but change can also have debilitating effects if that change is something like the loss of a job or the death of a loved one. This is where change can really be scary because it elicits feelings of anxiety and stress due to the unknown and a perceived lack of control.

Some people love change and some hate it. My dad was the kind of person who loved routine and was not one to seek out or embrace change as much as my mom. My mom, on the other hand, loved variety and travel and seeking out new experiences. Whenever my mom would suggest going to Ireland, my dad's natural tendency to prevent change would kick in with him saying, "Where are we going to stay? That's going to be expensive. How are we going to find the time to do that?" This is where our brains try to hijack us in order to keep us safe. But in actuality, it can keep us stuck and therefore unfulfilled.

After negotiating the airline tickets and the hotels and the places to visit, once we got to Ireland, my dad would inevitably have the time of his life and say, "We should do this more often!" The rest of my family and I would just smirk, knowing that the next time we suggested a trip, the safety mechanisms in his brain would try to prevent this again. People are as different about change as they are about any other behavior, and since all behavior is complex, there is no one silver bullet solution to accept it or deal with it.

As someone who has had to adapt to change, however, as a young kid with substantial moves, adapting to new environments and making new friends, having my home destroyed from 9 /11, being diagnosed with cancer twice, and pursuing careers in modeling, acting, and real estate development where change is a constant, I've had to learn some strategies to deal with and embrace change. These insights have helped me create an empowering context through which to move through these experiences with purpose and fulfillment instead of having them overwhelm me.

Any change can be difficult and from what I've recognized, change has been the most difficult when I have felt like I have no control over why it happened or what to do next. It's easy to plan for change, like when I know a TV show or a movie I'm working on is going to end, but when I was diagnosed with cancer and told I needed surgery in three days to alter my body forever, when the producers of Melrose Place called me on a random Wednesday morning to tell me that my character was too dark for the show, so they were writing me off, or when a friend of mine randomly texted me regarding The Client List, "Sorry that your show isn't getting picked up," news like this was stressful and debilitating mostly because I didn't know what was going to happen next, and my brain went right to the negative.

When something is great, we rarely want for it to change. However, I think it's easy for us to forget that when we become comfortable with the way things are, we can sometimes, almost arrogantly, expect them to stay that way forever. I've recognized that it's easy for us to take for granted that, in fact, everything "always" changes. Knowing and accepting this as a fact of life can help prevent us from being caught flatfooted and unprepared and enable for us to be more accepting of the rigors that often accompany change.

Furthermore, even if we don't like a situation and wish it would change, a lot of the time we don't take any action to modify our situation. This is because the fear of unknown is perceived to be more painful than actually doing anything about it. Why is it when child protective services comes to take a child away, often times, the child still clings to their abusive parent? It's because child protective services is a stranger, the unknown, and their parent is familiar, albeit dangerous. Familiarity can sometimes, mistakenly, be perceived to be a better alternative than the unknown.

The fear of the unknown can by paralyzing. What I have recognized is that whenever I have found myself in having to face change willingly or not, a big reason I feared the unknown is because, mistakenly, I thought I would lose control. As human beings, we relish in knowing and having power in a situation. Knowing a situation and being familiar with it gives us a sense of control. This is what makes us feel safe.

The harsh reality of control is that, as humans, as much as we desire it, will never be able to attain all the control we want. If by some miracle we do, it simply won't last forever. As soon as I truly recognized and embraced this, the easier it was for me to let things go. As kids, our natural inclination was to want to control our situation, and we would kick and scream if we didn't get it. We wanted what we wanted and if our moms wouldn't let us get Lucky Charms at the grocery store when we were three, we would make sure to let shoppers four aisles over know about it. Do you still do this in some subtle or not so subtle way?

The biggest shift for me with regards to dealing with a lack of control and change was to recognize that as adults, consciously or not, we have the ability to decide what we can control, what we can't control, and how we react to both. This, in its totality, is being in a place of empowerment and, ultimately, control. You are in control because you decide to be and, as such, you can do something about it.

I bring this up because the world is moving at hyper speed nowadays, and as such, things are constantly changing. New phones and computers come out with newer and faster capabilities, and people's jobs and livelihoods are being affected because of it. To be able to adapt to ever-changing conditions requires an incredible amount of agility. The reality is that a majority of people no longer work for one company their whole career, nor do they retire after fifty years with a pension and a gold watch.

According to the US Department of Labor's Bureau of Labor Statistics, as of 2017, the average person will change jobs about twelve times during his or her career. This is a major impetus for the need to be agile enough to adapt to change, especially when it comes to your vocation. It literally becomes a question of survival. The alternative is to be left in the past, no matter how good it may once have been.

To be an Agile Artist is more crucial now than ever. I myself have had to adapt and change in response to the entertainment industry, which, in the past few years, has gone through a huge evolution. With the invention of streaming platforms such as Netflix and Amazon Prime, in a matter of a few years, the amount of attendance at movie theaters in the US plummeted to a 25 year low in 2017, according to Box Office Mojo. The result is that fewer films are being made, an unfortunate casualty of which is that sequels to films such as Something Borrowed are not green lit. Their cost doesn't justify the return at the box office anymore.

Granted, there are more channels on television now and way more shows to watch than ever before. But, because of this volume of choice, the viewership for each has been so spread out that the advertising dollars spent per show has decreased to the point where most can no longer afford to pay actors what they used to. This makes it harder and harder for actors, including me, to make a living. Accordingly, I have had to look at alternative ways to make a living, which is why I transitioned to doing real estate in between my acting and producing gigs.

I have to admit, this change has not been the easiest to accept. After making a living as an actor for the last twenty years, I've had to face the harsh realities of needing to start over, so to speak, in a completely different field of work. Much as I love real estate and community development, acting is my passion. It's not something I'm giving up on by any means, but because of the huge changes in the industry, much like other people who have found themselves in similar situations, I have to rely on my creativity and ideas of how to keep moving forward to still be able to do what I love.

Instead of staying in Los Angeles and complaining about the state of the industry (which to me is as silly as the horse and buggy people complaining about the invention of the car) I decided to do something about it. While not an easy decision to leave LA, because in a way, I felt as if I was giving up on my dream and that I hadn't fully accomplished what I had set out to do when I first decided to move there, after taking a deep look inside myself, I realized in my heart that it was the right thing to do.

After twenty years being away from Chicago, I decided to pack up all my belongings, my dog James Taylor, and the rest of my whole life, rent a U-Haul and drive it all back. Full circle, baby! I decided to embrace change, full speed ahead, and to create an empowering context around it. By moving to Chicago, I knew I'd have a better chance of actively being able to grow my real estate business instead of sitting around, waiting in LA for my agent to send me on another audition where I would be allowing twenty other people in a Warner Bros. auditorium to control my fate.

I wasn't sure what was going to happen with my acting career, and was prepared to let it stay on hold for a bit while I was able to work on what I could control. But, as the universe has a way of conspiring with us when we are bold and commit to something that feels right in our hearts, the first week I was back in here in Chicago, I auditioned for and booked an independent film. Since then I've shot a TV pilot, two episodes of Chicago Fire, and I'm currently working on producing my first television show, a reality real estate show that shares an in-depth look inside the world or rehabbing homes hosted by yours truly! I had no idea what was going to happen when I came to Chicago other than that I knew I was creating an empowered context around it. As such, I'm creating more here than I was able to in twenty years going between New York and LA! I'm also writing this book, which would have never have been possible without the help of my amazing publisher who I met here in Chicago as well.

If you feel like you're stuck, you're not! It's the universe telling you it's time to embrace change and to look inside and ask yourself what you want out of life. Just because you don't know what change is going to look like, it doesn't mean you have to stay where you're at. Decide to be brave and ask, "WHO DO I NEED TO BE IN THE FACE OF WHAT I'M DEALING WITH IN ORDER TO CAUSE THE RESULT I'M LOOKING FOR?" Your spirit will answer you from this place!

LUCK

> *"Luck is believing you're lucky."*
> *– Tennessee Williams*

Whenever presented with a challenge or an opportunity, I find that sometimes it's worked out for me and sometimes it hasn't. Was I lucky on 9/11 when the towers came down and they didn't land on top of me? Was I lucky to have survived cancer? Was I lucky to have won the role of Dex in Something Borrowed? Was I unlucky when shows that I have been on got cancelled or when Battlestar Galactica went on to be a hit without me? Sometimes I've won, and sometimes I've lost, and I've always wondered how some people are able to turn most everything they touch into gold while others seem to struggle and be broke no matter what they try to do. Does luck have anything to do with it?

My mom is from Ireland. Does that mean she and the rest of my family are predisposed to possess the "the luck of the Irish?" Is that even a thing? Do the Boston Celtics win more games because their mascot is Lucky the Leprechaun? When I eat Lucky Charms (yes, I still do), why do I actually feel luckier and have a more positive outlook on things? And if luck really does exist, is it possible to become luckier by somehow harnessing the ways of the leprechaun or visiting Ireland more often?

I've never been a big gambler, and because I didn't play poker or blackjack enough to ever be good, I never thought that I was unlucky when I would show up at the casino only to have blown through $100 in ten minutes. In my mind, it had nothing to do with luck. It had to do more with the fact that I simply sucked at playing blackjack or poker. I didn't play enough to know the intricacies of the game to be able to know when to 'call' or 'stay' or know when to fold 'em. Compared to my college roommate and high school best friend, Chris, however, who would run the tables every night in our dorm at Illinois Wesleyan University where I went to school my freshman year, he seemed to have more luck in his pinky finger than most people did in their whole bodies.

More often than not, he would come back into our dorm room at 8 am, when I was waking up to go to class with a handful of cash and smirk on his face. Was he lucky? Knowing Chris as well as I did, luck or not, he just knew how to play the hell out of poker by not only being great at calculating odds, but by being a master at reading people. Similarly, the successful people I have met the world over, read about in numerous journals and magazines, and seen speak at TED Talks, all have the same thing in common: they are successful because they have worked and practiced to become masterful at what they do. They are able to take advantage of the opportunities that come their way, which also requires the courage to take risks.

We've all heard the expression, "luck is simply when hard work meets opportunity." I think most people would agree with this, but after listening to a professor named Tina Seelig who teaches entrepreneurship at Stanford University, I recognized that I truly am lucky, according to her analysis. She has spent the past two decades actually studying the concept of luck with the intention of trying to help her students take advantage of any small applications of leverage that can increase one's ability to be lucky.

Seelig describes luck as being similar to the wind. She says, "Sometimes it's calm, sometimes it comes in gusts, and sometimes it comes in directions that you never even imagined," and that successful people are those who have become very adept at capturing more of the winds of luck by "increasing the size of their sail."

In her studies, Seelig has discovered three concepts that she says have actually been shown to increase one's luck. The first, she says, involves changing your relationship with yourself by "taking small risks to stretch you out of your comfort zone." She continues to say that the problem is, the older we get, we less we do this. "We tend to lock down who we are and avoid taking risks." Much like how Ken Robinson mentioned that "kids are willing to give it a go" and as such, reap the rewards of learning things like how to ride a bike, so too as adults we need to stretch out of our norm by doing something different to see a different result. I'm sure you've heard the saying, "The definition of insanity is doing the same thing over and over again and expecting a different result." By trying something new or attending something that you wouldn't normally attend, a whole new world of possibilities can be opened to you.

I can't think of a better example of this than when I heard on the radio about the model search when I was in college. At first when I heard the ad, it sounded intriguing. Then the voice in my head kicked in, wondering if it was a scam and thinking that people would probably make fun of me if I had told them I was going. If I had I stayed in my comfort zone and let the voice in my head convince me not to go, I don't see how any of my journey to Hollywood and all the amazing things that have happened in my life ever would have come about. All because I showed up at a hotel on a Tuesday night from a radio ad. Was it out of my comfort zone? Yes. Was it worth it? Hell yes!!

Similarly, there have been several of these instances in my life that I can count as impactful. When I signed up for the real estate investment courses I took, a lot of people thought I was crazy for spending the money that it cost to go. Because I believed in the program and believed in myself and my dedication, I decided to do it. Since then I have rehabbed several houses, I own cash-flowing rental properties, have secured my mom's retirement income, and am helping revitalize communities. Out of my comfort zone? Yes. Worth it? Hell yes!!

This book is also a perfect example of how I am completely out of my comfort zone, but decided to take the risk anyway. This would have never have been possible if I had I hadn't had the fortune of meeting my amazing publisher, Melissa Wilson. How did I meet her? My social media manager, Dean DeLisle from Social Jack, introduced her to me. How did I meet Dean DeLisle? Through one of the biggest and most successful real estate agents in Chicago, Frank Montro. How did I meet Frank? I saw him speak at the real estate investment club I belong to. After his talk, when my friends were heading for the door to go have a burger and some beers, I headed in the opposite direction, up to the front of the room to introduce myself. After waiting for him to answer questions and talk to about ten other people who had huddled around him, I made my way up to him and asked him if he would have a coffee with me so we could chat and exchange ideas about real estate.

Get out and stretch! Start taking little risks. Do an intellectual risk like tackling a problem you've been avoiding. Take a social risk and strike up a conversation with the person sitting next to you on an airplane or bus. Take an emotional risk by telling someone how you authentically feel. Much like the lottery, there's no chance of winning unless you buy a ticket.

The second thing Seelig mentions to increase your luck is to change your relationship with other people. She says, "Everyone who helps you on your journey plays a huge role in getting you to your goals," and that if you don't acknowledge them, "not only are you not closing the loop, but you are missing out on an opportunity." By acknowledging them and showing appreciation, you actually are keeping the door open for further communication and possibilities.

Seelig runs three fellowship programs. She mentions that one day, she received a thank you letter from a student that she had turned down for one of the fellowships, not once, but twice. The note read, "I know I've been rejected for this program twice, but I want to thank you for the opportunity. I learned so much from the process of applying." She was so taken aback by this act of appreciation without asking for anything in return that she invited him into her office to meet with him. From that meeting, she got to know him and helped him to create a special independent study project that has since turned into a program called Play For Tomorrow. It teaches kids from disadvantaged backgrounds how to craft the lives they dream to live.

At the end of every day, Seelig says she reviews her calendar and all the people she met with that day and sends thank you notes, which she reports makes her feel grateful and appreciative. To this she writes,

"I promise you, it has increased my luck." I can't tell you how many casting directors I have sent notes and flowers to, not only after I have booked jobs, but for gestures I felt were worth recognition. I actually got the idea when I first started acting after reading an article about Ben Affleck and how he would do the very same thing. I remember reading how the casting director felt so appreciated, it made Ben stand out in her mind, which made her call him back in for subsequent auditions, which of course seems to have worked out for Ben quite nicely. Even though I haven't achieved the level of success Ben enjoys, I'm incredibly grateful for the opportunities and jobs that I have done. Who knows, I might be working with him someday soon.

The final concept Seelig talks about is that you want to change your relationship with ideas. She says most people, when faced with a new idea, will judge it as either bad or good, but she says the way to look at ideas is much more nuanced. She continues to say that, "Ideas are neither good or bad, and in fact, in the seeds of terrible ideas are often something truly remarkable." One of the things she has her students do is to look at bad ideas through the lens of opportunity, and inevitably, she says, within minutes, students are posing some incredible ideas simply because they took the time to look at them a little bit more deeply before writing them off.

Steven Spielberg, another epitome of an Agile Artist, once quipped, "All good ideas start out as bad ideas, that's why it takes so long." Coming from one of the most influential people in cinema history, Spielberg is not only an incredible filmmaker, he's a master at turning bad ideas (and bad situations) into gold.

From his book It's Not About the Shark, Dr. David Nevin tells the story of Spielberg as a budding 26-year-old filmmaker on the set of Jaws in Massachusetts, filming his first major studio movie, that almost ended before it even started. The mechanical shark for the film was built and tested in a freshwater tank back in California by some of the most experienced and talented designers in the business.

Unfortunately, the shark was now suffering the unforeseen corrosive consequences of the Atlantic saltwater.

According to Dr. Nevin, the mechanical shark "was a phenomenally complicated pneumatically powered colossus, attached to 150 feet of hose linking it to compressors floating above, on a barge. It took a small army of people—each working a different lever that controlled a fin, or the eyes, or the mouth—to make it go." However, the saltwater was preventing the mechanicals from working, and even worse, was starting to cause the outer synthetic skin to become bloated and waterlogged. Days and days of footage were unusable, and the rumblings from the studio was that this young filmmaker was in over his head as Spielberg had already blown through the entire film's original multimillion dollar budget on trying to fix the shark.

The whole premise of Dr. Nevin's work is how problems are best solved by focusing not on the problem, but on the solution. Dr. Nevin says, "Research shows that what we do most of the time is crawl deep inside our problems. We define everything on the problems' terms. We limit what we think is possible based on the boundaries the problems set for us. "

To this effect, what Spielberg did next is why he's considered one of the best in the business and why he can boast three Academy Award wins along with 189 others and counting. Spielberg, on the other hand, took the failure of his waterlogged shark as an opportunity to reimagine what he was doing. Instead of thinking of ways to fix the broken shark or ask the studio for more time and money that would likely not have been offered, instead, Dr. Nevins said Spielberg "flipped the situation on its head."

Spielberg has been quoted as saying, "What would Alfred Hitchcock do in a situation like this?" So, imagining a Hitchcock movie instead of a Godzilla movie, Spielberg, came up with the idea that the best solution to the problem was to make a shark movie without a shark.

"He had to invent, on the spot, another way of shooting,"

Richard Dreyfuss, who played Hooper in the film, mentions admiringly, "which was to imply the shark, which made an ordinary film into a great film."

With a final budget of $8 million, the film went on to earn over $470 million and was Universal Pictures' highest-grossing film to date. It has been named one of the greatest films of all time by the American Film Institute, and it's become one of a small handful of films permanently preserved by the Library of Congress as a cultural treasure. What Spielberg did was nothing short of brilliant, and by turning his attention to come up with a new idea instead of trying to change what couldn't be changed, Professor Seelig would say that Spielberg is absolutely lucky. On the matter of luck, Spielberg himself has said, "The shark not working was a godsend."

The moral of the story? By taking risks, expressing gratitude, and embracing ideas through the lens of opportunity, you will be expanding your sail to "capture the winds of luck" similar to the magical opportunities I've been blessed to have realized.

DISCIPLINE AND COMMITMENT

> *"Do. Or do not. There is no try."*
> *– Yoda*

Playing sports has taught me an immense amount about life lessons. One of them is that in order for a team to achieve its goals to score points, stop the other team, and ultimately win the game, an immense amount of preparation, discipline, and commitment is required. As a wide receiver, for me to score touchdowns, I spent hours upon hours practicing so that during a game, I could fly down the field at top speed, stop on a dime, and dart to one side, then have the football land perfectly in my hands at the exact right time, to then twist and turn...all the while keeping my balance and powering through tackles to then leap across the goal line.

To make things happen, you must be willing to show up at practice at 6 a.m. to run wind sprints and lift weights. You must be willing to take good care of yourself, feed yourself the best foods and avoid the ones that are bad for you. You must be willing to get plenty of rest. You must be willing to sacrifice a lot of things all because you want something bad enough. Much like an athlete, anyone who desires to do anything worthwhile and achieve greatness must be willing to adhere to a high level of discipline. Your focus must be consistently dedicated to doing every little microcosmic action necessary to stay headed in the direction that you want to go in and to take advantage of the smallest of opportunities, which can make all the difference.

A couple of years ago I went down to Cuba and visited where Ernest Hemingway lived. While visiting his house, the tour guide mentioned that Hemingway was so dedicated to his craft as a writer that he committed himself to write at least five hundred words a day. The tour guide further shared with us that Hemingway's passion for writing was matched only by his love for fishing. He went on to say Hemingway was so fiercely dedicated to his commitment that if he wanted to go fishing, he made sure to write one thousand words the day before so he could be free to take the next day off to angle for barracuda.

Success takes discipline and structure, especially if you want to turn your passion for art into a career whether as a writer, actor, graphic designer, fashion stylist, or artist. I have met many talented actors in my classes who never saw a minute of screen time or even the inside of a casting director's office. They either didn't believe in themselves or they lacked the discipline and drive to seek out an agent or a manager, or once they did, they couldn't seem to follow through to get new headshots or put together their demo reel.

Julia Cameron's great book The Artist's Way talks about the importance of developing discipline. She says many people have penned novels and screenplays simply by heading her suggestion of writing what she calls "morning pages." By making the time and committing to sitting down, putting pen to paper, and simply writing about whatever ideas come into your mind without editing or judgment, you will begin to rewire your brain. You do it even though you don't know what you're going to write; you don't know what's going to come out. You just do it because the mere act can of doing it has the potential to unleash some sort of creative spark that allows you to get closer to where you want to go. Simply getting in the habit of consistency can go a long way with creating the structure to turn things into a reality.

Much like Hemingway's, it's important to make a commitment, not only to yourself, but to others. Michael Levine shared that super successful people write down their plan, and they share it and announce it to friends, family, and even to the world in order to be held accountable for what they are up to. Then, they measure and track their performance and results to gain feedback on how to improve and make it better.

As Lady Gaga said in her empowered and heartfelt Oscar acceptance speech, "I've worked hard for a long time, and it's not about winning—but what it's about is not giving up." She followed it by saying, "If you have a dream, fight for it. There's a discipline for passion. And it's not about how many times you get rejected, or you fall down, or you're beaten up. It's about how many times you stand up, and are brave, and you keep on going." This is the Agile Artist's mantra.

Creating takes work, but if you love the work, and more importantly, if you are able to endure it's challenges while holding a high set of standards for yourself, then you're more likely to succeed.

World-renowned, multi-millionaire consultant Sam Ovens says, "We are not the highest version of ourselves which we can imagine. We are the lowest version of ourselves which we can accept. Understand that you will do nothing to achieve your dreams but fight like hell to not breach your standards. If you want to achieve your dreams and goals you must turn them into irrefutable standards."

I had the privilege of seeing The Rolling Stones live in concert a few years ago in LA. In addition to their amazing music, my friends and I marveled at the longevity these legends have created. Mick Jagger was jumping around the stage as if he were in his twenties. For them to be playing and touring for over FIFTY YEARS at such a high level is not by chance.

There's a great HBO documentary called Crossfire Hurricane I recently watched, which elaborates on their incredibly wild, creative, and enduring success. "It requires quite a bit of discipline to be a Rolling Stone," Keith Richards said. "Although it seems to be shambolic, it's a very disciplined bunch."

"No matter what was going on the outside, no matter how much we whooped it up," guitarist Ronnie Wood chimed in, "we felt a responsibility, and we still do, to make great music."

Richards went on to say that his relationship with Jagger, like any relationship, has had its ups and downs. Above all though, he says, "I've more and more respect for Mick's resilience. Being the frontman always is a little bit of an isolated position, it's like being the captain of a Royal Naval ship. He's very disciplined, almost to the point of insanity sometimes." It's been this discipline that has enabled the Stones to create over thirty studio albums and twentyfive live studio albums and garner millions of fans the world over.

According to Pollster, a publication that tracks live events, on their most recent tour in 2017, the Stones were making more money per night than any other band in the world, hauling in an incredible

$10 million per show. Not bad what a mix of creativity and discipline can do.

For me, my passion is acting and community development through real estate. Once committing to them and letting myself feel the excitement of each, it's this excitement and commitment that allow me to fulfill all the mundane crap that needs to be done in order for what I want to have and see done. There's the phone calls, the setting of appointments, going to the gym, reading scripts, and preparing for auditions, and looking for hours at potential houses to rehab, all so that I can get my next acting gig and next house to rehab. This stuff is not always fun, but knowing it's in service to what I am committed to and what lights me up, enables me to keep moving forward and accomplishing what simply needs to get done.

I decided very early on that I wasn't going to just dabble in each. I threw myself into both with full force and with a lot of energy. I'm really excited about all the things in my life that I have been manifesting, but there are still the things that have to get done that I'd rather not have to deal with. However, knowing why I'm creating all these things in my life, reminding myself of my commitment everyday by looking at my vision board and letting the excitement of knowing what it feels like to fulfill my dreams motivates me to make the calls, send the emails, and deal with all BS. Without belief, commitment, and discipline, nothing I have set out to accomplish could have happened.

Three Takeaway Action Tips:

1. Find out what your "why?" is. This involves a continuous exploration of what inspires and motivates you to achieve your goals.

2. Know that to be successful requires obsessive commitment and discipline.

3. Create your own luck by taking more risks.

07 SHARE LIKE YOUR LIFE DEPENDED ON IT

"Creativity is contagious, pass it on."
– Albert Einstein

With the proliferation of social media over the past few years, it's never been easier to share and connect with people. I'll admit, when MySpace, Facebook, Friendster, Instagram, Snapchat, etc. first came out, I wasn't really that active on them, mainly because I prefer to connect with people in person. I'm not big on the phone either. I'd much rather meet up where I can see someone's face, and read their body language and energy.

As my acting career continued to grow, however, I began to realize the power of social media and being able to connect and share with so many people. As I've become more active with social media, specifically Instagram, it's made me become more aware of the ability to truly make a difference in people's lives, and it has been amazing to see and hear back from people.

I've already mentioned that I love to make a positive difference in people's lives, and I love being inspired by others, which makes life so much more fulfilling. My victories wouldn't be as enjoyable if I wasn't able to share them with others. And when I've fallen down, it's been crucial to have the support from others to pick myself back up. For these reasons, I'm motivated to keep sharing and engaging with others to create a community of fellow, like-minded Agile Artists who support and inspire each other to live our best lives.

Social media has highlighted for me that to combine sharing with caring creates engagement. I'm excited to share all these insights I've learned over the years in hopes that you may use them to make your life more fulfilling too. John Travolta has, likewise, said about sharing, "As you get older, you have to force yourself to have new dreams. For instance, I've been flying for thirty-seven years, but now teaching others to fly is interesting for me. Sometimes you have to find new angles on life to keep you interested, like sharing successes and inspiring and helping others."

Throughout this book I have mentioned that the more authentic I have been when engaging with others, I've come to notice, the more impact I have been able to make. When early adopters of social media burst on the scene, such as Vin Diesel, it surprised me how many people responded to his posts about his personal life. It kind of scared me a bit to think that in order to be successful I had to show people what kind of coffee I was buying at Starbucks or where I lived.

Sharing who I am, what I've been up to, what my desires and fears are isn't something that I grew up feeling comfortable doing. Because I often had to take extra time to put my feelings into words, cohesively, from the time I was a little kid, I felt it easier simply to keep to myself. The idea of talking about what mattered to me, the things I liked, my fears, and my desires used to feel painfully unnatural. So I found it was easier and less risky to just bottle everything up and act like I didn't care. I now know that not only did this prevent me from being able to connect with others on a deeper, more fulfilling level, but it can also be unhealthy. We are social beings and we desire to feel connected with and close to others to fulfill our natural human needs, as Maslow has explained.

I also want to emphasize, again, that the more honest and open and willing to share with people I am, the more it tends to create a safe space for others to do the same. I think one of the main reasons I became an actor was because it provided for me a way to connect with others and express my feelings under the guise of being someone else. Acting provided for me a training ground and a template, if you will, for how to share my deepest, darkest, and most sensitive feelings by simply "plugging" into the character I was playing and injecting my personal feelings and desires into the role.

After years of playing so many different roles, even ones as ridiculous as being a transplanted fetus, my characters have had to convey and express all kinds of frustration, anger, fear, guilt, happiness, elation, and excitement. Becoming these other characters allowed me to regularly practice expressing all of these emotions. Doing so enabled me to open up to others which then translated into doing so, more naturally, in the real world. By opening up and sharing who my character was on stage, I was able to connect with the other actors in the scene as well as an audience, allowing us all to have a shared discovery. Acting class has served as a practice ground, if you will, for me to learn how to open up and connect.

Even if you're not an actor or don't ever plan to being one, what you can do to better connect with others is to start to take risks by being more authentic and honest about who you are in your daily life. Authenticity breeds authenticity, and the more you try to cover up your perceived faults and demons, the less likely you are to have the kind of fully realized and fulfilling life that could be possible.

I like being someone who can potentially inspire people to pursue what they truly want to. I can't tell you how many people I have met who say that I'm lucky or fortunate to be doing what I'm doing. I'm not going to say that the universe hasn't conspired with me or that everything I have accomplished was done with a lack of fortuitousness, but most of the time it has come down to me recognizing what I truly desire and am inspired by and sharing it with others, which anyone can do.

Whether you're unhappy in your current situation at work or in any kind of relationship, I've recognized that the more authentically you share, the more it creates the possibility for connection, change, and growth. By keeping silent and living a life of "quiet desperation" as Henry David Thoreau described, you prevent yourself from the chance of living a more fully realized life with more love and joy.

What I have loved seeing on my social media platforms is that the more I share, the more people seem to respond with heaps of gratitude for encouraging and inspiring them to do just the same. So as we begin to embrace this idea of the Agile Artist, may we lay down our swords and our shields, and may we encourage each other to pick up our pens and our paintbrushes to fulfill what's in our hearts from a place of love and passion.

Life is too short not to. As scary as my near-death experiences were, I wouldn't trade them for anything right now, for they have shown me the true path to fulfillment and gratitude. I don't think I would have the same appreciation for the fragility of life, which has motivated me to go out and do and accomplish and connect and build and inspire. I'm here to encourage you to do the same, and I invite you to dig deep, uncover those buried dreams or desires, dust them off, and begin to make them happen. Together I know we can do some amazing things.

Go ahead, start that book or screenplay you've always wanted to write, go learn how to surf, book that ticket to Europe and explore, get out of your comfort zone, and discover the world anew. There are so many incredible and amazing things in life to experience and create.

Nothing is worse than hiding that artist within you. I never wanted to be one day sitting in a retirement home and be plagued by regretful thoughts of "what if." Everyone has an artist inside of them, clamoring to create and share - to stretch, express, and grow. To live your dream life, I invite you to embrace the principles of the Agile Artist, and begin your life again. Let your inner artist have the freedom to do just that. Empower yourself!

We all have much more to offer than we recognize. We all are dealing with something and have overcome adversity in some form or another that, when shared, can help others. By creating this community, coming together, and sharing authentically, together, we can make a big difference. Creating a two-way street for mutual support through this venue will be incredibly empowering to us all.

Another great surprise I've realized through the writing of Agile Artist, is that since I've opened up and started sharing more about my writing process, a number of my Instagram followers have shared that they, too, are starting to do things that they haven't done before. People from all over the world are saying that they are creating again, which I'm both incredibly proud of and happy to hear.

Share like your life depends on it. Because it really does. For you to be able to succeed in life and really, truly create the life that you want to have, you've got to surround yourself with people who support you and are going to help contribute to whatever you're up to. By doing so, you will be provided with the opportunity to contribute to others, which is both incredibly gratifying and continues to perpetuate this growth. I'm excited to see all the amazing things that will be created through this journey, and I'm so very grateful for all of your support in making my dreams come true. If it wasn't for you buying movie tickets and watching TV, I wouldn't be able to do what I love to do. Each and every one of you has already contributed and made a positive impact, and I invite you to keep this thing going! Let's go—we have a lot of creating to do!

AGILE ARTIST AT WORK

"The only safe thing to do is to take a chance."
— Mike Nichols

One of the amazing parts of my job is having the opportunity to meet and work with some incredibly talented and special people. Whether it's been a casual introduction at a party or actually being on set working with and getting to know some of the legends in this business, there's always been something to inspire me or reaffirm my commitment to pursue my ambition of working at a very high level. One of those exchanges was with none other than the incredible Gary Oldman in a film called *The Space Between Us*. One of the film's stars is Asa Butterfield, who plays a kid who was born on the planet Mars and comes back to Earth as a teenager in search of his father. Also featured is the beautiful and talented Britt Robinson, Carla Gugino, and Janet Montgomery.

Harry Potter fans will know Gary best as Harry's godfather, Sirius Black, and he recently won an Academy Award for playing Winston Churchill in *The Darkest Hour,* but my favorite role that Gary brought to life was a rastafarian drug dealer named Drexl Spivey in Quentin Tarantino's cult classic *True Romance*. Not only is *True Romance* one of my favorite films, but Gary happens to be one of my favorite actors. In the brief time that I got to meet and work with him, he shared not only what his interests and passions were with me, but something incredibly special about who he is an artist.

We were shooting *The Space Between Us* in an insanely beautiful house in Malibu, right on the beach. The main house was right off the Pacific Coast Highway, and the guest house, where we shot, was down a steep driveway toward the beach. Asa and Britt had quite a bit of coverage' to shoot before Gary, Carla, and I were needed for our scenes, so we had quite a bit of time to hang out and wait. Being the curious, risk-taking person I am, I took advantage of our downtime to get to know Gary and his manager, Doug Urbanski, who has represented Gary for the entirety of his career.

Upon my arrival at the palatial Malibu spread where we were shooting, I was greeted by the second assistant director. He led me down to the beach guest house and into a room that had been set up as the makeshift "holding pen" for us actors to hang out in and wait. There were three folding chairs, so I went over to one, set my bag down next to it, and proceeded to head out to the beach where the film crew was busy setting up. After talking with Asa, Britt, and the director, Peter Chelsom, for a bit, I decided to go back inside to the holding pen room to look over my script and the scenes I would be doing that day.

When I walked into the room, I expected it to be empty as when I left. Instead, catching me off guard, there were three people sitting in folding chairs, one of whom looked like Gary Oldman. Holy shit, yep, it was him. What struck me was how polite and attentive he was when I walked in. He immediately stood up and introduced himself in a gentle and gracious manner. There he was, looking exactly the part of a true bohemian artist with his beard, trademark chunky glasses, and linen scarf and jacket. I replied in kind, trying to hold back a good deal of my excitement.

What he did next was something I couldn't possibly have expected. Here I was, standing in front of one of my favorite actors, who just so happens to also be one of the highest-grossing actors of all time. Gary's been in the *Batman* franchise, *Armageddon*, *Lost in Space*, and the *Harry Potter* films, all of them Hollywood blockbusters. And what did he do? After introducing me to his girlfriend and his manager, who were occupying the two other chairs, he said, "I'm sorry, am I sitting in your seat?" and proceeded to offer me his chair.

Are you kidding me? I have to admit, I was a bit surprised by such a generous and considerate gesture to offer his chair, which was the only remaining unoccupied chair in the room, just so that I would have a place to sit. This was the first time we had met, and I hadn't even had a chance yet to tell him I was acting in the film with him. As far as he knew, I could have been a production assistant or any of the other support staff who commonly come into the holding rooms to let the actors know the shooting status and where they are needed next.

I politely declined and told him I was happy to sit on the floor, and so I did. I'm not saying I was expecting Gary to be a jerk, I've been around quite a few successful people, in many different industries throughout my travels and experiences; it's rare that I have been greeted with such humbleness and consideration from someone so accomplished.

After exchanging some pleasantries and letting them know who I was playing in the film, we settled in and grabbed my script to work on my scene. What I couldn't help notice, though, when I was sitting on the floor, was that from this lower vantage point, almost hidden under the bottom of his baggy trousers, were a pair of pastel pink socks peeking out. This made me smile on the inside and I couldn't help thinking what a nice creative complement to his artistic self-expression they were.

Gary, his girlfriend, and Doug began talking about a variety of different topics, such as art, theatre, and politics. I sat and listened until Doug asked me some questions about where I was from and where I lived. Now that I felt invited into the conversation a bit more, we all began chiming in on some recent films and theatre we had seen. It was amazing just listening to Gary talk so artistically and deeply about plot, performances, and themes and how moved he was by each with regard to the project he was talking about. What drew me in about Gary and his descriptions was how passionate he was, how authentically he shared what the projects had meant to him on a personal level, and how they had made him feel.

I remember feeling almost pulled into the vivid world of imagery and impression he was painting for us in the room. It was by far one of the more memorable moments of my career. After a while, I couldn't help myself. At a certain point at a break in the conversation, I just had to know.

"Gary, I'm sure you get this a lot, but as a fellow actor who appreciates character development," I began, "I can't help but be curious about Drexl in *True Romance*. Was that how Tarantino wrote him on the page? Was it his idea for you to look like that or did you come up with it? Because it was all so specific and random. Did

Tarantino tell you to get a fake eye and dreadlocks or was a lot of that your creation?"

I almost winced a bit afterward, thinking he might not want to answer but at this point, after our lead up, I think he could tell I was genuinely interested from an artist's point of view. Regardless, by now, I had a good feeling he'd be at least generous enough to appease a fan geek's curiosity. His answer was better than I could have ever imagined and one that solidifies for me why Gary Oldman is the epitome of an Agile Artist.

For those of you who don't know Drexl Spivy, the Jamaican pimp that Gary played in *True Romance*, you're in for such a surprise with this juicy display of cinematic and artistic genius who was only on screen for a mere seven minutes. For someone like Gary Oldman who is all of about 5'9", rather slight in frame, and comes across as an English workingman's gentlemen to completely transform into something so opposite was remarkable. Drexl is vicious, reptilian, and vile with a penchant for violence and Chinese food. He sports gold teeth, dreadlocks, and a milky 'dead' eye (which to me was truly marvelous), which is why I had to know how Drexl came about.

A slight grin began to form on his face, as if I had unlocked an amusing memory. He then regaled that on the page, Tarantino had written Drexl as "a white guy who wanted to be black, but that was about it." Gary went on to say that at the time he got the offer for the role from Tony Scott, the director, he was shooting another film (*Romeo is Bleeding*) in New York.

While in his trailer in between scenes for the film he was shooting, Gary would work on how to make Drexl stand out since he wasn't in the film that much and Gary wanted to make him memorable. He went on to describe how he thought of the idea to have Drexl have dreadlocks and that he called a wigmaker he had worked with on the film *Dracula* who made him the wig, then he decided to create the dead eye to make Drexl look more frightening (I found out later was the eye he used in *Dracula*) and even went to a dentist while he was in New York to have the set of gold teeth made.

When I asked Gary if he had changed any of the dialogue that Tarantino had written, Gary went on and explained with no less acuity than what I would describe as being in tune with the acting gods; manifesting, creating, and being open to receive from the universe. This is what I've come to recognize true master artists do in their work and how they live their lives.

For context, what makes Gary's response so unique is that in between scenes and setups, most actors will go back to their trailers, mini apartments if you will, to rest up, change, and create a space where they can relax and work on their scenes. As such, they will keep the door to their trailer closed for privacy. In one of my earlier acting classes, however, one of my acting teachers gave me a piece of advice once by saying, "When you start working, and you will start working, keep your trailer door open as much as possible to encourage a feeling of welcoming people in and inviting them to collaborate, bond, and build trust."

He said, "Keeping an open door on the set sends a subconscious signal to the rest of the cast and crew, and to the project itself that you are not 'above' anyone else, and that you are open to give and to receive." I would argue that this could be applied to any door in any office or home. Of course, privacy is important, especially when changing into a nude-colored speedo on the set of *The Client List* right before arresting a Russian prostitute, or when you're needing to avoid distractions to complete something. But, for the most part, I try to heed my teacher's advice by pushing back against my natural introverted tendencies and keeping my doors open, not just in my trailer, but with my creative doors as well.

Similarly, when Gary answered my question about the wording and 'voice' of Drexl, he said his trailer was parked on a street in Brooklyn with the door open to it so that he could hear people on the sidewalk as they walked by. He continued, "As I was working on the scenes, I heard a voice outside of my trailer that sounded just like what Drexl should sound like." In true Austin-Kleon style, Gary decided to "steal," or in this case, actually asked to borrow, this kid's "voice." He said he invited the young man into his trailer and explained to him that he was working on a character for a new movie who was a pimp and a drug dealer. Gary then asked if the kid wouldn't mind taking a look at it to give him his thoughts on it, particularly asking, "Does this seem authentic?" Gary said the kid read it over, then started correcting some things and making suggestions for how to say some others. What came of it was nothing short of a genius creative collaboration.

Gary encapsulates the essence of being an Agile Artist. By creatively searching for an answer, keeping doors open, taking a risk to ask others for help and "stealing" ideas, he effectively expanded his sails and captured more of the "winds of luck." His efforts to do so resulted not only in one of the most memorable characters in cinema, but also one of the most creative.

GRATITUDE IS THE ATTITUDE

> *"When I started counting my blessings, my whole life turned around."*
> *– Willie Nelson*

I've learned quite a bit, having been afforded the privilege of meeting hundreds of people throughout my extensive travels, and rehearsing for thousands of hours on the stage. I've gained tremendous insight and exposure to different ways of thinking by reading even thousands more pages of scripts and plays, and filming movies and TV shows around the world, including Thailand, Vancouver, South Africa, and Brazil. I've also been blessed with many incredible experiences. Being an honorary guest of Prince Albert of Monaco at his Palace, having dinner with Elton John, Cate Blanchett, and a Spice Girl, and doing Gianni Versace's last fashion show are among them. Working with my boyhood idol, Sylvester Stallone, and representing some of the top fashion brands in the industry are all dreams come true for which I have profound gratitude. While all this has been both incredibly rewarding and fulfilling, none of it would mean anything if I didn't feel like I was giving back or paying something forward. I have had so many people in my life who have supported and believed in me, and it all started with my family.

My mom came to America from Ireland when she was ten years old. She was one of five kids and the second oldest, so she took a lot of the responsibility at an early age of helping raise her siblings. My mom has worked as an office manager at the Board of Trade in Chicago, and has owned her own business, Ice Cream Village, where I worked in high school. After my brother and sister and I finished college, she, herself went back to college, got her degree in psychology, and then went on to get her masters to become a family therapist. When I was younger, she would regularly come into my room, sit on my bed, and make the effort to connect with me. In high school like most boys, I was pretty quiet and private and didn't say much most of the time. When she would ask me how my day was, I'd respond with the typical, teenage, boyish, monosyllabic response of, "fine" or "good."

Regardless, she'd sit there, and if I wasn't much for talking, which was most of the time, my mom would tell me about her day and share with me what mattered to her and whom she had met. As much as I didn't feel like opening up to her, it made me feel good knowing that she cared and that she was at least making the time and giving me the opportunity to connect if I wanted to. My mom has always been an incredible inspiration with her attitude toward possibilities. I remember when I got the acceptance letter to Illinois Wesleyan University, the school I really wanted to be able to attend. My father was concerned with how we were going to afford it because it was private school. In typical Mom fashion, she replied, "We'll find a way."

My mom is one of the most daring, caring and unpredictable people I know and also one of the most altruistic. As a kid, I observed her regularly delivering meals to the homeless and she would bring us to soup kitchens where we would help serve. Coming from a relatively meager upbringing, my mom has always expressed an appreciation for everything she has worked for and for what she was given. Her curiosity for life and new things rubbed off on me and made me realize that people are truly similar through and through. My mom has also taught me that no matter who you are or where you come from, everyone deserves to be treated with dignity and respect. That is true no matter what color someone's skin is, no matter where people come from, or how much money they do or don't have.

My mom is now my real estate partner. I'm so grateful that she has always believed in me as much as she has, and so am really excited to be growing our real estate business together based on the principles and 'can-do' attitude I learned by watching her while I grew up. Recently, she gave me a framed picture of James Dean that now hangs on my wall. The picture has a quote on it that reads, "Dream as if you'll live forever, live as if you'll die today." It's hard to believe that James Dean was only twenty-four years old when he died, but if you pose the one-hundred-year legacy paradigm to his life, in his short time on earth, James Dean made the most of it. He has left his mark, continually inspiring people like me to go after and pursue the things in life that matter most to them. My mom knew I would find this special.

I think kids learn way more from watching than by being taught. Watching the way my parents did things, how they treated others and one another for their forty-five years of marriage until the day of my father passed, taught me a lot about patience, forgiveness, and love. They aren't perfect people by any means and have made their fair share of mistakes. But the way in which they handled the setbacks and how they were always there for each other no matter what imbued my understanding of what it takes to be there selflessly for someone else.

My father was an obstetrician and gynecologist who delivered over 9,000 babies over the course of his career. All of the people he ever worked with and the patients he treated have never had anything but amazing things to say about him. This makes me incredibly proud. My dad was also very creative and was an artist himself. One of my prized possessions, which also hangs on my wall, is a drawing he did from one of my high school football games, of me catching a pass with a defender close by. He would help us with our homework and taught us how to play sports and was our biggest champion when we were out on the field. The image of him with his VHS video camera on his shoulder, filming my brother and I scoring touchdowns, will forever be etched in my memory. He was one of the kindest and most caring people I have ever met. It broke my family's heart, especially my mom's, when he passed away. My father's legacy of being a caring husband and father lives on. It has had a tremendous influence on how I live my life.

One of the most memorable things my dad did for me was during a particularly difficult time in college. Like many other kids experience in their early twenties, I was feeling the pressure of deciding what my career path was going to be for the rest of my life. But truthfully, I didn't even really know who I was yet.

My dad sent me a note giving me some encouragement. Part of it read, "I hope things are going better for you this week. I wish I could make it better for you but as you know, this is just something you have to wade through and sort things out. Fear of the unknown and uncertainty of the future can be an overwhelming thing, but I know you can get through it as hard as it may feel." At the end of the note, he wrote a quote by Gil Atkinson, "No one can really predict to what heights you might soar. Even you will not know until you spread your wings." Sometimes it's the smallest gestures like this that can make a huge difference in people's lives and encourage them to spread their wings too. My dad's simple but powerful reminders of my possibility have always kept me going. They continue to inspire me to spread my wings as wide as they can be.

My sister, Kerry, worked as a successful sales rep for several media companies, representing magazines such as *Elle* and *Details,* and is the mother of four beautiful girls. Growing up, she used to take me shopping, making sure I sported the latest fashions from Generra and Ralph Lauren and making sure that we listened to the latest offerings from *Wham* and *Prince.* I'll never forget her trying to feather my hair with her curling iron in the morning before school in sixth grade, giving up after a few days because my hair would never stay. Kerry has always been one of my biggest influences as it relates to going out into the world and living life to the fullest. An early thespian, Kerry is the one responsible for introducing me to the world of the theatre and inspiring my first performance as a cuckoo bird. I will forever be grateful to her and her amazing husband, Tom, and their family for their incredible support and friendship.

My brother, Sean, is a captain for Southwest Airlines. One of the things that I admire about him is his appreciation for and boldness with life. He's married to a beautiful wife, Tammy, they have three kids together, and anyone who knows him will tell you he is the life of any party. Sean has more enthusiasm and positivity than anyone I know, and it all stems from him loving the life that he has created. He is the perfect example of someone who found what he loved to do, pursued it, found the woman that he loved, pursued her, and has slowly but surely built an incredible career and a beautiful family. Even though he is four years younger than me, Sean continually inspires me by reminding me that when you love what you do and who you're with, life is truly fun and one big karaoke song.

Finally, I'd like to thank my Godparents, my Uncle Gary and Aunt Eileen, who have always supported and believed in me. I'm forever grateful to my nieces and nephews who allow me to be their

"Funcle."

There are so many other people in my life who I am thankful for. One of the most important things I've learned in life is that the smallest acknowledgement of gratitude can go a long way towards making a positive difference in someone else's. Acknowledging someone for something they did or, even just for who they are can have a profound effect on making that person feel valuable, but even more so, that their existence has meaning to you. This, in turn, will likely motivate them to support you and what you're up to in life. This is just one touchpoint on the power of community and how, collectively, we make more of a difference than were we to try to accomplish things on our own. It's a feedback loop that can perpetually create and then multiply it's positive effects.

When gratitude is lacking however, whether in a personal or professional scenario, much like a plant starved of water, any chance of connection or growth, dies. We see it time and time again. One main reason for any relationship going south is the lack of appreciation from one side or another. Looking at life through a lens of gratitude is the juice and energy that keeps relationships alive and thriving! Personally, I have learned, it's one of the single most important things I can do to elevate my own mood, no matter what is happening around me. Giving thanks is simple, but, unfortunately, it's also one of the most overlooked practices out there. Why is that?

A common theme I have discovered throughout my life is that gratitude is a key element to happiness. When I first went to see Wendy Spiller, as I earlier mentioned, writing out all the things I was grateful for was the exercise that she had me do on her couch. Similarly, when I was going through my cancer experience, a lot of what I read about self-healing and the power of positive thinking had to do with harnessing the beneficial effects of gratitude.

Recently, I was watching a TED talk about gratitude given by a Benedictine Monk named David Steindl-Rast who speaks about the relationship between happiness and gratitude. He began by positing that most people in the world share, in common, the pursuit of some variation of happiness. He went on to say that "It's not happiness that makes you grateful." But rather, the other way around, he argues that "It's gratefulness that makes you happy." Thus, he says people base the way they live on an erroneous belief when they say, "if only I had a million dollars then I'd be happy and that would make me grateful." The problem with this orientation, at base, is that people unceasingly want more and more in order to find happiness. Compare this, he says, with people who have next to nothing, but they are able to find their inner peace through gratitude for what they have, regardless of how simple or meager.

He argues, "There are plenty of people who have everything it would take to be happy, and they are unhappy because they want something else or want more of the same." By contrast, he continues "We all know people who have lots of misfortune and they are deeply happy, because they are grateful."

Steindl-Rast's explanation that gratitude occurs when something is both valuable and freely given, really resonated with me, having lived through my cancer experience. He goes on to say that we can manifest gratitude, and thus happiness, whenever we want and in any given moment by simply looking at every moment as a gift that has been freely given. When we are given something we deem valuable, with no strings attached, it is the seed from which gratitude springs. Thus, even though we may be faced with a difficult challenge in our lives, whether it be the loss of a job, disease or being confronted with the loss of a loved one, we can be grateful in any given moment for the opportunity to decide how we choose to respond.

Looking back, I'm grateful for the adversity I had to face in my life. It offered me the opportunity to become the man that I have always wanted to be. Much like pressure turns coal into a diamond, were it not for the adversity, I wouldn't have had to rise to the challenge and become who I am today.

Similarly, by stopping to reflect on any given moment, most especially the good things in life that we often take for granted, such as a relationship or our current school or work situation, SteindlRast says we have the opportunity to truly change our perspective on life. He continues to suggest that when we are grateful, we act from a place of abundance. This leads to sharing because we are acting from a place of "enough."

Joel Wong and Joshua Brown published an article based on a study of 300 people seeking mental health counseling in *Greater Good Magazine*. In it, they share their discovery that, compared to a control group, participants who were asked to write gratitude letters to another person, in addition to their therapy, "reported significantly better mental health four weeks later and even more so 12 weeks after the exercise ended."

Another study by UC Davis psychologist Robert Emmons, author of *Thanks!: How the New Science of Gratitude Can Make You Happier*, shows that simply keeping a gratitude journal—regularly writing brief reflections on moments for which we're thankful—can significantly increase well-being and life satisfaction.

"The more grateful I am, the more beauty I see." – Mary Davis

As Jack Canfield says, "Gratitude is the single most important ingredient to living a successful and fulfilled life.

Deepak Chopra adds, "Gratitude opens the door to the power, the wisdom, the creativity of the universe."

With all this profound insight into the benefits of gratitude available to us, why then do we not practice acknowledging what we are grateful for and reap it's proven benefits?

One main reasons is that we are not used to doing so and as such, it can make us feel both uncomfortable and vulnerable. After reading about Brian Doyle's near-death experience and watching him give a talk about how it made him appreciate his life on a whole new level, it was evident to me that saying "thank you" can be harder than we think while paradoxically more rewarding than we think as well.

What Brian decided to do was each day, for 365 days, he was either going to call or meet with someone he knew to say "thank you" for the meaning they had in his life. He said it was a very different way to look at life at first, but that after a while, he would wake up every morning, motivated to think about who he was going to call or meet with, that day, to thank and for what. Brian said this made him focus on searching for the good which he says, "is everywhere."

Brian also says that one of the most prominent things he discovered during this exercise is that "people don't know we appreciate them unless we show it. Unless we verbalize it. We hope that they know, we think that they know and we assume that they know. But they honestly don't until we tell them."

Brian felt that one of the most significant offerings of gratitude was to his Dad. Brian had previously revealed to his dad that he is gay but he went on to explain how voicing his appreciation his my dad was more "nerve wracking and more stressful" than sharing with his own father about his sexuality. He said this was because it was so foreign to him and something he was not used to doing. Ever since, Brian said, he feels like something "unlocked" with his father and that he feels more open and happier as a result. By taking a risk and sharing something that he was at first nervous to do, Brian has proven that by being vulnerable and courageous, it's possible to have a better and stronger connection with someone.

Steindl-Rast contributes that another reason we don't offer as much gratitude to others is simply because we are too busy to take the time to reflect to do so. A simple anecdote he shares is to "stop, look, and go" when it comes to offering thanks. By taking even a few minutes out of your life each day to think about who you can offer gratitude to and then doing so, he says your life can change profoundly.

My own experience with cancer and the World Trade Center, and all the ups and downs in between, have made my appreciation for the people I care about in life immensely more profound. A big part of this is because I have shared my gratitude for what these people mean to me more than ever before. Perhaps this, too, will help "unlock" something and inspire you to share with people in your life what they mean to you more authentically. Most likely this will perpetuate and magnify the miracle effects of gratitude, not only for yourself but for others as well.

LET'S DO THIS!

> *"Nothing would mean anything if I didn't live a life of use to others."*
> *— Angelina Jolie*

Completing the exercises that my real estate instructor had us perform during that weekend seminar helped me identify the real reason why I get out of bed every morning. Dealing with the one hundred mundane but necessary things we all have to deal with in order to be able to realize our dream life is essential to achieve our goals. By chipping away every day, little by little, my dream of being able to "have the freedom in my life to live the lifestyle I want to have to be able to provide for the people I love" is what it's all about.

I love what I do as an actor and also as a real estate developer. I love the excitement of being on set and co-creating with amazing actors, the travel, the events, and the Oscar parties. Equally, I love building my real estate development company, Stage 2 Properties, by transforming houses into beautiful homes. As much as I love these things, it's my "Why?" that makes all the difference.

I've also always loved being part of a team. Whether it was playing baseball or soccer when I was little, or football in high school and college, I've long cherished being a part of a diverse group of people who share common goals. As I've gotten older, I've found I still love to compete, which is why I participate in marathons and triathlons, but it's not the same as looking over at my teammate after a hard-fought battle, knowing that win or lose, he or she had my back.

This is yet one more of the reasons why I love to work in entertainment and to rehab houses. It's all about the team. Each and every person has a specific area of expertise and is there to work collectively to make something happen, and we're all dependent on each other for the project to come together. That being said, it amazes me how people can sometimes take others for granted, particularly in the workplace, where each and every job and responsibility is crucial to getting anything done.

On the set of any project, no one person is more important than the other for things to work. Just because someone might be incredibly famous and command a high salary, they're no less crucial than the grip. It's the grip that scales up and down ladders, hangs off the sides of buildings and runs all over the place to position the lights where they need to be so the star is lit perfectly and can be seen. Equally critical to the success of a production is the boom mic operator. They're the ones who climb all over the other crew members, hiding under desks, behind curtains, and on top of walls to record what the actors are saying, all the while making sure that the microphone isn't seen in the shot. Then there's the numerous production assistants and transportation crew members who show up hours before anyone, leave hours after everyone, and quite often operate on two to three hours of sleep.

No production would be possible without each person performing their specific task. Whenever I'm working, I try to get to know each and every one of them by name so I can thank them for what they do. I'm living my dream as an artist to be able to create with them on that film set. I feel it's a part of my job to recognize their contribution.

The same thing goes for working on the houses that I rehab. Over the past few years, I've compiled a great team of incredible men and women. Together we have done quite a bit of work that I'm extremely proud of. Whether it's other brokers, attorneys, lenders, home inspectors, appraisers, and of course, contractors and subcontractors, I love having a team to rely on and support so we can conduct our projects and get to the finish line. Not only do we rehab houses and provide beautiful new homes for families, but in the process, we also provide employment opportunities for local residents while helping clean up neighborhoods specifically in the South Side of Chicago.

When I first started rehabbing houses, I began looking at areas that made sense to work in. I talked to a lot of people, including real estate brokers, attorneys, other real estate investors, friends, and colleagues in both Los Angeles and Chicago. Everything in LA that I considered was incredibly expensive, and most of the time, overpriced. Since I'm from Chicago and was traveling back to visit family and friends quite a bit, I started to take a more serious look at the possibilities there each time I came back. My curiosity piqued, I went to real estate investment meetings and seminars, and started meeting the serious investors here. I consistently found that quite a few people were both investing and working in Chicago's South Side.

Growing up in a sleepy farm town called Crete, about a twentyfive minute drive away, I was no stranger to what was going on with regard to the violence and crime that has plagued the South Side for decades. It's not uncommon to see headlines such as:

"At least 72 shot, 13 killed in Chicago over violent summer weekend, police department says"'

USA Today - August 6, 2018

"In less than 7 hours, 41 shot, 5 fatally as violence rips Chicago"

Chicago Tribune - August 6, 2018

When I was younger, I remember that my parents would watch the news at night. A lot of the time, the anchor's cold open was the description of another shooting or homicide in the area. When I heard real estate investors were actually working and rehabbing houses in these same neighborhoods, I was nervous and skeptical at best. However, I decided to take a closer look and check out some houses through a local real estate agent who had been working in some of these areas to investigate and experience the area myself.

The agent assured me that despite the violence that is reported in the news, there are many areas in the South Side where commercial development and investment had been made by established companies and retailers to help support the need for more quality housing. These companies, such as Walmart, Whole Foods, and Home Depot had started to revitalize some neighborhoods and were creating jobs. Affordable housing for their growing workforce was a logical next step.

After repeated visits to the South Side and looking at several homes in several neighborhoods, I was struck by how normal most areas seemed. Despite some pockets of run-down blocks and certain streets sporadically set in and around different neighborhoods, more often than not, I discovered beautiful neighborhoods and charming houses. Most of the homes in the South Side had been built at the turn of the last century, during Chicago's Industrial Golden Age when immigrants from all over the world came to Chicago because of the vast employment opportunities. As a result, the homes are close to, if not more than, a hundred years old. Mostly made of brick, with the Chicago bungalow style being the most popular, the bones of the houses are solid and aesthetically beautiful. A lot of them could use a bit of a facelift here and there, but are, for the most part, really nice. What I found, also, while exploring, is that the violence and crime are relatively contained in certain pockets. A majority of the areas are normal neighborhoods with folks who are simply trying to go about their day like everyone else.

According to fbi.gov, special agent Michael Anderson in charge of the Chicago division says, "Chicago's Communities are being hijacked by a relatively small percentage of people. The overwhelming majority of residents are hardworking citizens going to work, going to school, trying to go about their daily lives. These communities are under siege, and they are desperately looking for help."

Of Chicago's 22 police districts, the majority of violent crimes are taking place in a cluster of neighborhoods on the South and West Sides. "A handful of districts—probably five or six—are responsible for the disproportionate number of homicides and shootings," Anderson said.

According to the *Chicago Tribune*, by 2010, Chicago's homicide rate had surpassed that of Los Angeles (16.02 per 100,000) and was more than twice that of New York City (7.0 per 100,000). By 2016, Chicago had recorded more homicides and shooting victims than New York City and Los Angeles combined. Chicago's violence spiked in 2016 to a degree not seen since the late 1990s. The Chicago Police Department said 4,331 people were shot and 762 were killed.

With the implementation of a task force in conjunction with the FBI in 2016 in response to this violence and a concerted community outreach program, Chicago has seen a drop in crime. "Since we put the task force in place," says Chicago Police Department Superintendent, Eddie Johnson says, "we've seen significant drops in gun violence. We are making some real positive gains. By no means are we declaring success, but we have seen some really encouraging results." Unfortunately, Johnson says that kids at ever earlier ages are getting involved in this carnage. "We've seen kids as young as 10 and 11 with firearms."

I began to speak with more people in the real estate community who work in these areas, community leaders and advocates, alderman and residents themselves, to learn more about the neighborhoods. While doing so, it became apparent to me that a lot of kids in these areas lack mentorship and oversight, most of the time because parents are working or are nonexistent. This is a ripe breeding ground for kids to see their natural need for belonging fulfilled.

Even if kids are not involved with gang activity, frequently, innocent residents including kids find themselves caught up in the crossfire of gang rivalries or drug deals gone bad. Regardless of how the circumstances originated, they have resulted in a disproportionate amount of kids being left unsupervised for extended periods of time. Bottom line is, kids need safe places with positive and productive activities to engage with in order to help curb their involvement in nefariousness. Kids shouldn't be punished and neglected for the reasons that are out of their control.

Many schools' budgets have been reduced so substantially that after school programs and activities like sports, music, and art have been eliminated, leaving kids to their own devices and looking for things to do. All too often this leads to their involvement with gangs and senseless misguided displays of power fueled by unrewarded, basic self-esteem needs. In an interview conducted by CNN, Aisha Pullen, a mother of two, says it's too dangerous to let her two children play outside after school hours. "Sometimes it's not about flying bullets. They (gang members) jump on kids if they don't want to join gangs. I don't want my kids subject to that type of violence," Pullen says. "Free time, empty hours, empty minutes without anything to do—that's what gang members look for, kids with no business."

Again, I'm not a psychologist and I don't claim to be an expert when it comes to solving inner city crime. However, having worked with kids in the past and knowing how important it was for me, growing up, to have mentors and parents to look up to for guidance, support, and discipline, you can see the writing on the wall. It doesn't take an expert to recognize that the residents who have grown up in this cycle simply need some support if anything is ever going to change.

The more time I spent in the South Side and doing my research, the more I started to see an amazing opportunity. It's not simply from a real estate redevelopment perspective but to be able to make a direct and positive impact in some of these neighborhoods. Where some might see fear and violence, I saw a chance to heal. Where some might see little hope, I saw the opportunity to partner with some philanthropic groups who are already making a big difference to lend them more support for the great work they are doing.

Organizations such as I Grow Chicago, Neighborhood Housing Services, The Safer Foundation, and Good City, along with community leaders such as Kareem Wells, are just some that are making the effort to curb the violence and crime. Kareem in particular is instrumental in regularly promoting peace parades. He supports neighborhood groups by providing opportunities to local residents, especially kids, that are sorely lacking. Peace House is one particular place that Kareem took me, where he introduced me to the folks who run this veritable oasis of safety, education, and creativity.

Located in Englewood, which is statistically one of Chicago's more crime-ridden areas, the founder is an amazing woman by the name of Robbin Carroll. Along with her directors, one of whom was once one of the more prominent gang leaders in the area and is now one of the area's more established mentors. Peace House is instrumental in community development in the area. Created out of Carroll's desire to fulfill a need within the community she saw as urgently lacking, Peace House was founded to help kids deal with the stresses of growing up surrounded by violence. Robbin's journey is rooted in her work to understand how the body moves to heal trauma and her belief in collaborative community engagement to foster hope and healing. After earning a degree in biochemistry from UCLA and running her own business for thirty-five years, she completed her kundalini yoga teacher certification, along with training in Street Yoga, YogaKids, Radiant Child Yoga, Brain Gym, and Heart Math.

Looking to provide some relief from the stress and trauma of continual exposure to violence, Robbin began volunteering as a yoga teacher for children at an Englewood community school. She soon found that the children she most wanted to engage and impact were outside the classroom. They were either sitting in the hallway, suspended, or expelled. The root causes of trauma, experienced outside of school walls and by people of all ages, meant expanding her efforts. The result of her work is I Grow Chicago (igrowchicago.org), the organization behind the actual Peace House itself.

Robbin told me the story of how in 2014, she found an abandoned house in Englewood, bought it, and rehabbed it with her own money. Now with the help of executive director, Tameka Lawson, she conducts the outreach of I Grow Chicago. She said the rehabilitation of the house has created economic opportunity, job and life skills training, and a new sense of hope for residents. It also provides intergenerational programs that foster wellness and empowerment for all.

Residents can come and get food, kids can get help with homework, and yoga and art classes are regularly conducted there. Across the street, the group has planted a garden, and the whole front of the house is adorned with art and murals.

Then as now, Robbin and her staff work to integrate the practices of restorative justice, artistic expression, mindful movement, and community development to create a new model of social change, and from my visits there, I see the direct impact I Grow Chicago and so many other organizations that are making similar efforts are having in these communities.

In a *Chicago Tribune* article written by Barbara Brotman about I Grow Chicago, Brotman interviewed Karl Mables, a twenty-fouryear-old resident of Englewood who works to help maintain Peace House. When asked about the impact I Grow Chicago and the Peace House have had on him, he replied that without I Grow Chicago, "we'd probably be dead or in jail. Robbin and Tameka, they saved our lives."

In the article Carroll talks about how yoga is central to I Grow Chicago's mission. "Yoga has been shown to have a powerful impact on people suffering from trauma," said Robbin. When she taught at the Montessori School of Englewood, she was struck by how badly the children needed it.

"The little kids, their bodies were so tense and rigid," she said. "They couldn't open their fists."

After implementing yoga into the program at the beginning of the summer a few years ago, by summer's end, it had become a treasured part of the day.

"That yoga thing, it's made such a difference," said Mables.

Many of the young men who work with I Grow Chicago have criminal backgrounds and gang ties. The organization partners with One Summer Chicago Plus, the city's summer employment antiviolence program for young people at higher risk for involvement with gun violence. Neighborhood residents say that Peace House has, in fact, brought peace to its immediate surroundings.

"This whole block is at peace," said Mables. "I feel very safe here." Other streets could feel tranquil too, he said.

"If you come and pay attention, you can change things on your block," said Mables. Ora Bradley, 62, who has lived on the block for more than 40 years, said she sees clear changes.

Young people are walking away from quarrels instead of getting caught up in them, she said. Some even step forward to cool down other people's tempers.

"They try to interrupt what's going on," she said. "That's Peace House."

"If I could change, I'm pretty sure anybody could," said resident, Clarence Franklin, who learned to paint in jail and is now painting murals for Peace House.

Why is Lawson so committed to the impact she is making? "If I don't do it, I'm just another person turning my eyes away from the problem," she said.

Robbin, too, is undeterred by the gun violence surrounding Peace House.

"We would like it to stop," she said. "But that's what we're here for."

To date, I Grow Chicago has:

- Served more than 24,000 meals to Englewood residents

- Provided over 2,000 coats to community residents

- Delivered 650 turkeys to community residents

- Gifted over 3,500 Christmas presents to neighborhood families

- Taught yoga and mindfulness to 3,000 children

- Supplies thousands of household and personal hygiene supplies through community pantry for anyone in need

- Transformed 3 vacant lots into 3 community spaces (Peace

- Garden and a safe outdoor play area for children)

- Created 10 pieces of positive public art for the community

- Partnered with the city of Chicago to provide hundreds of summer jobs to the city's youth, every summer from its inception in 2012

This is real impact! After meeting with Robin Carroll and several other organizations and other community advocates, I was inspired to help and saw an opportunity to legitimately make a difference. What I learned from my investigation into the southside is one of the large contributors to my decision to move back to Chicago from LA It's my desire to contribute and be a part of something that I see as an amazing team that I want to help win. I love Chicago and feel a sense of community and pride in here. I absolutely have embraced the city since moving back, have embraced the city as much as I feel it has embraced me in return.

In many of the projects I have conducted in the past several years, I have had the opportunity to provide employment to former gang members who continue to be a part of my construction team. With my mom as my business partner, we look to continue to provide more employment opportunities. This, when coupled with our plan to promote home ownership among local residents with low income down payment assistance programs and opportunity zone investments, is our planned contribution to the neighborhood. I'm encouraged by all the support of so many special people and have made it my mission to let others know there is a lot more work to be done.

My parents fostered in me an interest to want to give back from a very early age. They made me well aware that just because I was fortunate to have food on the table, someone to help me with my homework and to throw a baseball in the backyard with me, that there were many other families in the world where this was not the case. My parent's influence has served as a huge impetus for me to work in the inner cities of Chicago, New York, and LA as a tutor, community advocate, and real estate developer. Accordingly, I have seen firsthand that regardless of how bright, motivated, or hopeful someone is, when people are struggling to fulfill their basic human physiological needs, safety needs, and need to belong, it's insurmountably difficult to pursue self-actualization.

From the outside looking in on certain communities, it may appear that cycles of poverty and self-perpetuating sabotage keep being played over and over again. We can assume it's due to a lack of education or a lack of drive and motivation toward self-improvement. After spending time in communities such as the South Side of Chicago, however, I've discovered firsthand that regardless of how motivated people are or desirous of peace and economic growth, it's virtually impossible to perform beyond mere survival when literally dodging bullets to go home from school or work. I believe that we, as a nation, can do better than this and provide opportunities for all of the people of our communities to pursue their dreams.

This, essentially, is why one of my central focuses has been to support groups like I Grow Chicago, Neighborhood Housing Services. My current mission is to create a youth center in Chicago's Roseland area where a permanent home will be provided for an organization called Art On the Loose (artontheloose.com). There, art and creativity are used to heal, grow, and teach kids about the career opportunities that exist in the world of creativity.

Art On the Loose was founded and run by an incredibly generous and altruistic man named Vernon Lockehart. He has been a beacon in the South Side, pioneering in his efforts to expose kids to the career opportunities available in art, design, advertising, and marketing. Vernon and I have assembled a team, identified the building, and have put the plans together to convert an empty 10,000 sq. ft. building into a thriving hub for the community, similar to what *Peace House* is achieving in Englewood. Witnessing *Peace House's* direct community impact has cemented my goal to further this thrust by providing the same inspirational safehaven in the Roseland neighborhood. Though the task is an uphill one, I'm a firm believer that by enrolling enough people to join in our "Why?" to provide better opportunities for the children and families that populate these neighborhoods, together, *We can do this!*

My parents also instilled in me the belief that when you make the effort to get to know someone, you have the chance to discover something unique and extraordinary not just about them, but about yourself. From working with, tutoring, and getting to know people in the communities that I focus on, I see the results and difference a little bit of effort can make, and it is incredibly rewarding knowing that we have had such a positive impact. WITH YOUR HELP, WE CAN DO SO MUCH MORE!

I wouldn't be where I am today were it not for the hundreds of people in my life who helped support me to get here. Even when things didn't turn out the way I had hoped, the fact that the support was there is what made all the difference.

In my darkest hour, sometimes all I needed to know was that I wasn't alone and that someone cared. Having been blessed with people who showed such concern, I recognize that it's time now for me to step it up and give back in a big way. But again, I can't do it alone. I want to make a difference, and with your help I know we can. Not just in a 'thoughts and prayers' kind of way, but actual boots on the ground to make a tangible difference.

There is a solution to end the violence, crime, and fear here in Chicago and everywhere else in the world. To borrow from what Tameka Lawson says, if we don't do it, we're just "another person" turning our eyes away from the problem. Let's turn our eyes and our hearts toward the problem and make a difference. By purchasing this book, you have already contributed in a small way, for which I am incredibly appreciative. If you'd like to find out how to help in a bigger way and join the Agile Artist Community in making this art center happen and supporting hundreds of kids pursue their dreams, please go to my website, colinegglesfield.com, and sign up for my email newsletter for updates and more information. Let's work together to provide more than hope, but also a real place for kids and adults to feel safe, supported, and inspired to realize their dreams as well! LET'S DO THIS!

DO IT ANYWAY

> *"The Force will be with you. Always."*
> *— Obi-Wan Kenobi*

I'm not a religious person per se, but you may have picked up at this point that I'm a firm believer in spirituality and connecting directly with what I like to call "source." You may refer to source as God or Allah or what have you, but regardless of your beliefs, there are a few prayers that I find insightful and inspiring. One such prayer was a modified version of *The Paradoxical Commandments* by Dr. Kent M. Keith that Mother Teresa had written on the wall in her office. I'd like to simply leave you with this. Before I do, let me say thank you for your time and willingness to read my story. I hope you've learned something or gained a little bit of inspiration with which you can manifest and pursue your dream life. All my love to you and yours on your artistic journey!

People are often unreasonable, irrational, and self-centered. Forgive them anyway.

If you are kind, people may accuse you of selfish, ulterior motives. Be kind anyway.

If you are successful, you will win some unfaithful friends and some genuine enemies. Succeed anyway.

If you are honest and sincere, people may deceive you. Be honest and sincere anyway.

What you spend years creating, others could destroy overnight.

Create anyway.

If you find serenity and happiness, some may be jealous. Be happy anyway.

The good you do today, will often be forgotten. Do good anyway.

Give the best you have, and it will never be enough. Give your best anyway.

In the final analysis, it is between you and God. It was never between you and them anyway.

BEFORE YOU GO: THE GREAT INVITATION

We've all come a long way in life. We've been dealt with a lot and have overcome a lot. We all have our unique challenges and our special circumstances and stories, and we all know what it means to succeed and fail. We know what it means to love and to be hurt, and we know the importance of forgiveness. We know what it feels like to be hopeful and give it your all, and we know what it feels like to be disappointed. At the end of the day, these are the experiences that allow us to decide who we want to be. An important thing I've realized, however, going through all the experiences I have so far in life, is that no matter what I was dealing with or going through, I couldn't and didn't want to do it alone.

There's so much that people collectively share with one another that can be so beneficial to so many others if we just take dare to take the risk of opening up and sharing who we are, authentically. This is why I'm making The Great Invitation to join the Agile Artist Community. We will embark on a journey of self-exploration and creativity, a journey where we help each other overcome the obstacles we are faced with that prevent us from living our dream lives!

I invite you to visit my website, www.colineggleslfield.com, to sign up for my newsletter and to join the Agile Artist Community.

In it, we will be holding webinars, workshops, and seminars centered on cultivating more creativity, balance, and empowerment in our lives. The more connected we become, the more we will be able to share ideas, support each other, and create accountability for the things we seek to achieve. Collectively, not only can we help each other to grow and learn, we can also make a difference and have a positive impact in the lives of so many and be of service to countless others too! Come join us!

Much love,

Colin

ACKNOWLEDGMENTS

I've already acknowledged quite a few people, but I'd like to thank my family once again for always offering their unending support and encouragement. This is especially true of my mom and dad for their never-ending belief in me and for teaching me to always dream. I'd like to also thank them for teaching me how to pick my head up even when I struck out. I'd like to thank my sister, Kerry, for introducing me to the crazy world of entertainment by letting me tag along to her play auditions when we were little, and my brother, Sean, for always inspiring me to be a better person and the life of the party. To my amazing publisher, Melissa Wilson at Networlding Publishing, without whose guidance, encouragement, patience, and belief in me this wouldn't be possible. Thank you to all my friends, including Lisa, Jeremy, and Todd for the laughs, the tears, and the Negronis. Thank you Jeremy as well for your tireless work editing this book and for your constant reminders about how to use a comma properly. This book wouldn't have been possible without you. Thank you to Dean DeLisle, Frank Montro, and everyone else who helped to conspire to make this book happen!

Thank you to all my acting coaches and teachers, including the amazing and beautiful-inside-and-out Margie Haber for all the oatmeal and blueberries you would feed me when I would come over to rehearse in the mornings. Thank you Larry Moss for showing me how to be a true professional and for the encouragement when I needed it most and for reminding me to breathe! Thank you Jackie Segal for your infectious love and passion for the theatre. Thank you Susan Batson, Penny Templeton, Terry Schreiber, Chris Fields, Ivana Chubbuck, and all of the hundreds of fellow thespians I have had the privilege to share the stage and screen with. A special thank you to Molly Smith and Hilary Swank for believing in me and to Emily Giffin, not only for creating an amazing story and the best character ever in Dexter Thaler, but for your love, support, and encouragement as well!

Thank you to Sebastian McWilliams, Roger LaRose, Spencer Salley, and all of my other numerous modeling agents who helped support my dream. Thank you to all of my amazing agents and managers who helped create my career and believed in me, including Suzette Vasquez, Larry Taube, Colton Gramm, Chris Fioto, and Darren Boghosian. Thank you to Joe at Budget Car Rental and all the other serendipitous exchanges with people who have inspired me along the way on my journey. Thank you to all the amazing doctors, nurses, staff members, and research scientists who have provided me with a second and third chance to continue to live my dream life.

Thank you to everyone else who has been a part of my incredible journey and especially to all of you out there who have supported me by watching my movies and my TV shows and for being the best fans ever! And thank you to everyone who has read *Agile Artist* and is looking to make more of a difference in their life and in communities around the world. Let's bring more creativity and fulfillment, not only to ourselves, but to people in our communities who need the support to do it as well.

Let's do this! Colin

PAYING IT FORWARD

Throughout *Agile Artist* I have shared my belief in the importance of supporting an individual's exploration of their creativity for what it can contribute to the greater good of humanity. I believe this starts, at the very core, by empowering our youth to explore their many talents so they may find a healthy comfort zone with which to contribute their "WHY?" to the greater good. As such, I have chosen to dedicate 10% of the proceeds from this publication to the not-for-profit organization *Art on the Loose* based in Chicago's south side.

– Colin

ENGLEWOOD

Englewood and I Grow Chicago by the Numbers

EMPLOYMENT 2017

- Per-capita income: $10,559

- Households below poverty level: 32.3%

- Unemployment rate: 34.7%

- No high school diploma: 30.3%

SAFETY

- Second most violent community in Chicago

- Of Chicago's 4,379 shootings in 2016, Englewood accounted for 441 of them (10%)

- Population ever arrested: Male 59%, Female 16%

- Felt unsafe alone in neighborhood in the daytime: Male 30%,

- Female 39%

- Felt unsafe alone in neighborhood in the nighttime: Male 46%, Female 47%

HUNGER

- West Englewood has the second-highest food insecurity rate and lowest income per capita

- Hunger-insecure residents: 48%

- Used emergency food resources in the past year: 44%

- Received food stamp benefits in the past year: 73% Poverty and lack of opportunity leads to violence, trauma, and collective hopelessness.

From the I Grow Chicago website:

I Grow Chicago started in the streets, is supported by the streets, and is transforming the streets. We are creating a culture of hope in Englewood, where a community is ready to make a difference for themselves, their neighbors, and their children. We engage and employ residents to build their vision of their community and collaboratively work together to lead our five service areas:

- Mentorship and skill building

- Restorative justice and community building

- Yoga and mindfulness

- Creative expression

- Sustainability and urban farming

ABOUT THE AUTHOR

While studying pre-med, Colin went to a model and talent search on a whim. Soon he was working with some of the top designers and photographers in the world, letting fashion lay the groundwork for his acting career.

After moving to New York he starred in the long lived daytime drama, 'All My Children' playing the son of Erika Kane which soon led to roles on, 'Rizzoli and Isles' and the romantic comedy, 'Something

Borrowed' with Kate Hudson.

In 2014, with his passion for wanting to make a positive social impact and a desire to get into the world of real estate, Colin started his own real estate investment company, Stage 2 Properties and began rehabbing houses in the south side of Chicago. He is currently working with community leaders and developers including a nonprofit called 'Art on the Loose.' One of their main goals is to help revitalize underserved communities including the creation of a youth community center that teaches inner city kids about careers in art and design.

These experiences and more have shaped Colin and taught him a lot about life, success, and making a difference, the impetus for his book. In 'Agile Artist,' he shares his rich life stores and provides plenty of inventive strategies to help you, too, break through to your creative, true self.

*10% of proceeds from "Agile Artist" will go towards the development of the 'Art on the Loose' youth center.

CPSIA information can be obtained
at www.ICGtesting.com
Printed in the USA
LVHW012341020919
629744LV00009B/683/P